W9-CEH-091

Gotcha for Guys!

Gotcha for Guys!

Nonfiction Books to Get Boys Excited About Reading

**Kathleen A. Baxter and
Marcia Agness Kochel**

A Member of the Greenwood Publishing Group

Westport, Connecticut ● London

Library of Congress Cataloging-in-Publication Data

Baxter, Kathleen A.
  Gotcha for guys! : nonfiction books to get boys excited about reading / by Kathleen A.
Baxter and Marcia Agness Kochel.
        p. cm.
  Includes bibliographical references and index.
  ISBN 1-59158-311-X (pbk : alk. paper)
  1. Boys—Books and reading—United States. 2. Children—Books and reading—United States.
3. Book talks—United States. I. Kochel, Marcia Agness. II. Title.
Z1039.B67B39 2007
028.5'5—dc22   2006030667

British Library Cataloguing in Publication Data is available.

Copyright © 2007 by Kathleen A. Baxter and Marcia Agness Kochel

All rights reserved. No portion of this book may be
reproduced, by any process or technique, without the
express written consent of the publisher.

Library of Congress Control Number: 2006030667
ISBN: 1-59158-311-X

First published in 2007

Libraries Unlimited, 88 Post Road West, Westport, CT 06881
A Member of the Greenwood Publishing Group, Inc.
www.lu.com

Printed in the United States of America

The paper used in this book complies with the
Permanent Paper Standard issued by the National
Information Standards Organization (Z39.48–1984).

10 9 8 7 6 5 4 3 2

To the new boy readers in our lives
Ethan and Owen Comiskey and Will Kochel

Contents

List of Figures ix
Introduction xv

Chapter 1—Around the World 1
  New and Notable 1
  Not to Be Missed 10
  Worth Reading 18

Chapter 2—American History 23
  New and Notable 23
  Not to Be Missed 40
  Worth Reading 48

Chapter 3—Prehistoric Creatures 51
  New and Notable 51
  Not to Be Missed 57
  Worth Reading 58

Chapter 4—Science 67
  New and Notable 67
  Not to Be Missed 79
  Worth Reading 84

Chapter 5—All Things Gross 95
  New and Notable 95
  Not to Be Missed 104
  Worth Reading 112

Chapter 6—Animals 115
  New and Notable 115
  Not to Be Missed 128
  Worth Reading 138

Chapter 7—Creepy-Crawly Creatures: Bugs, Reptiles, and Amphibians 159
  New and Notable 159
  Not to Be Missed 163
  Worth Reading 166

Chapter 8—Action and Innovation: Sports, the Military, Machines, Buildings, and Inventions 175

   New and Notable...175

   Not to Be Missed 184

   Worth Reading 188

Chapter 9—Disasters and Unsolved Mysteries 205

   New and Notable...205

   Not to Be Missed 211

   Worth Reading 217

Chapter 10—Hot Topics: Magic, Riddles, Games, and Puzzles, Art and Drawing, Fascinating Facts and Reference Books 223

   Magic 223

   Riddles, Games, and Puzzles 224

   Art and Drawing 227

   Fascinating Facts and Reference Books 230

   Acknowledgments 233

   Author/Illustrator Index 243

   Title Index...251

List of Figures

What If You Met a Pirate? by Jan Adkins..2

Pirates & Smugglers by Moira Butterfield. 3

How to Be a Medieval Knight by Fiona MacDonald. 6

Remember World War II: Kids Who Survived Tell Their Stories
    by Dorinda Makanaonalani Nicholson. 7

Adolf Hitler: Evil Mastermind of the Holocaust by Linda Jacobs Altman. 18

The D-Day Landings by Sean Connolly. 19

The Colosseum by Leslie DuTemple. 19

Spies by Clive Gifford...20

Ancient Greek War and Weapons by Haydn Middleton...21

Pirates and Privateers of the High Seas by Laura Lee Wren......................................22

Freedom Riders: John Lewis and Jim Zwerg on the Front Lines of the Civil
    Rights Movement by Ann Bausum...24

Kid Blink Beats The World by Don Brown...26

The Battle of the Alamo by Matt Doeden...28

Let It Begin Here! Lexington & Concord: First Battles of the American
    Revolution by Dennis Brindell Fradin. 29

The Remarkable Benjamin Franklin by Cheryl Harness. 30

Onward: A Photobiography of African-American Polar Explorer
    Matthew Henson by Dolores Johnson. 31

Counting Coup: Becoming a Crow Chief on the Reservation and Beyond
    by Joseph Medicine Crow. 34

The Journey of the One and Only Declaration of Independence by Judith St. George.........37

You're On Your Way, Teddy Roosevelt! by Judith St. George.....................................38

Read about Crazy Horse by Stephen Feinstein...49

Wyatt Earp: Wild West Lawman by Elaine Landau...50

True Tales of the Wild West by Paul Walker. 50

Boy, Were We Wrong about Dinosaurs by Kathleen Kudlinski. 54

How Dinosaurs Took Flight: The Fossils, the Science, What We Think We Know, and the Mysteries Yet Unsolved by Christopher Sloan. 55

Feathered Dinosaurs of China by Gregory Wenzel. 56

Mammoths: Ice-Age Giants by Larry D. Agenbroad and Lisa Nelson. 59

Pteranodon: The Life Story of a Pterosaur by Ruth Ashby. 59

Dinosaur Discoveries by Gail Gibbons. 60

Flying Giants of Dinosaur Time by Don Lessem. 62

Triceratops: Mighty Three-Horned Dinosaur by Michael W. Skrepnick. 64

National Geographic Prehistoric Mammals by Alan Turner. 64

Little Book of Dinosaurs by Cherie Winner. 65

Fireworks by Vicki Cobb. 68

Genius: A Photobiography of Albert Einstein by Marfé Ferguson Delano. 69

Guinea Pig Scientists: Bold Self-Experimenters in Science and Medicine by Leslie Dendy and Mel Boring 70

Investigating Murders by Paul Dowswell. 71

Home on the Moon: Living on the Space Frontier by Marianne J. Dyson. 72

In Your Face: The Facts about Your Features by Donna M. Jackson. 74

Leonardo da Vinci by Kathleen Krull. 76

Science Verse by Jon Scieszka. 79

The Amazing International Space Station. 84

Tornadoes: Disaster and Survival by Bonnie Ceban. 85

Robotics by Helena Domaine. 85

Electricity and Magnetism Science Fair Projects: Using Batteries, Balloons, and Other Hair-Raising Stuff by Robert Gardner. 86

Forces of Nature: The Awesome Power of Volcanoes, Earthquakes, and Tornadoes by Catherine Grace. 87

Robots Slither by Ryan Ann Hunter. 87

Planet Patrol by Marybeth Lorbiecki. 88

An Extreme Dive under the Antarctic Ice by Brad Matsen. 88

Zzz…: The Most Interesting Book You'll Ever Read about Sleep by Trudee Romanek........89

Junk Lab by Michael Elsohn Ross. 90

Why Does My Body Smell? And Other Questions about Hygiene by Angela Royston. 91

Microscopic Life by Richard Walker. 92

Avalanches by Anne Ylvisaker. 92

Curse of the Pharaohs: My Adventures with the Mummies by Zahi Hawass. 97

Tutankahmun: The Mystery of the Boy King by Zahi Hawass. 98

Outside and Inside Mummies by Sandra Markle. 100

Achoo! The Most Interesting Book You'll Ever Read about Germs by Trudee Romanek. ...101

What's Living in Your Bedroom? by Andrew Solway. 103

Bog Mummies: Preserved in Peat by Charlotte Wilcox. 112

What's Living inside Your Body? by Andrew Solway. 113

A Platypus, Probably by Sneed B. Collard III. 115

Rickie and Henri: A True Story by Jane Goodall. 119

The Best Book of Wolves and Wild Dogs by Christiane Gunzi. 120

Great White Sharks by Sandra Markle. 123

Hyenas by Sandra Markle. 124

Killer Fish by Andrew Solway. 126

Exploring the Deep, Dark Sea by Gail Gibbons. 131

Grey Wolf by Jill Bailey. 138

Hermit Crabs by Tristan Boyer Binns. 139

Untamed: Animals around the World by Steve Bloom. 139

Little Gorillas by Bernadette Costa-Prades. 140

Critter Riddles by Marilyn Helmer. 142

Powerful Predators by Tim Knight. 145

Gross and Gory by Elizabeth Laskey. 146

Vultures by Wayne Lynch. 147

Sea Creatures by Tiffany Peterson. 150

Caribou by Susan E. Quinlan. 151

Killer Carnivores by Andrew Solway. 152

Gray Wolves by Lynn M. Stone. 154

Asian Elephant by Matt Turner. 155

Wild Horses by Julia Vogel. 156

Seahorses by Sally M. Walker. 156

Vampire Bats by Anne Welsbacher. 157

Outside and Inside Killer Bees by Sandra Markle. 160

The Bumblebee Queen by April Pulley Sayre. 161

Mosquito Bite by Alexandra Siy. 162

Creepy Crawlies by Jim Bruce. 167

Yellow Sac Spiders by Eric Ethan. 168

Lizards: Weird and Wonderful by Margery Facklam. 169

Snakes by Adrienne Mason. 170

Deadly Spiders and Scorpions by Andrew Solway. 172

*Everything Bug: What Kids Really Want to Know about Insects and
      Spiders* by Cherie Winner. 173

Young Thomas Edison by Michael Dooling. 177

Freeze Frame: A Photographic History of the Winter Olympics by Sue Macy. 180

Smokejumpers: Battling the Forest Flames by Diana Briscoe. 184

Tae Kwon Do by David Amerland. 188

U.S. Army Fighting Vehicles by Richard Bartlett. 188

The World's Fastest Indy Cars by Glen Bledsoe and Karen Bledsoe. 189

Extreme Mountain Biking Moves by Kathleen Deady. 190

BMX by Scott Dick. 191

An International Soccer Star by Ben Godsal. 192

Attack Fighters by Ian Graham. 192

Crime-Fighting Aircraft by Henry M. Holden. 194

Cars by Nancy Smiler Levinson. 195

Trucks and Big Rigs by Arlene Bourgeois Molzahn. 196

Eureka! Great Inventions and How They Happened by Richard Platt. 197

The Best Book of Martial Arts by Lauren Robertson. 198

Scooters and Skateboards by Wendy Sadler. 198

Stunt Planes by Jeff Savage. 199

The World's Fastest Pro Stock Trucks by Jeff Savage. 199

Transformed: How Everyday Things Are Made by Bill Slavin. 200

Karting by Graham Smith. 201

How to Build Your Own Prize-Winning Robot by Ed Sobey. 201

Bulldozers by Linda D. Williams. 203

The Lost Colony of Roanoke by Jean Fritz. 206

Vanished by Judith Herbst. 207

Fooled You! Frauds and Hoaxes through the Years by Elaine Pascoe 208

Mysteries of History by Robert Stewart. 209

Secrets of a Civil War Submarine: Solving the Mysteries of the H.L. Hunley
    by Sally M. Walker. 210

1906 San Francisco Earthquake by Tim Cooke. 218

Myths and Monsters: Secrets Revealed by Katie Edwards. 219

The Short and Bloody History of Ghosts by John Farman. 219

Spooky Riddles by Marilyn Helmer. 220

Games: Learn to Play, Play to Win by Daniel King. 225

Eye Guess: A Foldout Guessing Game by Phyllis Limbacher Tildes 227

Drawing with Your Fingerprints by Godeleine De Rosamel 228

Ed Emberley's Drawing Book of Trucks and Trains by Ed Emberley. 228

Ed Emberley's Drawing Book of Weirdos by Ed Emberley. 229

Ralph Masiello's Bug Drawing Book by Ralph Masiello. 229

Introduction

I do not think I will ever stop talking about and recommending books. Thank heaven for that! In the twenty-first century, Americans are concerned about the "dumbing down" of our society and, particularly, of our kids. Boys especially often claim no interest in and no time for reading. Their time is like that of adults: overscheduled. When did we all become so busy? And what can we do to get them to prioritize reading as an important part of their time?

There is one solution on which all the experts agree: **Let them choose.** Make a good selection of books on appealing topics at different reading levels available to them and watch what happens.

The problem can be one of gender. Let's face it, books on topics that appeal to boys often have little appeal (on the surface, at least) to females. Gross stuff? Not our thing. Weapons and the military? No way. Cars and other vehicles? You've got to be kidding. And that's just the beginning. Over and over I've read about and talked to men who went to libraries to find reading material about the things they love only to be put down by female librarians who disdained their choices. The books girls want to read are good, and the books boys want to read are bad. You want a book or magazine on wrestling? Can't you think of a topic more worthy of your time?

The teaching and library professions are dominated by women. We choose what to purchase for our collection, and we choose what to display and recommend. We have our standards, and frequently our standards bear little relation to what most boys want to read.

I have a fun section in my booktalk programs on gross books for boys. You'll find them all listed here in Chapter 5. Most of my audience of teachers and librarians is with me all the way, laughing, making faces, and having a grand time of it. I even saw a man jump up and down in his seat once!

But there are always a few who sit stony-faced, disapproving, appalled that I would even consider mentioning the word "poop." You know that the boys in their classes and libraries, who find those books so irresistible, will not find the books there. Some of these women (never, ever men) even talk to me afterward, letting me know that I am way out of line talking about these things in public.

Well, lighten up. What we have been doing all of these years to turn boys off of reading has worked brilliantly. The failure of boys in our schools is a national crisis. What can we do to bring them back?

First of all, make the books that they want available to them. Then show off those books! Display them, set them apart, and watch them fly out the doors. If they don't want to read an award winner, let them choose not to. If the book is lower than their reading level, it does not matter. If they want the same book over and over and over again, let them have it. Somehow, most boys have determined that reading is a task, a chore, an assignment. It is now our job to teach them that reading is fun; reading is something pleasurable that we can all enjoy doing.

Second, we need to talk about the fun we have when we read. When we talk to kids about the great time we have while reading, we are opening the door to their realization that reading is not just a chore. Tell them about the great new fact you learned yesterday, or that you stayed up way past bedtime because you could not put down the book you were reading. I like to tell my audiences anything that communicates to them that reading is enjoyable. I tell them that my husband liked Jack Gantos's *A Hole in My Life* so much that he loaned it to his best friend, Greg, whose career is in scrap metal. Greg gave it back the next week, remarking that it was ridiculous that such a great book was written for teenagers. Any book this good, he declared, should be for adults! In fact, Greg was so taken with Jack Gantos that he went out and bought all of the Joey Pigza books for himself—to read more books by this great author.

When I first saw *The Race to Save the Lord God Bird* by Philip Hoose, I just plain wasn't interested. Long books about extinct birds are not my thing. But my job is reading the new nonfiction, and I was stuck. My husband had led the way; he is interested in birds and read and loved the book before I started it.

But I should have trusted Philip Hoose! What a wonderful read that book was. I was bummed out for days after I finished it. And the next year, when I was traveling and picked up the copy of *USA Today* that was lying in front of my hotel room door, I started crying when I read the news article that said the Ivory-Billed Woodpecker had been sighted in Arkansas. I was so thrilled I called my spouse, and he started crying too! And this is something I need to tell kids, too: a book that did not look appealing to me was, in fact, a huge pleasure to read. A male teacher told me that when he first saw *A Single Shard,* the Newbery Medal winner by Linda Sue Park, he thought "You've got to be kidding! *I* have to read a book about medieval Korean pottery? Boorrring."

But he read it and he loved it, and he introduced it to his class just that way. He said they absolutely loved it when he read it aloud, and he thinks telling them that the topic did not do much for him at first glance really helped pave the road to their enjoyment.

Third, let's bring in any men or boys we can find to read to our classes and libraries and talk about the books they enjoy. Boys' academic lives are dominated by women in control. It is a rare thing for a man to be in charge of a class or a school media center or public library children's department. Boys need desperately to see male reading models. A lot of them see reading as something only females do. If you can bring in a popular member of your high school sports team to read to boys or talk to them about books he enjoyed, you are making a major contribution to boys' reading. *Any* male reading model is good.

Finally, let them choose what to read, how long it should be, what reading level it should be, whether to just read the photo captions, and where to read it; accept and allow almost any source of reading material (we do understand that *Penthouse* magazine might not be the best option). Supply graphic nonfiction as well as graphic novels. Make sure you have a selection of reading material that is almost irresistible. Have you ever seen *anyone* who turned down a chance to browse through *The Guinness Book of World Records*?

Most of the booktalks in this book are short and sweet. Some have longer information. Pick and choose what works for you. We no longer believe that anyone has an attention span anymore. Keep your booktalks moving. If you don't like what I am talking about right now, never fear: it will change soon.

There are three types of listings in this book. First, we (my partner Marcia Kochel and I) include booktalks of the type you have come to expect from the previous *Gotcha* books. All of these are published here for the first time. They are found at the beginning of each chapter under the heading "New and Notable."

Second, there are annotations of books that are popular with boys. Many of these have booktalks written in *Gotcha!, Gotcha Again!,* or *Gotcha Covered!.* You may refer to the earlier *Gotcha* books for complete booktalks on these titles should you desire them (the *Gotcha* title in which previous booktalks appear can be found at the end of the annotations). They are found in each chapter under the heading "Not to Be Missed."

Third, there are lists—long lists—of books with guy appeal that we may not have seen or read but that have received positive reviews in major library reviewing sources—*School Library Journal, Booklist of the American Library Association,* or *The Horn Book Guide.* If the books were reviewed in the *Horn Book Guide,* they received a number score of at least 4, and perhaps higher. *Horn Book Guide,* I have been assured, does consider that a good review. There are many books from series publishers on these. They are found in each chapter under the heading "Worth Reading."

Series publishers include Heinemann, Raintree, The Child's World, Rosen, Capstone Press, Lerner, ABDO, and many others. Series publishing presents a problem for booktalkers. Most of the books are products, assembled quickly, using stock photographs and, often, not the best writers. The books are usually sold directly to librarians, rather than through jobbers such as Follett, BWI, and Baker and Taylor. Discounts are small, and prices are high.

Please look for a good review before you purchase a series book. Their quality varies wildly. Make sure that someone somewhere in some major reviewing source has read and recommended the book before you spend your hard-won tax money on it. And, remember, just because one book in a series receives a good review does not mean that *all* of the titles in that series are equally worthy. Be careful about spending your oh-so-limited funds on poor-quality materials. And consider purchasing books on popular sports and entertainment figures only in paperback. The information dates so quickly that you should feel no hesitation about throwing much-outdated titles away—and a book for which you paid a lot of money can be hard to toss.

What is most important is that we have a strong collection of titles available in our schools and libraries that boys will want to grab and read. Where we get these titles is not nearly as important as that we somehow acquire them and have them available.

There is no magic bullet for getting boys to start reading. We only wish there were. But providing exciting books on appealing topics is a great way to start, and Marcia and I hope this edition of *Gotcha* leads you to some irresistible books for guys.

Good luck!

—Kathleen Baxter

Chapter 1

Around the World

This chapter encompasses everything from pirates to wars, ancient cities to exotic places, even hunting for gold. Boys with a sense of adventure and imagination should find plenty of excitement in the pages of these books from around the world and throughout history.

NEW AND NOTABLE

Adkins, Jan. *What If You Met a Pirate?* Roaring Brook Press, 2004. ISBN 1596430079. 32 p. Grades 2–8.

    This book looks small, but it is packed with great information. Here are some facts to share with your listeners:

- Pirates did not spend a lot of time being pirates. Most of the time they were dirty, smelly sailors who had hard, monotonous work to do.

- Most pirates were not all that illegal. A country would give them something called a letter of marque (pronounced "mark"), which gave them the right to steal from regular ships from certain other countries—as long as they gave the first country half of everything they got.

What If You Met a Pirate? **by Jan Adkins.**

- Pirates made short trips, not long voyages, and they were packed tightly into their small ships.

- Most people did not choose to become pirates. They were forced into it, one way or another.

- Many pirates dealt in the business of slaves.

- Most pirates died long before they grew old. Most of them died from diseases.

- There are no records of pirates making anyone walk the plank. Apparently a famous artist, N. C. Wyeth, made up that story.

You'll find these facts and lots more to entice the boys in your library or classroom.

Bartoletti, Susan Campbell. *Hitler Youth: Growing Up in Hitler's Shadow*. Scholastic Nonfiction, an imprint of Scholastic, 2005. ISBN 0439353793. 176 p. Grades 5–up.
Long before Hitler came to power in Germany, there was a Hitler Youth group.
It began in 1926, and over the next six years, fourteen Hitler youth were killed in street fights. They believed in their leader, and they worked hard to make sure that Nazi candidates got elected. In July 1932, their efforts paid off—the Nazis became the largest political party in Germany. Hitler's party had much to accomplish, and this is the story of the young people who helped it to both fail and succeed in achieving its goals.
Germany had suffered much after it surrendered following World War I. The economy was terrible. German citizens were angry at the countries that had defeated them and then forced Germany to pay large amounts of money in reparation for causing the war and for the damage it had done. A lot of adults wanted revenge—and so did a lot of kids.

They could begin helping by joining the Hitler Youth. At first it was not something everyone did, but, as time went on, young people were virtually forced to join. There were two groups, one for boys ages ten to fourteen and one for girls of the same age. Applicants to join had to get a pass that proved their racial heritage. No people with Jewish names could apply. Even Jews who had converted to Christianity were not allowed to join. People who could not join were outcasts. And, of course, as Hitler became more and more powerful, even worse things happened to them.

By 1934, Hitler was both the chancellor and president of Germany. His soldiers harassed the Catholic Church, persecuted the Roma people (commonly known as Gypsies), and sent Jehovah's Witnesses to concentration camps. The members of Hitler Youth were taught how to fight a war. They were extremely disciplined and were not allowed to disagree with anything. Many of them hated that. They were even supposed to turn in their parents if they did not think they were good Nazis—and some of them did.

This is the story of several real kids who were Hitler Youth, and some who quit and died because they hated Hitler. Show students the photos of all twelve young people on pages four and five to start off your booktalk. Then pose the question, "What do you think you would have done if you had been pressured to join the Hitler Youth?" *Hitler Youth* was named a 2006 Newbery Honor Book as well as a 2006 Sibert Honor Book.

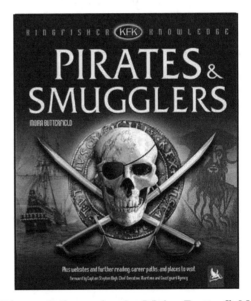

Pirates & Smugglers by Moira Butterfield.

Butterfield, Moira. *Pirates & Smugglers* (Kingfisher Knowledge). Foreword by Captain Stephen Bligh. Kingfisher, 2005. ISBN 0753458640. 64 p. Grades 4–8.

Children will learn the truth about pirates and their long history when they read this book. Pirates have been around for a long, long time. Their lives may look exciting and full of adventure to young readers, but that was not often the case. They lived grim, hard lives, and most of them were (or became) terrible criminals.

Even in ancient times, pirates in the Mediterranean Sea attacked ships transporting goods. Merchant ships tried to stick as close to shore as possible because of the danger. Not only were they in danger of losing their goods and their lives, they could also be captured and sold into slavery.

Capturing people and selling them into slavery—or just making them slaves—was one of the main things pirates did through much of history. In the 1400s and 1500s, Muslim pirates, who were called corsairs, captured up to one million Europeans to be slaves. Many of the men became naked galley slaves, chained to their benches where they rowed the ships, and were beaten mercilessly. Most of them did not live long. Many of the women were sold into harems. "At one time there were said to be so many Christian slaves in Algiers that you could buy one for the cost of an onion" (p. 13).

In the 1500s, many European pirates became legal! The rulers of the countries in which they lived hired them to disrupt enemy sea trade. They were pirates, and the rulers got a share of whatever treasure they got. It was a win-win situation!

But the golden age of pirates was between 1690 and 1730. That was when the most famous pirates lived—people like Henry Morgan, William Kidd, and Blackbeard. Blackbeard put burning fuses into his hair and beard when he attacked. This was frightening. But Blackbeard did not end up well. When he was killed by a British navy expedition, they cut off his head and hung it on their ship as a warning to others.

This book is jam-packed with great information and wonderful pictures of pirates and smugglers.

Harness, Cheryl. *Ghosts of the Nile.* Simon & Schuster Books for Young Readers, 2004. ISBN 0689834780. Unpaged. Grades 3–8.

Zachary goes to the special "Egypt of the Pharaohs" exhibit with his parents and his spooky old great aunt, Allie, who has, it seems, unusual talents and mysterious powers.

Allie and Zachary are suddenly sent through time, in the company of a mysterious cat—probably the mummified one they saw on a desk in the "Staff Only" area. Khi, the cat, tells Zachary that he serves the scarab amulet Aunt Allie always wears and takes him on a tour of the pyramids and an educational lesson on how they were built.

Share these facts with your readers:

- The Egyptians believed that the body had to last for all eternity because it was always the home for the soul, no matter how often the soul left it.

- The priests who made mummies pulled out the body's brain through the nose, using a special hook.

- Falcons, crocodiles, and jackals were also mummified.

This colorful book is packed with illustrations and extraordinary information.

Jeffrey, Gary, and Kate Petty. *Julius Caesar: The Life of a Roman General* (Graphic Nonfiction). Illustrated by Sam Hadley. Rosen, 2005. ISBN 1404202390. 48 p. Grades 4–up.

Boys might have heard the name Julius Caesar, but who was he? And what did he do? This book looks like a comic, but it is filled with excellent information about one of the most famous people of all time.

Julius was born in Rome more than 2,100 years ago. His family was fairly important, but he wanted power—and lots of it. And he was not too fussy about how he got it. Taking it by force worked fine for him.

He was a power-hungry man. He wanted to be in charge of everything—to be treated as the most important person in the whole Roman Empire, to conquer unconquered lands, and to destroy all of his enemies.

And he pretty much got what he wished for.

This is the story of the battles he fought and the power he struggled for—and, in the end, died for. Show boys the comic format, and they will be hooked.

Lawton, Clive. *Hiroshima: The Story of the First Atom Bomb*. Candlewick Press, 2004. ISBN 0763622710. 48 p. Grades 4–8.

In 1905, Albert Einstein published his theory of relativity, which claimed that huge amounts of energy are locked inside atoms. In the years to come, scientists proved that the theory was correct. They discovered that by splitting an atom of the metal uranium, they could start a chain reaction that would release huge amounts of power.

By 1938, the Nazis in Germany, from whom Einstein had fled, were invading various parts of Europe. Einstein was worried that they might make a bomb based on his theory. He wrote a letter to U.S. President Franklin Roosevelt urging him to beat Germany in the race to build a bomb.

Roosevelt approved the plan, and in December 1941, he implemented it after Pearl Harbor was attacked and the United States was pulled into World War II. A group of scientists lived and worked in Los Alamos, New Mexico, studying how to make the bomb.

This book describes the beginnings of the project, how conflicted the scientists felt when they realized what they were creating, and how the decision was made to use the bomb to end the war in August 1945 when the United States dropped two bombs on Japan.

There are all sorts of interesting facts to share with your listeners, such as the following:

- The attack on Pearl Harbor made many Americans hate all Japanese people.

- The Japanese treatment of their prisoners, Americans and their allies, made people furious. Germany treated its prisoners much better than the Japanese treated theirs.

- Japan used kamikaze pilots, whose goal was to commit suicide by flying into enemy ships. Unless you could shoot them down, they were very effective, and many Americans died because of their attacks.

- Scientists were not sure that the bombing crew would not blow up when the atom bomb they dropped exploded.

It is a fascinating book with many photographs to pull in young readers.

How to Be a Medieval Knight
by Fiona MacDonald.

MacDonald, Fiona. *How to Be a Medieval Knight* (How to Be series). Illustrated by Mark Bergin. National Geographic, 2005. ISBN 079223619x. 32 p. Grades 3–8.

What was it really like to be a knight? Was it fun? Glamorous? Exciting?

This book tells us what the job requirements were to be a knight, what kinds of knights there were—and the fact that you needed a lot of money if you wanted to be a knight.

A knight had to be:

• A boy (Forget about it, girls, women were not knights)

• Pretty well off or, better yet, rich

• Well trained—they had to do a lot of grunt work to work their way up to knighthood

You had to have the right equipment: armor, weapons, horses, a tent, and baggage. And you had to pay for the equipment for the soldiers who went off to war with you, too.

You had to be really tough and not think too much about all the damage you were doing to the lives of the innocent people—like the peasants whose food was taken so you and your men could eat, knowing the peasants would starve.

This book tells about the different kinds of fights knights were involved in and the weapons they used. In general, it provides a lot of good information about what it took to be a knight.

Millman, Isaac. *Hidden Child*. Frances Foster Books/Farrar, Straus & Giroux, 2005. ISBN 0374330719. 73 p. Grades 3–up.

The cover of this book shows a photograph of a little boy set inside a drawing of a six-pointed gold star. That boy is Jewish, and that boy grew up to be an artist who tells us the story of his hidden childhood in this amazing book.

Isaac Millman lived in Paris with his beloved mother and father, but when he was seven years old, the Nazis invaded the city, and they started making life difficult for Jewish people. There were all sorts of new laws that said Jewish people could not go to the movies, or the park, or shop until almost all of the food in the stores was gone.

It was not long before the Nazis came and arrested Isaac's father, who was sent to a prison camp in France, and then to the infamous Auschwitz concentration camp.

Isaac's mother tried to escape to a safe part of France with her son, but she did not make it. Isaac was left all alone, with no one, it seemed, to help him—until he met a wonderful woman, also Jewish, who helped him go into hiding to survive World War II.

This is an incredible, true story. Show your listeners any one of the author's full-page spreads of artwork.

Remember World War II: Kids Who Survived Tell Their Stories by **Dorinda Makanaonalani Nicholson.**

Nicholson, Dorinda Makanaonalani. *Remember World War II: Kids Who Survived Tell Their Stories*. National Geographic, 2005. ISBN 0792271793. 60 p. Grades 4–up.

Who is a better person to write about what it is like to be a kid during a war than a person who was a kid during a war?

Author Dorinda Makanaonalani lived in Hawaii and was six years old when the Japanese attacked Pearl Harbor, so she knows what it was like. She talked to lots of other people who were also kids during the war, and in this interesting book, she shares some of their stories.

Kathy's All-Time Favorite Nonfiction Books to Booktalk to Boys

- Lauber, Patricia. *What You Never Knew about Tubs, Toilets, and Showers.*

- Settel, Joanne, Ph.D. *Exploding Ants: Amazing Facts about How Animals Adapt.*

- Jackson, Donna M. *The Wildlife Detectives: How Forensic Scientists Fight Crimes against Nature.*

- Yolen, Jane, and Heidi Elisabet Yolen Stemple. *The* Mary Celeste: *An Unsolved Mystery from History.*

- Goodman, Susan E. *The Truth about Poop.*

- Jackson, Donna M. *The Bone Detectives: How Forensic Anthropologists Solve Crimes and Uncover Mysteries of the Dead.*

- Capuzzo, Michael. *Close to Shore: The Terrifying Shark Attacks of 1916.*

- Lauber, Patricia. *The True-or-False Book of Dogs.*

- Crowe, Chris. *Getting Away with Murder: The True Story of the Emmett Till Case.*

- Walker, Sally M. *Secrets of a Civil War Submarine: Solving the Mysteries of the H. L. Hunley.*

- Sloan, Christopher. *How Dinosaurs Took Flight: The Fossils, the Science, What We Think We Know, and the Mysteries Yet Unsolved.*

From *Gotcha for Guys! Nonfiction Books to Get Boys Excited About Reading* by Kathleen A. Baxter and Marcia Agness Kochel. Westport, CT: Libraries Unlimited. Copyright © 2007.

Hedi Wachenheimer, who was Jewish and lived in Germany, had to leave her parents and go to England on the Kindertransport, which was a way to take Jewish children out of Germany to protect them from the Nazis. She never saw her parents again—they died at Auschwitz.

Fred Losch had to join the Hitler Youth.

Solange Berger was five years old when the Nazis invaded her hometown in Belgium. She and her family tried to leave, but there was no place to go. They went back to their home and had to share it with Nazi officers for almost five years.

Fourteen-year-old Lilly Lebovitz spent years at Auschwitz.

In the Philippines, Joy Crichton and her British family were put into an interment camp when the Japanese invaded. They spent the next three and a half years there, with barely enough to eat and in terrible living conditions

In the United States, citizens of Japanese descent, such as seventh-grader Allan Hida, were moved into camps in remote places. The U.S. government was afraid these people would spy on and injure the country.

Readers will identify with these young people and hope that they never have to survive a war.

Provensen, Alice. *Klondike Gold.* Simon & Schuster Books for Young Readers, 2005. ISBN 0689848854. Unpaged. Grades 4–up.

Slightly fictionalized, *Klondike Gold* is based on the true story of a young American, Bill Howell, whose friend Joe talked him into going with him in the Klondike Gold Rush in 1897.

Hardly anyone even really knew where the Klondike was, but Joe and Bill were game. They were going to be rich!

But to get rich, they had to spend a lot of money just getting to the Klondike and invest a lot of money in basic supplies. Think of carrying around with you things like 200 pounds of beans, two 80-pound boxes of candles, 40 pounds of salt, 30 pounds of nails, and a lot more (see the list on the third double-page spread). And to get to the Klondike in below-zero weather, climbing up mountains and crossing frozen lakes, was hard, hard work. Many gave up, and many died.

This is an amazing story, with a surprising ending and lots of good pictures to show to young readers.

Ross, Stewart. *Ancient Rome* (Tales of the Dead). Illustrated by Inklink & Richard Bonson. DK, 2005. ISBN 0756611474. 32 p. Grades 3–8.

This book is just jam-packed with interesting information.

First of all, if you follow along the sides and the bottom of the pages, you will see a story about two kids from Africa whose father served with the Roman army and is now lucky to be a Roman citizen. Right off the bat, the kids are in big trouble when their village is attacked and it looks as though their father is dead. They are taken away to be sold as slaves—and the chance of escape is almost zero.

Featured above and between the text are a lot of information about and pictures of the ancient Roman Empire—how and where people lived, how they stored and prepared their food, how they fought, how they traveled, how slaves lived, and a lot, lot more.

It is a fun look at an incredibly interesting time in world history. Show any one of the two-page spreads to entice your readers.

Whiteman, Dorit Bader. *Lonek's Journey: The True Story of a Boy's Escape to Freedom.* Star Bright Books, 2005. ISBN 1595720219. 141 p. Grades 5–8.

In August 1939 in a town called Jaroslaw, Poland, an eleven-year-old boy named Lonek found that his life had changed permanently.

Lonek's father warned him that the Germans—the Nazis—were stationing troops on the Polish border, and it looked as though Germany might invade Poland. His father dressed in a soldier's uniform, and the family worried because they knew that Hitler, Germany's leader, hated Jewish people—and Lonek's family was Jewish.

The worst happened. The Nazis invaded on September 1 and promptly defeated the Poles. Lonek's father was missing for a few days then showed up at home worried sick about the family's safety. He arranged to escape from the prison area where the Nazis put him, and then he got his family away with him into hiding.

But hiding was a dicey thing. It was not safe anywhere. The family kept moving on and eventually ended up in the horribly crowded Lvov, Poland, as refugees. There they lived in a room that held sixty people. And there, in the middle of the night, in June 1941, they were ordered out of their room and onto the cattle car of a crowded, filthy train headed for a prison in Siberia. The Russians had captured them, and they were warned that no one ever escaped from the Gulag, as the Russian prison system was called.

Lonek had begun his journey, but he had much further to go before he could be free and happy and have enough to eat.

This is an amazing true story about a kid who had to do everything he could just to survive—including separate from his beloved family.

NOT TO BE MISSED

Adler, David. *Child of the Warsaw Ghetto.* Illustrated by Karen Ritz. Holiday House, 1995. ISBN 0823410919. 32 p. Grades 3–8. *Gotcha.*

This is the story of Froim Baum, a poor Jewish boy who had to work hard from a very young age to help support his family. Conditions went from bad to worse when the Nazis invaded Poland and he was put in a ghetto, and then in one concentration camp after another. Despite all of this, he managed to survive and come to live in the United States.

Adler, David A. *Hilde and Eli: Children of the Holocaust.* Illustrated by Karen Ritz. Holiday House, 1994. ISBN 0823410919. 32 p. Grades 3–8. *Gotcha.*

This is the story of two children who did not survive the Holocaust. We know of Hilde and Eli because their siblings told us about them. Good pictures accompany the horrifying story.

Aliki. *William Shakespeare & the Globe.* HarperCollins, 1999. ISBN 006027820X. 48 p. Grades 3–8. *Gotcha Again.*

Most kids probably don't realize that, to the world, William Shakespeare is still a mystery man. And most kids probably think he is boring. But open this book, start reading, and you will be delighted at the man, the story, and the wonderful words he was the first to use or invent. An attractive and entertaining introduction to the world of Shakespeare.

Ash, Russell. *Great Wonders of the World.* Illustrated by Richard Bonson. DK, 2000. ISBN 0789465051. 64 p. Grades 4–up. *Gotcha Again.*

A long time ago, writers chose the "Seven Wonders of the World." Only one of those ancient constructions is still standing. Can your listeners guess which one? Ash describes all seven of them and then compares them to modern wonders of the world. With lots of pictures, this is a great book for browsing.

Berger, Melvin, and Gilda Berger. *The Real Vikings: Craftsmen, Trades, and Fearsome Raiders.* National Geographic, 2003. ISBN 0792251326. 60 p. Grades 4–9. *Gotcha Covered.*

The legend of the Vikings is a fierce one, probably because they scared the living daylights out of a lot of people during the Middle Ages. But they were more than fierce warriors and raiders. They had a unique and rich culture, and their influence is still felt in many of the words we use today. Excellent photographs to entice young readers.

Blacklock, Dyan. *The Roman Army: The Legendary Soldiers Who Created an Empire.* Illustrations by David Kennett. Walker, ISBN 0802788963. 48 p. Grades 4–9. *Gotcha Covered.*

It looks like a comic book—graphic nonfiction at its best—but it tells, in interesting detail, the story of the greatest army in the ancient world and what life for the troops was like.

Blumberg, Rhoda. *Shipwrecked: The True Adventures of a Japanese Boy*. HarperCollins, 2001. ISBN 0688174841. 80 p. Grades 4–8. *Gotcha Covered.*

Alas, they are not going to pick up this one by themselves, but the ones whom you can talk into giving it a try will be surprised at what a ripping good true story this is. A teenage Japanese boy is shipwrecked in the mid-1800s, picked up by an American whaling ship, and embarks on an astonishing new life.

Bramwell, Martyn. *Polar Exploration: Journeys to the Arctic and Antarctic.* Illustrated by Marje Crosby-Fairall and Ann Winterbotham. DK, 1998. ISBN 0789434210. 48 p. Grades 4–8. *Gotcha Again.*

Kids who are interested in the polar regions of the globe will be delighted by this browsing book detailing the history of our coldest areas and expedition members who have tried (and sometimes failed) to discover its mysteries. Includes lots of photos.

Coburn, Broughton. *Triumph on Everest: A Photobiography of Sir Edmund Hillary*. National Geographic Society, 2000. ISBN 0792271149. 64 p. Grades 4–8. *Gotcha Again.*

With his Sherpa guide Tenzing Norgay, a New Zealander named Edmund Hillary (who had been a weird kid) climbed the world's tallest mountain, Mount Everest. Norgay and Hillary were the first in history to reach the summit, and Sir Edmund was made a British knight, while Tenzing Norgay was pretty much ignored. Hillary thought this was wrong and has spent much of his life trying to help the Sherpas. This photobiography has lots of visual appeal.

Cooper, Margaret. *Exploring the Ice Age*. Atheneum Books for Young Readers, 2001. 0689825560 93 p. Grades 4–8. *Gotcha Covered.*

The cavemen were a lot more developed and creative than a lot of us ever imagine. About thirty-five thousand years ago, during the first Ice Age, they were living well in incredibly cold conditions in much of the world (Manhattan Island lay under a thousand-foot sheet of ice) and even creating art. An excellent look at a fascinating topic.

Corbishley, Mike. *The World of Architectural Wonders*. Peter Bedrick Books, 1996. ISBN 0872262790. 45 p. Grades 3–8. *Gotcha Again.*

This book contains color photos and drawings of some of the most amazing sites in the world, including some that are not well known: the city of Petra in Jordan, the Great Zimbabwe, and many more. Corbishley tells us how and why these structures were built.

Drez, Ronald J. *Remember D-Day: The Plan, the Invasion, Survivor Stories.* National Geographic, 2004. ISBN 079226668. 60 p. Grades 4–9. *Gotcha Covered.*

The story of the D-Day invasion and the events leading up to it is told irresistibly here. Filled with great information and loaded with wonderful photographs, this is a history and military buff's dream book.

Giblin, James Cross. *Secrets of the Sphinx.* Illustrated by Bagram Ibatoulline. Scholastic, 2004. ISBN 0590098470. Unpaged. Grades 4–8. *Gotcha Covered.*

When Jesus Christ was born, the Sphinx was already 2,500 years old. It has been staring across the desert for thousands of years, but, alas, the desert is no longer so empty. Now it stares about two hundred yards before it sees souvenir shops and hotels. This is the story of its construction and its hastening destruction, largely due to environmental issues. Lots of pictures illuminate the story.

Giblin, James Cross. *The Life and Death of Adolf Hitler.* Clarion Books, 2002. ISBN 0395903718. 256 p. Grades 5–up. *Gotcha Covered.*

The winner of the Sibert Award for the best nonfiction book of the year, this is a compelling, readable biography of one of the most horrifying men in history. It's not an easy read, but it's a fine one.

Gold, Alison Leslie. *A Special Fate. Chiune Sugihara: Hero of the Holocaust.* Scholastic, 2000. ISBN 0590395254. 176 p. Grades 5–8. *Gotcha Again.*

Chiune Sugihara was the Japanese consul in Lithuania, but he had a lot in common with the more well-known hero of the Holocaust, Oskar Schindler. Both tried to save the lives of the people the Nazis hated most—the Jewish people. Sugihara made a hard decision—he would save as many Jews as he could, and he knew he would probably be punished for that decision. He wrote about six thousand visas that enabled the Jews to leave Lithuania, where they would have certainly been killed. A powerful true story with lots of photographs and illustrations.

Jenkins, Steve. *The Top of the World: Climbing Mount Everest.* Houghton Mifflin, 1999. ISBN 0395942187. Unpaged. Grades 3–8. *Gotcha Again.*

A lot of people who set out to climb Mount Everest never make it to the top—and a significant percentage of them die while trying. This is a picture book with great color illustrations, but it also has riveting factual information about the mountain, the cold, and the difficulty of the climb.

Kaplan, William, with Shelley Tanaka. *One More Border: The True Story of One Family's Escape from War-Torn Europe.* Illustrated by Stephen Taylor. Groundwood Books, 1998. ISBN 0888993323. 60 p. Grades 3–8. *Gotcha Again.*

This is a true story about a Jewish family that was helped by Chiune Sugihara, a Japanese official who gave the father and his two sons exit visas. Through a combination of circumstances, the mother did not get one. She escaped—but would any other country let her in? One of the sons who escaped wrote this suspenseful account of their adventure.

Kent, Peter. *Go to Jail! A Look at Prisons through the Ages.* Millbrook Press, 1998. ISBN 0761304029. 30 p. Grades 3–8. *Gotcha Again.*

The history of prisons is not pleasant. In general, conditions today are better than in the past, but most of us would just as soon never be a prisoner. This shows pictures of some of the worst prison conditions of the past, and each two-page spread includes a "find-the-prisoner" game that will delight readers.

Krull, Kathleen. *They Saw the Future: Oracles, Psychics, Scientists, Great Thinkers, and Pretty Good Guessers.* Illustrated by Kyrsten Brooker. Atheneum Books for Young Readers, 1999. ISBN 0689812957. 108 p. Grades 5–8. *Gotcha Again.*

It would be a wonderfully handy skill to be able to predict the future, and a lot of people have become famous for their seeming ability to do just that. The only trouble is that most of them were wrong at least as often as they were right. But this is a fun book with humorous illustrations and a lot of interesting facts that will make anyone wonder.

Langley, Andrew, and Philip de Souza. *The Roman News.* Candlewick Press, 1996. ISBN 0763600555. 32 p. Grades 4–8. *Gotcha.*

This is so jam-packed with facts about ancient Roman life that you'll have a hard time putting it down. In the form of a newspaper, including ads, it gives us all sorts of excellent information.

Lawton, Clive. *Auschwitz.* Candlewick Press, 2002. ISBN 0763615951. 48 p. Grades 4–8. *Gotcha Covered.*

Auschwitz was the most infamous of the Nazi death camps, and this book is loaded with horrifying photographs, many from an album rescued by a Jewish prisoner on the day the concentration camp was liberated by American soldiers. It is filled with compelling information on a horrifying topic.

Lekuton, Joseph Lemasolai, with Herman Viola. *Facing the Lion: Growing Up Maasai on the African Savanna.* National Geographic, 2003. ISBN 0792251253. 127 p. Grades 5–8.

This autobiography draws readers in with descriptions of life in Kenya for a Maasai boy. Lekuton's quest for an education and his eventual graduation from Harvard are an inspiration to children of all ages.

Levine, Ellen. *Darkness over Denmark: The Danish Resistance and the Rescue of the Jews.* Holiday House, 2000. ISBN 082341477. 164 p. Grades 5–up. *Gotcha Again.*

The Danes were extraordinary in their efforts to protect their fellow citizens, the Jewish people that Hitler's invading Nazis despised and wished to exterminate. This is their story and the story of the Resistance movement that helped defeat the German army.

Logan, Claudia. *The 5,000-Year-Old Puzzle: Solving a Mystery of Ancient Egypt.* Illustrated by Melissa Sweet. Melanie Kroupa Books, Farrar, Straus & Giroux, 2002. ISBN 374323356. 41 p. Grades 3–8. *Gotcha Covered.*

In the 1920s, searching for mummies was all the rage, inspired by interest in King Tut's tomb. Young Will Hunt joins his archaeologist parents on a trip to Egypt to do a dig, and learns all sorts of interesting things—including how boring a lot of the expedition can be. Grand, colorful illustrations show us what the dig was like in this mixture of fact and fiction.

Lourie, Peter. *The Mystery of the Maya: Uncovering the Lost City of Palenque.* Boyds Mills Press, 2001. ISBN 1563978393. 48 p. Grades 4–up. *Gotcha Covered.*

The Mayan Indians built the city of Palenque in what is now central Mexico in around A.D. 431 and abandoned it in 799. It is enormous, and little of it has been excavated. Lourie assisted with a recent dig and took many fine photographs. Budding archaeologists will be entranced.

Lourie, Peter. *Tierra del Fuego: A Journey to the End of the Earth.* Boyds Mills Press, 2002. ISBN 156397973X. 48 p. Grades 4–8. *Gotcha Covered.*

The legendary Tierra del Fuego is the tip of South America. It is as close to Antarctica as you can get without actually being there, and it is a remote land with terrible weather and dangerous waters. Lourie took this journey by ship and tells an exciting story of the journey, illustrated with many beautiful photographs.

Mann, Elizabeth. *Machu Picchu: The Story of the Amazing Inkas and Their City in the Clouds* (A Wonders of the World Book). With illustrations by Amy Crehore. Mikaya Press, 2000. ISBN 0965049396. 48 p. Grades 4–8. *Gotcha Again.*

Many people believe that Machu Picchu, the city in the clouds, is one of the most beautiful places on Earth. Built by early inhabitants of the Andes Mountains, it was never destroyed by the Spaniards because they never found it. Hardly anyone but the local natives even remembered that the ruins were there until it was discovered by an archaeologist in 1911—and pretty soon the rest of the world wanted to see it, too. This is its story.

Mann, Elizabeth. *The Panama Canal: The Story of How a Jungle Was Conquered and the World Made Smaller* (A Wonders of the World Book). With illustrations by Fernando Rangel. Mikaya Press, 1998. ISBN 0965049345. 48 p. Grades 4–8. Gotcha Again.

After people started settling the west coast of the United States, travelers faced a huge problem. Before the railroad connected east and west, all travel had to be done by horse or foot. It took a long time. Another option was to go by sea, but look at a map: any ship that needed to get to the Pacific Ocean from the Atlantic Ocean (or vice versa) had to go all the way around the huge continent of South America. There was one narrow place, the Isthmus of Panama, where everyone wanted to build a canal, but it seemed impossible—there was too much disease, too much heat, too much jungle in the area. This is the story, with lots of pictures, of the staggeringly difficult building of the Panama Canal.

Mann, Elizabeth. *The Great Pyramid: The Story of the Farmers, the God-King and the Most Astounding Structure Ever Built.* Illustrated by Laura Lo Turco. Mikaya Press, 1996. ISBN 0965049302. 48 p. Grades 3–8. *Gotcha.*

Huge, colorful pictures, including foldouts, add enormously to the entertainment value of this enlightening book, which explains exactly how the pyramids were made and who built them (it wasn't slaves).

Mann, Elizabeth. *The Great Wall: The Story of 4,000 Miles of Earth and Stone That Turned a Nation into a Fortress.* Illustrated by Alan Witschonke. Mikaya Press, 1996. ISBN 0965049329. 48 p. Grades 3–8. *Gotcha.*

Thirty feet high and thousands of miles long, the Great Wall of China is so big that many people lived and worked on it to defend the borders of their country. This is its story, including the information that today most of the wall is gone, eroded and ruined.

Mann, Elizabeth. *The Roman Colosseum: The Story of the World's Most Famous Stadium and Its Deadly Games* (A Wonders of the World Book). With illustrations by Michael Racz. Mikaya Press, 1998. ISBN 0965049337. 48 p. Grades 3–8. *Gotcha Again.*

It's one of the most famous buildings of all time, and it is still there, although it is almost two thousand years old. It is the Colosseum, in Rome, and building it was an extraordinary feat, especially so long ago. But it was built, and it hosted fifty thousand people being entertained by gladiators killing each other and other gory games. This is the story of the building and its construction, with lots of excellent pictures.

McDonough, Yona Zeldis. *Peaceful Protest: The Life of Nelson Mandela.* Illustrations by Malcah Zeldis. Walker, 2002. ISBN 0802788211. Unpaged. Grades 2–8. *Gotcha Covered.*

A fighter, a dreamer, a leader, Nelson Mandela spent much of his life in prison, suffering because of his political belief that the native people of South Africa deserved to be treated equally with the white people who had taken over their land. Lots of color pictures help tell us the almost unbelievable story of his life.

Meltzer, Milton. *Piracy and Plunder: A Murderous Business.* Illustrated by Bruce Waldman. Dutton Children's Books, 2001. ISBN 0525458573. 96 p. Grades 4–up. *Gotcha Covered.*

The stories that make pirates look glamorous are wrong—completely wrong. They were common criminals, with no sense of honor. In fact, most money pirates made was from selling slaves. The truth about the pirate life is better than the stories.

Marcia's All-Time Favorite Nonfiction Books to Booktalk to Middle School Boys

- Jackson, Donna M. *The Bone Detectives: How Forensic Anthropologists Solve Crimes and Uncover Mysteries of the Dead.*

- Armstrong, Jennifer. *Shipwreck at the Bottom of the World: The Extraordinary True Story of Shackleton and the* Endurance.

- Nelson, Pete. *Left for Dead: A Young Man's Search for Justice for the USS* Indianapolis.

- Warren, Andrea. *Surviving Hitler: A Boy in the Nazi Death Camps.*

- Paulsen, Gary. *Guts: The True Stories Behind Hatchet and the Brian Books.*

- Fulghum, Hunter S. *Don't Try This at Home.*

- Jackson, Donna M. *ER Vets: Life in an Animal Emergency Room.*

- Crowe, Chris. *Getting Away with Murder: The True Story of the Emmett Till Case.*

- Lekuton, Joseph Lemasolai, with Herman Viola. *Facing the Lion: Growing Up Maasai on the African Savanna.*

From *Gotcha for Guys! Nonfiction Books to Get Boys Excited About Reading* by Kathleen A. Baxter and Marcia Agness Kochel. Westport, CT: Libraries Unlimited. Copyright © 2007.

Millard, Anne. *A Street through Time: A 12,000 Year Walk through History.* Illustrated by Steve Noon. DK, 1998. ISBN 0789434261. 32 p. Grades 4–up. *Gotcha Again.*

You can spend a long time engrossed in this book. Starting with a two-page spread of a settlement of Stone Age people along a riverbank, it takes the same place and depicts it at different times throughout its history. In every picture, can you find Henry Hyde, a modern-day traveler who gets to see the place in all of the scenes.

Nir, Yehuda. *The Lost Childhood: A World War II Memoir.* Scholastic, 2002. ISBN 0439163897. 284 p. Grades 5–up. *Gotcha Covered.*

Polish, Jewish, and eleven years old, Yehuda Nir was definitely in the wrong place at the wrong time in 1941. After his father disappeared in 1941, he, his mother, and his sister went into hiding—but what was extraordinary is that they hid in the open. They pretended to be Catholics and managed to survive the war.

O'Connor, Jane. *The Emperor's Silent Army: Terracotta Warriors of Ancient China.* Viking, 2002. ISBN 0670035122. 48 p. Grades 3–8. *Gotcha Covered.*

In 1974, a Chinese peasant farmer digging in a field made one of the most important discoveries of all time. He found the pottery head of a soldier, and, when the archaeologists came to investigate, they found an unbelievable treasure—seven thousand life-sized soldiers, each different from the others, buried in the tomb of an emperor. Color photographs show us the amazing sight.

Robertshaw, Andrew. *A Soldier's Life: A Visual History of Soldiers through the Ages.* Lodestar/Dutton, 1997. ISBN 0525675507. 48 p. Grades 4–8. *Gotcha.*

A great browsing book, this shows what soldiers wore through the ages, what they ate, and what kind of weapons they used.

Rumford, James. *Seeker of Knowledge: The Man Who Deciphered Egyptian Hieroglyphs.* Houghton Mifflin, 2000. ISBN 039597934x. Unpaged. Grades 3–8. *Gotcha Covered.*

Jean-Francois Champollion was only eleven years old when he discovered his life's work. While visiting a famous scientist who had been in Egypt with Napoleon's army, he saw a house stuffed with Egyptian treasures, many of which had something that was obviously writing on them. But no one could read that writing, and Jean-Francois made up his mind that he would be the man who would figure it all out—and he did just that, although it took him many years to achieve his goal.

Salkeld, Audrey. *Climbing Everest: Tales of Triumph and Tragedy on the World's Highest Mountain.* National Geographic, 2003. ISBN 0792251059. 128 p. Grades 4–8. *Gotcha Covered.*

For decades people were not even sure you could climb Mount Everest. If you got up that high, would you just die? Today many people have climbed the mountain successfully, but many have also died in the attempt. *National Geographic*'s wonderful photographs help tell the incredible story of the successful—and failed—attempts.

St. George, Judith. *So You Want to Be an Explorer?* Illustrated by David Small. Philomel Books, 2005. ISBN 0399238689. 53 p. Grades 2–8.

In the style of the Caldecott-Medal-winning *So You Want to Be President?* St. George cheerfully describes what it takes to be a successful explorer. "Explorers have a middle name—Curiosity," she tells us on page 12. They are enthusiastic, determined risk takers, and they need maps—just as mapmakers need them. Good ones respect the natives and learn from them. Some of them make great discoveries and do not even realize what they have discovered (think Christopher Columbus). David Small's delightful illustrations add zest and humor to the mix.

Stanley, Diane. *Michelangelo*. HarperCollins, 2000. ISBN 0688150861. Unpaged. Grades 4–8. *Gotcha Again.*

    Michelangelo was dirty, smelly, and hard to get along with. He was stubborn and rebellious. And he was one of the greatest geniuses of all time. He considered himself a sculptor first and foremost, but his painting of the Sistine Chapel ceiling is one of the most famous works of art in the world. This is a beautifully illustrated book about an extraordinary man.

Stanley, Diane. *Saladin: Noble Prince of Islam.* HarperCollins, 2002. ISBN 0688171354. Unpaged. Grades 4–8. *Gotcha Covered.*

    Kids who love knights and crusades will be drawn to this colorful biography of Saladin, the most famous warrior of his time. He beat the crusaders in 1185. This book looks like a collection of Persian miniatures.

Steele, Philip. *Knights.* Kingfisher, 1998. ISBN 0753451549. 64 p. Grades 4–up. *Gotcha Again.*

    A lot of boys find the subject of knights mesmerizing, and this is filled with colorful, useful information—how knights lived, how they rode, how they got their armor, and more.

Tanaka, Shelley. *D-Day: They Fought to Free Europe from Hitler's Tyranny: A Day That Changed America.* Paintings by David Craig. Historical Consultation by Joseph Balkoski. Hyperion Books for Children/A Hyperion/Madison Press Book, 2003. ISBN 0786818816. 48 p. Grades 4–8. *Gotcha Covered.*

    The stories of some of the individual soldiers as well as of the overall invasion plan and the events of the day are told with excellent photographs and compelling illustrations.

Tanaka, Shelley. *In the Time of Knights: The Real-Life Story of History's Greatest Knights.* Illustrations by Greg Ruhl. A Hyperion/Madison Press Book, 2000. ISBN 0786806516. 48 p. Grades 4–6. *Gotcha Again.*

    Loaded with color illustrations, this tells the story of one of the most remarkable knights ever to carry a sword, William Marshal, born in 1146.

Tanaka, Shelley. *Lost Temple of the Aztecs.* Illustrations by Greg Ruhl. A Hyperion/Madison Press Book, 1998. ISBN 0786804416. 48 p. Grades 4–6. *Gotcha Again.*

    In 1519, a group of Spaniards led by Hernando Cortes marched into what is now Mexico and were welcomed as gods. The Aztecs had made a terrible mistake: the men they originally believed to be gods destroyed their city and their civilization. The great temple of Tenochtitlan was destroyed and buried in what is today Mexico City.

Warren, Andrea. *Escape from Saigon: How a Vietnam War Orphan Became an American Boy.* Melanie Kroupa Books/Farrar Straus & Giroux, 2004. ISBN 0374322244. 110 p. Grades 4–8. *Gotcha Covered.*

    The son of an unknown American soldier and a young Vietnamese woman, Long seemed destined to live in poverty in a war-torn country. But when he was seven years old he was taken to the United States at the end of the war in Vietnam, and he became an American boy. This one is hard to put down and is well illustrated with photographs.

Warren, Andrea. *Surviving Hitler: A Boy in the Nazi Death Camps.* HarperCollins, 2001. ISBN 0688174973. 144 p. Grades 4–8. *Gotcha Again.*

Jack Mandelbaum was only twelve years old when his life changed forever. Jack was Jewish, and the only member of his family to survive World War II, even though he spent years of it in a concentration camp. This is a riveting, eye-opening read for young people.

Watkins, Richard. *Gladiator.* Houghton Mifflin, 1998. ISBN 039582656x. 88 p. Grades 4–8. *Gotcha.*

A crowd pleaser from the word go, this not only tells who the gladiators were, what their lives were like, what they fought with, and what they wore but also includes a number of deliciously gruesome true stories from their horrible history.

Wright, Rachel. *The Viking News.* Candlewick Press, 1998. ISBN 076360450X. 32 p. Grades 4–up. *Gotcha Again.*

Looking somewhat like a color newspaper, this is filled with great facts about the warriors and other Vikings who terrified much of Europe for centuries. Read this book to find out what the word "berserk" means.

WORTH READING

Nonfiction books with "boy appeal" that have received positive reviews in *Booklist, Horn Book Guide,* and/or *School Library Journal.*

Adams, Simon. *Life in Ancient Rome* (Kingfisher Knowledge). Kingfisher, 2005. ISBN 0753458632. 64 p. Grades 4–6.

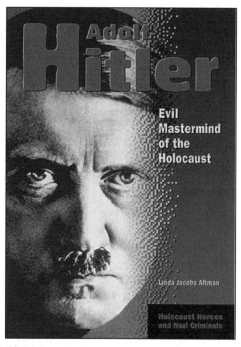

Adolf Hitler: Evil Mastermind of the Holocaust
by Linda Jacobs Altman.

Altman, Linda Jacobs. *Adolf Hitler: Evil Mastermind of the Holocaust* (Holocaust Heroes and Nazi Criminals). Enslow, 2005. ISBN 0766025330. 160 p. Grades 7–up.

Califf, David J. *Battle of Actium* (Great Battles through the Ages). Chelsea House, 2003. ISBN 0791074404. 118 p. Grades 5–up.

Chrisp, Peter. *Ancient Egypt Revealed*. DK, 2002. ISBN 0789488833. 38 p. Grades 4–up.

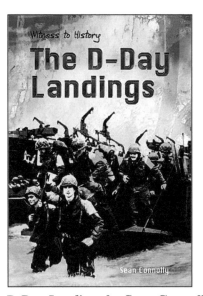

The D-Day Landings by Sean Connolly.

Connolly, Sean. *The D-Day Landings* (Witness to History). Heinemann Library, 2003. ISBN 1403445672. 56 p. Grades 4–8.

Crompton, Samuel Willard. *The Third Crusade: Richard the Lionhearted vs. Saladin* (Great Battles through the Ages). Chelsea House, 2003. ISBN 0791074374. 118 p. Grades 5–up.

The Colosseum by Leslie DuTemple.

DuTemple, Leslie A. *The Colosseum* (Great Building Feats). Lerner, 2003. ISBN 0822546930. 96 p. Grades 4–8.

Farman, John. *The Short and Bloody History of Knights* (Short and Bloody Histories). Lerner, 2002. ISBN 0822508419. 96 p. Grades 4–8.

Farman, John. *The Short and Bloody History of Pirates* (Short and Bloody Histories). Lerner, 2002. ISBN 0822508397. 96 p. Grades 4–8.

Farman, John. *The Short and Bloody History of Spies* (Short and Bloody Histories). Lerner, 2002. ISBN 0822508451. 96 p. Grades 4–8.

Spies **by Clive Gifford.**

Gifford, Clive. *Spies* (Kingfisher Knowledge). Kingfisher, 2004. ISBN 0753457776. 64 p. Grades 4–8.

Grant, Neil. *Everyday Life in Ancient Rome* (Uncovering History). Illustrated by Manuela Cappon. Creative/Smart Apple, 2003. ISBN 1583402497. 46 p. Grades 4–8.

Grant, Neil. *Everyday Life of the Celts* (Uncovering History). Illustrated by Manuela Cappon. Creative/Smart Apple, 2003. ISBN 1583402527. 46 p. Grades 4–8.

Greenblatt, Miriam. *Charlemagne and the Early Middle Ages* (Rulers and Their Times). Benchmark Books, 2002. ISBN 0761414878. 80 p. Grades 4–8.

Harris, Nathaniel. *The Rise of Hitler* (Witness to History). Heinemann Library, 2004. ISBN 1403448663. 56 p. Grades 4–8.

Harward, Barnaby. *The Best Book of Pirates* (Best Book of). Kingfisher, 2002. ISBN 0753454491. 32 p. Grades 3–6.

Holub, Joan. *Valley of the Golden Mummies* (Smart about History). Grosset & Dunlap, 2002. ISBN 0448428172. 32 p. Grades 3–5.

Hooper, Meredith. *Stephen Biesty's Castles.* Illustrated by Stephen Biesty. Enchanted Lion, 2004. ISBN 1592700314. 48 p. Grades 3–up.

Hynes, Margaret. *The Best Book of Early People* (Best Book of). Kingfisher, 2003. ISBN 0753455773. 32 p. Grades 3–6.

Lassieur, Allison. *The Ancient Romans* (People of the Ancient World). Franklin Watts, 2004. ISBN 0531123383. 112 p. Grades 5–up.

Malam, John. *Gladiator: Life and Death in Ancient Rome* (DK Secret Worlds). DK, 2002. ISBN 078948532x. 96 p. Grades 4–up.

Malone, Caroline, and Nancy Stone Bernard. *Stonehenge* (Digging for the Past). Oxford University Press, 2002. ISBN 0195143140. 48 p. Grades 4–8.

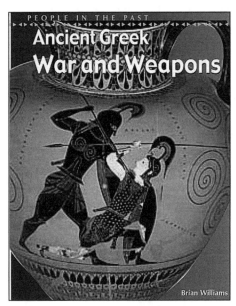

Ancient Greek War and Weapons
by Haydn Middleton.

Middleton, Haydn. *Ancient Greek War and Weapons* (People in the Past). Heinemann Library, 2002. ISBN 1588106357. 48 p. Grades 4–8.

Morris, Ann, and Heidi Larson. *Tsunami: Helping Each Other.* Millbrook Press, 2005. ISBN 0761395016. 48 p. Grades 2–4.

Shapiro, Stephen. *Battle Stations! Fortifications through the Ages.* Annick Press, 2005. ISBN 1550378899. 32 p. Grades 5–up.

Sherman, Josepha. *Your Travel Guide to Ancient Israel* (Passport to History). Lerner, 2003. ISBN 0822530724. 80 p. Grades 4–8.

Simon, Seymour. *Pyramids & Mummies* (See More Reader). Chronicle/Sea Star, 2004. ISBN 1587172402. 40 p. Grades K–3.

Solway, Andrew. *Rome: In Spectacular Cross-Section.* Illustrated by Stephen Biesty. Scholastic Press, 2003. ISBN 0439455464. 32 p. Grades 4–8.

Waldman, Neil. *Masada.* Boyds Mills Press, 2003. ISBN 1590780639. 64 p. Grades 4–8.

Walker, Kate. *Spies and Their Gadgets.* Creative/Smart Apple, 2003. ISBN 1583403418. 32 p. Grades 4-8.

Wheatley, Abigail, and Struan Reid. *The Usborne Introduction to Archaeology: Internet-Linked.* (Archaeology). EDC/Usborne, 2005. ISBN 0794508086. 128 p. Grades 6–9.

Woolf, Alex. *Assassination in Sarajevo: June 28, 1914* (Days That Shook the World). Raintree, 2003. ISBN 0739860488. 48 p. Grades 4–8.

Woolf, Alex. *Death and Disease* (Medieval Realms). Gale/Lucent, 2004. ISBN 1590185331. 48 p. Grades 5–up.

Worth, Richard. *Heinrich Himmler: Murderous Architect of the Holocaust* (Holocaust Heroes and Nazi Criminals). Enslow, 2005. ISBN 0766025322. 160 p. Grades 7–up.

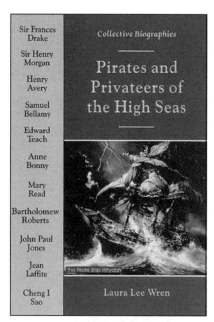

***Pirates and Privateers of the High Seas*
by Laura Lee Wren.**

Wren, Laura Lee. *Pirates and Privateers of the High Seas* (Collective Biographies). Enslow, 2003. ISBN 0766015424. 104 p. Grades 5–up.

Chapter 2

American History

There is much in American history to interest and excite boys. Often the trick to getting them reading is to stimulate some initial interest in the topic at hand. Get familiar with these history books, but when you talk about them to boys, focus not so much on the historical details as on the action, humor, and the occasional gore involved.

NEW AND NOTABLE

Armstrong, Jennifer. *Photo by Brady: A Picture of the Civil War.* Atheneum Books for Young Readers, 2005. ISBN 0689857853. 147 p. Grades 5–up.

If you know something about the U.S. Civil War, you probably know that Matthew Brady took amazing documentary photographs of it and that it was the first American war to be photographed.

The second half of that sentence is true. The first is not.

Matthew Brady was a famous photographer who decided early on that he was going to photograph history. He lived in New York City and was renowned for his portraits of famous people. He was a real artist who took great photographs. But by the time the Civil War started, Brady was having major problems with his vision, and most of the famous photographs we see were, in fact, taken by photographers working in his studio or by competitors. The legend of Brady photographs became so huge, though, that most of us believe he himself took most of the photographs.

It was hard work to take those photographs. There were no such things as action shots. The picture-taking process lasted at least thirty seconds, which seems like forever when you're trying to stand still. People had to have their heads clamped so they would not accidentally move them when they were being photographed!

Photography was still new and untested, and not only was taking the pictures difficult, but finding the right light to take the pictures was iffy, and developing and hauling around the equipment was a complicated and time-consuming process.

This book is loaded with a lot of those Civil War photographs. Most of them were staged. The photographers frequently posed dead bodies to get a good effect. This is loaded with great information.

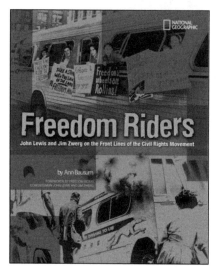

Freedom Riders: John Lewis and Jim Zwerg on the Front Lines of the Civil Rights Movement **by Ann Bausum.**

Bausum, Ann. *Freedom Riders: John Lewis and Jim Zwerg on the Front Lines of the Civil Rights Movement.* National Geographic, 2006. ISBN 0792241738. 80 p. Grades 5–up.

African Americans were ready for change. As long as they had been in America, they had faced discrimination. Although the Supreme Court had ordered the integration of the schools, conditions had not been improving very rapidly. African Americans were sick of being separate, not equal.

In 1960, African Americans—especially young African Americans—started taking real action. Doctor Martin Luther King, their most influential leader, urged nonviolence. No matter what happened to them, they decided, they would not react violently.

At first they started sitting at segregated lunch counters, quietly insisting on being served.

Then, in 1961, the Freedom Rides took place. Bus companies were still insisting that black passengers ride in the back of the bus and white passengers in front. If there were not enough seats, blacks had to give up theirs. Whites and blacks rode together through the deep South on a Freedom Ride to protest this policy, and John Lewis, a young African American (now a U.S. congressman) was the first to be beaten. One of the buses was burned in Anniston, Alabama.

On May 20, another bus drove from Birmingham to Montgomery, Alabama. John Lewis was back on the bus, and so was a young white man from Appleton, Wisconsin, named Jim Zwerg. The two young men were among those severely beaten when they arrived in Montgomery. Zwerg's suffering was especially disturbing to many Americans. No ambulance driver, white or black, would take him to a hospital—and no white hospital wanted him as a patient. He was afraid he would be lynched. He lay, beaten senseless, for more than two hours before someone finally found a hospital to accept him.

And that was just the beginning.

As the Freedom Riders increased their numbers and dedication, they put their names on pieces of paper inside their clothes in case they were killed—they wanted their bodies to be recognized. They knew when they got on a bus, that they were likely to be jailed, beaten, or killed for what they were doing. But they kept on doing it.

This is an incredible true story that you will have a hard time putting down.

Bobrick, Benson. *Fight for Freedom: The Remarkable Revolutionary War*. A Byron Preiss Visual Publications, Book/Atheneum Books for Young Readers, 2005. ISBN 0689864221. 96 p. Grades 4–up.

Kathy's Favorite American History Books to Booktalk

- Crowe, Chris. *Getting Away with Murder: The True Story of the Emmett Till Case.*

- Bausum, Ann. *Freedom Riders: John Lewis and Jim Zwerg on the Front Lines of the Civil Rights Movement.*

- Fradin, Dennis. *Bound for the North Star: True Stories of Fugitive Slaves.*

- Chandra, Deborah, and Madeleine Comora. *George Washington's Teeth.*

- Drez, Ronald J. *Remember D-Day: The Plan, the Invasion, Survivor Stories.* National Geographic, 2004. ISBN 079226668. 60 p. Grades 4–9. *Gotcha Covered.*

- Fradin, Dennis Brindell. *The Signers: The Fifty-Six Stories behind the Declaration of Independence.*

- Krull, Kathleen. *Harvesting Hope: The Story of Cesar Chavez.*

- Schanzer, Rosalyn. *George vs. George: The American Revolution as Seen from Both Sides.*

- Walker, Sally M. *Secrets of a Civil War Submarine: Solving the Mysteries of the* H.L. Hunley.

- Warren, Andrea. *We Rode the Orphan Trains.*

From *Gotcha for Guys! Nonfiction Books to Get Boys Excited About Reading* by Kathleen A. Baxter and Marcia Agness Kochel. Westport, CT: Libraries Unlimited. Copyright © 2007.

If you are at all interested in the war that Colonial Americans fought against Great Britain to create a new country, completely different from the one that had ruled over them since the beginning, this is a fine place to start exploring that period in our history.

Each two-page spread has one colorful, fine picture that fills an entire page, and then a page of text and another illustration. Each of the important battles is described, and some surprising facts are offered:

- Six terrified British soldiers surrendered to an old woman who was digging up weeds near Concord, Massachusetts. This made the colonials laugh. They asked, "If an old lady can capture six [British soldiers], how many soldiers will King George need to conquer America?" (page 12).

- Three whole British regiments were made up entirely of criminals who were pardoned for their crimes upon enlisting.

- Benjamin Franklin's home in Philadelphia was sacked by the British. They took away all of his scientific instruments and much of his library.

- Nathanael Greene was considered the best American general, second only to George Washington. He said, "We fight, get beat, rise, and fight again" (page 84). It was not a glamorous strategy, but it worked.

- The British tried to capture Thomas Jefferson, who was living in Charlottesville. He escaped just in time.

Filled with interesting information, this book is great for assignments and for fun reading.

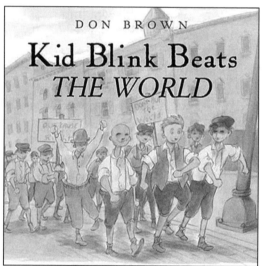

Kid Blink Beats **The World by Don Brown.**

Brown, Don. *Kid Blink Beats* The World. Roaring Brook Press, 2004. ISBN 1596430036. Unpaged. Grades 1–3.

One of the most famous strikes in U.S. history took place in 1899. And it was all about kids and money. The kids won, more or less!

The strike leaders were all kids. The most famous ones were Kid Blink, Race Track Higgins, Tiny Tim, Crutch Morris, and Crazy Arborn. They sound like quite a gang!

The kids were "newsies." They sold newspapers. They bought them, five newspapers for ten cents, and their goal was to sell every one of them. They could make decent money doing this, but they had to work hard for it. They were all poor kids, living in terrible housing conditions in poor neighborhoods, and the money they made really helped their families to survive.

Then two of the newspapers decided to raise their rates. They wanted to charge six cents for ten copies, and the kids knew they could not make enough money that way. So they went on strike.

This is a fine, true story.

Caputo, Philip. *10,000 Days of Thunder: A History of the Vietnam War.* A Byron Preiss Visual Publications Book/Atheneum Books for Young Readers, 2005. ISBN 0689862318. 128 p. Grades 6–up.

"The Vietnam War has three dubious distinctions: It was the longest and the most unpopular war in American history and the only war America ever lost.

"Whether as advisors to the South Vietnamese Army or as combat troops directly engaged in fighting the Viet Cong and the North Vietnamese Army, U.S. soldiers served in Vietnam from 1959 to 1975, making the war twice as long as the War of Independence" (page 6).

Philip Caputo was a young soldier who served in Vietnam, so he knows firsthand about his topic. He tells us that one good thing about serving there was that you were there for only a period of time (usually thirteen months), not until the war ended, which had been the way in the two world wars. Medical care was also much better, and superior American airpower was also good.

But it was a guerilla war. It was hard to find the enemy and hard to fight them. It proved to be a war that it was impossible to win.

And another bad thing about serving there was that some people hated you when you got back to the United States. Many Americans hated the war and took out their hate on the young men who had to fight in it. They sometimes called them baby killers, because many innocent civilians, including children, were killed in the war. American soldiers did not really know who was an enemy and who was not—and they made mistakes.

The war was really about the Cold War between Soviet Union and the United States and its allies. Americans were terrified that Communists would take over the world, and it looked as though the Communists in North Vietnam were making a good start at it. Americans felt they had to be stopped. So first they sent in military advisors, and then they started sending in troops. The United States never actually declared war on Vietnam, which meant that the young men who were captured by the enemy were treated horribly.

Many things happened during the Vietnam era. The war itself was a terrible tragedy, and the opposition to the war back in the United States created more tragedies. It was a difficult, terrible time in our history.

Boys with an interest in war will find this story fascinating and the many photographs riveting. Show the one of the captured American prisoner on page 90.

Clinton, Catherine. *Hold the Flag High.* Illustrated by Shane W. Evans. Katherine Tegen Books, An Imprint of HarperCollins Publishers, 2005. ISBN 0060504293. Unpaged. Grades 1–4.

In January 1863, right in the middle of the Civil War, President Lincoln signed the Emancipation Proclamation. Many slaves, who were now free, flocked to join the Union Army. They were not treated fairly, and their commanding officers were all white people, but they showed the world how brave they were—especially at the Battle of Fort Wagner, which nearly destroyed their regiment, the Massachusetts Fifty-fourth. (If you have seen the movie *Glory,* you will know about this story.)

William Carney was black and an officer, although not a commander. He had one important goal during the battle. He vowed that the Union flag—the American flag—would never touch the ground—no matter what. And this is the story of his courageous fight.

Show the actual photograph of Carney at the end of the book.

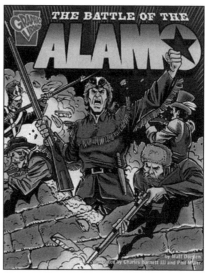

***The Battle of the Alamo* by Matt Doeden.**

Doeden, Matt. *The Battle of the Alamo* (Graphic Library: Graphic History). Illustrated by Charles Barnett III and Phil Miller. Capstone Press, 2005. ISBN 0736838325. 32 p. Grades 3–9.

The Americans who went to live in Mexican territory weren't happy that they had no say in how their country was run. They wanted to start their own country—but the Mexicans didn't like that idea at all. The Texans took over an old church mission called the Alamo and made it their headquarters. There, in 1836, one of the most famous battles in U.S. history took place.

Today no one is sure exactly what happened there or how many people were involved, but the Mexican defeat of the Texans was the beginning of a great victory for the Americans.

This book looks and reads like a comic book. Readers will learn a lot of interesting history in a fun way.

Let It Begin Here! Lexington & Concord:
First Battles of the American Revolution
by Dennis Brindell Fradin.

Fradin, Dennis Brindell. *Let It Begin Here! Lexington & Concord: First Battles of the American Revolution.* Illustrations by Larry Day. Walker, 2005. ISBN 0802789455. Unpaged. Grades 2–5.

Have you ever heard of "the shot heard round the world"? If you have, do you know where it was fired? And when? And who fired it?

The answers to the first two are easy, and famous. It was fired in Lexington, Massachusetts, on April 19, 1775. But no one knows who fired it.

It was the beginning of a war, the war that became the American Revolutionary War, in which the people of the American colonies of Great Britain united to declare their freedom from the country that had created those colonies. At first, it did not look like the colonists could possibly win a war against such a mighty nation as Great Britain, but they surprised everyone, maybe even themselves.

This is the story of the first battles of that war, in Lexington and Concord, Massachusetts, and of what happened the famous night before those battles, when Paul Revere made one of the most famous rides in history. It's an excellent read.

Giblin, James Cross. *Good Brother, Bad Brother: The Story of Edwin Booth and John Wilkes Booth.* Clarion Books, 2005. ISBN 0618096426. 256 p. Grades 5–up.

They were both famous, considered two of the best actors of their day. They were brothers. And one of them, John Wilkes Booth, assassinated Abraham Lincoln. What would it feel like to be his brother? How would you feel if you found out that your little brother had killed the president? How would you feel if you started getting death threats because people wanted to kill *you* to retaliate?

Edwin was five years older than John, and they had four other siblings. Their father was a famous actor too—Junius Booth, who performed throughout the country and made a good and happy home for his family, although he was an alcoholic and sometimes had periods of demented behavior. Edwin started acting because he traveled with his father to keep him in line and prevent him from drinking. He decided he loved the stage and went into acting himself. John also decided to be an actor, and they both made a big success of it, making a lot more money than most people at that time.

Edwin, like his father, became an alcoholic, although he stopped drinking fairly young, realizing it was ruining his career. He always remained close to his family, although he married twice. He felt he never knew John all that well, though, and was horrified to learn that he had killed Lincoln.

John hated Lincoln, loved the South, and thought his assassination of Lincoln might reverse the outcome of the Civil War. He was impetuous and impulsive and once got out of an acting job to go watch the hanging of the well-known abolitionist John Brown. He loved women, and at the time of his death, he was engaged to the daughter of a senator. He was flamboyant and handsome and organized a group of companions to kill the president and a few people in the cabinet. It was a disastrous night—the only thing that happened anywhere close to as planned was Booth's killing of the president in Ford's Theater. Even that did not go as expected, because Booth broke his leg when his spurs caught on a flag hanging on the presidential box. The writer takes us with him on his desperate escape from Washington, D.C., and describes his dramatic death and those of his fellow conspirators.

This is compulsive reading. These were fascinating people, and Giblin tells us a great true story.

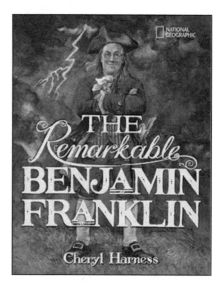

***The Remarkable Benjamin Franklin*
by Cheryl Harness.**

Harness, Cheryl. *The Remarkable Benjamin Franklin.* National Geographic, 2005. ISBN 0792278828. 48 p. Grades 2–5.

Benjamin Franklin is one of the most beloved people in American history. When he died in 1790, 20,000 people came to his funeral. He was an old man, eighty-four years old, and he had lived a full life; he was a great scientist *and* a great patriot. This, with a lot of wonderful illustrations, is his story.

Benjamin was the tenth child of his parents, and he loved to read. He did not have much formal schooling, but he learned a lot from books. When he was twelve years old, he was apprenticed to his older brother James. James was a printer, and Benjamin became a fine printer, too, but he could not stand working for James, even though he got some of his writing published. He fled from his hometown of Boston to Philadelphia, where he got a job in a print shop—and an opportunity to start his own printing business. He also fell in love with a girl, but lost her temporarily when she married someone else while he was seeking work in England.

On the way home, he started measuring something that he called (and we still call) the Gulf Stream. It was one of his big scientific experiments, and he did a lot of them. He invented helpful things, too, such as the lightning rod.

Benjamin was world famous by the time the American Revolution started, and he saw no problem with using his fame to help his people win the war. And he did.

He was an amazing human being. You'll enjoy learning about his life.

Show the picture of the young Ben at sea on page 13.

Onward: A Photobiography of
African-American Polar Explorer
Matthew Henson **by Dolores Johnson.**

Johnson, Dolores. *Onward: A Photobiography of African-American Polar Explorer Matthew Henson.* National Geographic, 2006. ISBN 079229714x. 64 p. Grades 4–up.

Matthew Henson's parents were not slaves, but they were almost as bad off financially as slaves. They lived on a tiny sharecropper farm in Maryland, and they worked hard to earn barely enough to stay alive.

Matthew was born in 1866, the year after the Civil War ended, and by the time he was thirteen, he was an orphan. He got a job as a dishwasher and then met a retired sailor named Baltimore Jack who convinced him that he ought to go to sea. He walked forty miles to the city of Baltimore and boldly asked an elderly white sea captain for a job as a cabin boy. The captain hired him immediately and spent two hours a day teaching him reading, writing, history, geography, carpentry, and how to navigate by the stars. With him, Matthew sailed the world.

But when Captain Childs died in 1883, Matthew quit. He found a series of low-level jobs where people would not discriminate against him because he was African American. In 1887, he was working as a stock boy in a hat store, and his luck changed. A young naval lieutenant name Robert Peary needed a manservant, and the owner of the shop recommended Matthew.

Thus he began the greatest adventure of his life.

First he spent some time with Peary in the jungles of Nicaragua, but Peary had a big dream. He wanted to be the first person ever to reach the North Pole. And Matthew became a big part of that dream. Together, the two of them traveled to Greenland, where they recruited Inuit people to help them in their quest.

That quest took years and was full of tragedies and failures. In 1898, for instance, Peary's feet became so frostbitten, eight of his toes snapped off at the first joint when he took off his boots. All but his little toes had to be amputated.

Both men fathered sons by Inuit women, and there are pictures of Henson's son and grandson in the book.

All the struggling and all of the failures were, in the end, worth it, because Peary and Henson became the first two men to reach the North Pole. But when they came back to the United States, they found another adventurer had claimed he got there first. It took months for their competitor, Frederick Cook, to be declared a fraud.

By then Henson and Peary were no longer speaking—and no one knows why, even today.

Henson was an astonishing hero, and what is even more wonderful is that he was a model for people of color everywhere. He lived to be a very old man. This is his riveting story.

Jurmain, Suzanne Tripp. *George Did It.* Illustrated by Larry Day. Dutton Children's Books, 2006. ISBN 0525475605. Unpaged. Grades K–3.

Practically everybody has heard of George Washington. He was, of course, the first president of the United States of America. But he did not *want* that job. He'd been busy for a long time fighting a war—the Revolutionary War. He was commander in chief of the armed forces, and it was hard work. It did not always look as though he would win, either.

He hadn't been home much, and now he was fifty-seven years old and *wanted* to be home for a while. He loved his wife and his farm, and he loved to go hunting with his dogs. He didn't like the thought of being president—it made him nervous just to think about it. But George Washington had a long history of doing whatever his country needed him to do, and we know what he did about being president. Much of this story isn't well known, and this humorous book puts a human face on a famous American.

Lasky, Kathryn. *John Muir: America's First Environmentalist.* Illustrated by Stan Fellows. Candlewick Press, 2006. ISBN 0763619574. 42 p. Grades 3–6.

John Muir's last name means "wild land" in Scottish, and John was born in Scotland in 1838. Growing up there, his favorite thing to do was something called a "scootcher," a dare or a dangerous stunt. He loved to crawl out his bedroom window and hang by his hands—or by one hand—or by maybe even a finger. He scared his little brother a lot.

John loved the birds, flowers, animals, plants—everything about the outdoors. When his family moved to Wisconsin in 1848, he loved to look at the country he called "wonder-filled." His father made him work very hard, sixteen hours a day, clearing the land, and helping out on the farm, and he left home when he was twenty-two years old to find out what he really wanted to do.

What John Muir really wanted to do was save the land and the wilderness and to protect nature. He said that people need "beauty as well as bread, places to pray in, where nature and cheer give strength to the human body and soul alike" (page 27).

John walked thousands of miles in his quest to save the wilderness and to admire and enjoy it. He founded the Sierra Club to try to build a strong conservation policy, and he was instrumental in creating America's national parks and wilderness areas.

This is his story, illustrated with beautiful pictures. Show the one of John doing a scootcher in the picture facing page 1.

McDonough, Yona Zeldis. *The Life of Benjamin Franklin: An American Original.* Paintings by Malcah Zeldis. Henry Holt, 2006. ISBN 0805078568. Unpaged. Grades 1–3.

Ben Franklin not rich and famous when he was born. His father made soap and candles in Boston and he had thirteen brothers and sisters. Ben liked to read, and he wrote a poem when he was seven. This was unusual, and his parents sent him to school, which was also unusual—in those days, children from families without much money often didn't have the chance to go to school. He loved to read and write, but he failed arithmetic. When he was twelve years old, his parents apprenticed him to his older brother James, who was a printer.

Ben loved printing, but he hated working for James, and the moment he could, he ran away—to another colonial American city, Philadelphia. There Ben fell in love, got married, and found the work which was clearly right for him. He became a printer, a writer, and an inventor. By the time he was forty-two years old, he had made enough money to retire from a regular job, and his goal in life was to help people improve their lives. Ben helped set up the first lending library in the colonies, founded the first fire department, and helped establish the country's first hospital. Plus he started inventing all sorts of useful things, including the lightning rod, bifocals, and the Franklin stove. And he also became interested in politics.

Ben became one of the most important men in the American Revolution. He assisted in writing the Declaration of Independence and also the Constitution.

Read this colorful book that tells his story.

Show the picture of Ben signing the Declaration of Independence.

Counting Coup: Becoming a Crow Chief
on the Reservation and Beyond
by Joseph Medicine Crow.

Medicine Crow, Joseph, with Herman J. Viola. *Counting Coup: Becoming a Crow Chief on the Reservation and Beyond.* National Geographic, 2006. ISBN 0792253914. 128 p. Grades 5–up.

There certainly cannot be many people alive today who had a grandfather who was a scout for General Custer at the Battle of Little Bighorn. One of them is the man who wrote this wonderful book about what it was like growing up on an Indian reservation and making his way in the white world, including becoming a soldier in World War II.

Joseph Medicine Crow belongs to the Crow tribe of Native Americans. He was born in 1913, on a reservation in Montana. He was truly brought up in the old, revered Indian ways. Among those ways, he tells us right off the bat that there were the four kinds of war deeds a warrior had to perform to become a chief:

• Sneak into an enemy camp unnoticed and steal a prized horse. Usually the horse would be found in front of the owner's teepee. Then the warrior had to bring the horse home, and this was considered the most important coup.

• Touch the first enemy to fall in a battle. This could be very dangerous, because even if an enemy had fallen, he might still have a weapon and be ready to fight.

• Take away the weapon of an enemy.

• Lead a successful war party.

Joseph became a chief, and this is his story, including how he counted his four coups in World War II.

Myers, Walter Dean, and Bill Miles. *The Harlem Hellfighters: When Pride Met Courage.* HarperCollins, 2006. ISBN 0060011378. 152 p. Grades 5-9.

As Walter Dean Myers tells us right away, black people have participated in all of America's battles. In Colonial America, they helped fight the Native Americans. During the Revolutionary War, more than five thousand blacks fought for freedom—but usually not their own freedom, for many were slaves.

Black soldiers were never treated as equals. They never had the same rights and privileges as white people. And they hated that. They wanted to show the world that they were as capable as any men anywhere. When the United States finally entered World War I, they thought they had a chance at that.

The United States had not wanted to enter the war, but then Germany attacked ships carrying American passengers. The Germans hated that Americans were giving aid to the British and the Allied powers. They even proposed to Mexico that they become allies, promising that they would help Mexico get back the territory it had lost in Texas, New Mexico, and Arizona. In April 1917, the United States declared war on Germany.

Blacks were ready. In New York, black people wanted to form their own regiment, complete with black officers at every level. But it was not to be. It was clear that there would be no black regiment unless most of the officers were white. African American leaders and recruiters were disappointed, but they accepted the reality of the situation and made sure that there was an opportunity for black officers to be trained.

Many young black men were patriotic and enlisted. There were racial problems in many parts of the country, especially the Deep South, where the treatment of black people was frequently horrible. When regiments were sent there for training, the black soldiers suffered terribly. Their problems were increased by the fact that their white leaders instructed them never to do anything that could cause additional animosity, no matter how unjust their treatment.

The 369th Infantry Regiment finally ended up in the front lines of the war in Europe and proved they had everything it took to be considered great soldiers. This is their wonderful story.

O'Brien, Patrick. *Duel of the Ironclads: The* Monitor *vs. the* Virginia. Walker, 2003. ISBN 0802788424. Unpaged. Grades 2–5.

Two ships, the *Monitor* and the *Virginia,* often called the *Merrimack,* were something new. They were ships, but their makers tried something different. They made them ironclad. Wooden ships were easily destroyed by enemy fire, but not ironclad ships. Guns didn't do much good against ironclads. Neither did cannons.

In the Civil War between the states, the Confederates came into possession of an old northern ship, the *Merrimack.* When the Northerners had to abandon her, they set her on fire—but she was rescued before she was completely destroyed. The Confederates realized that what was left, the engine and the bottom part of the hull, could still be used. They built an ironclad ship on top of that old engine and hull. It could hold 260 men and keep them pretty safe from enemy fire. The Confederates knew they were creating a new and powerful weapon, and when the Yankees heard about it, they decided they needed one, too. Theirs was completely different from any ship ever built, and it rode very low in the water. It could hold fifty-eight men, and it headed off to stop the *Virginia* from destroying Union ships.

This is the story of the battle between the two strange-looking ships and what happened to them. Show students the two-page spread that pictures them both. It's quite a tale.

Penner, Lucille Recht. *Eating the Plates: A Pilgrim Book of Food and Manners*. With illustrations selected by the author. Aladdin Paperbacks, 1991, 1997. ISBN 0689815417. 117 p. Grades 3–up.

As it says on the cover of this book, "The Pilgrims thought about food all the time. They had to!"

They called themselves "Saints." They called others who did not share their religious beliefs "Strangers." They had to live together in a strange new land. "When the *Mayflower* sailed for America, the Pilgrims knew less about their destination than our astronauts did when they blasted off for the moon" (page 117).

One thing they found out quickly and that they all had in common was that they almost never had enough to eat. They were hungry all of the time. And their eating habits, and living habits, were not like ours.

Here are some of the interesting things young readers will learn in this book:

• It was crowded and dirty on the *Mayflower*. Probably no one changed clothes. They were covered with lice and fleas.

• Everybody drank beer—even children. They hated water.

• Without the help of the Native Americans, especially a man named Squanto, they almost certainly would have starved to death. Squanto taught them to plant corn, which became their main source of food.

• The first houses were horribly cold—built right on the ground with no insulation and fireplaces that sent the heat right up the chimney.

• Pilgrims thought water and soap were bad for people.

• They did not have socks, and their feet were always cold.

• Most food was served in one pot on the table. Everyone reached in and grabbed their food. Poor people might not have had plates at all. Their food might be served on plate-shaped bread—and after they ate the rest of it, they ate their plates.

• Dishes never really got clean. They were just wiped off and put away. (Yuck!)

• Some people used turkey wings as brooms.

This is great stuff to share with your listeners.

***The Journey of the One and Only Declaration of
Independence* by Judith St. George.**

St. George, Judith. *The Journey of the One and Only Declaration of Independence.* Illustrated by Will Hillenbrand. Philomel Books, 2005. ISBN 0399237380. Unpaged. Grades 2–5.

The one we think of as the *real* Declaration of Independence was not even signed until August 2, 1776. It was engrossed. That means it was written in parchment in large, clear letters. The twenty-five copies that were around earlier had just been printed in an ordinary fashion. This copy looked good, and for a piece of parchment it had a lot of adventures.

Philadelphia was a great place to store it until it looked like the British were going to take over the city in December of 1776. Charles Thomson, the secretary of the Congress, rolled it up and fled with it out of the city. When the threat of the British passed, the Declaration was brought back and then removed again when the threat returned. It went to York, Pennsylvania, this time. And that was just the beginning of its travels.

It went to New York City. It went to Washington, D.C., and it was rescued when the British invaded in 1812.

It hung in a window, exposed to direct sunlight, which is never a good idea for precious documents. It faded. It went back to Independence Hall in Philadelphia for the nation's centennial celebration in 1876.

And it kept on moving after that—read to find out where.

This is a fun, true story with good pictures. You'll learn a lot.

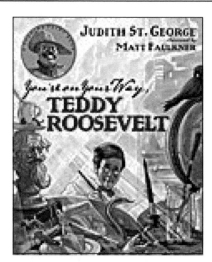

You're On Your Way, Teddy Roosevelt!
by Judith St. George.

St. George, Judith. *You're On Your Way, Teddy Roosevelt!* (Turning Point Book). Illustrated by Matt Faulkner. Philomel Books, 2004. ISBN 0399238883. Unpaged. Grades 1–4.

Many people believe that Theodore Roosevelt was one of our greatest presidents. But he wasn't always great. In fact, when he was a young boy, he was so sickly that his parents were afraid he was going to die very early in life.

He simply could not breathe. He had a very severe case of asthma and had a hard time sleeping. He was thin and pale. He had nightmares, sometimes about werewolves crouching on his bed.

But although he was sick, he was interested in everything. He loved the wild animals he saw around the city and made a collection of them. It drove his mother crazy. One day he came home with the head of a seal that he got outside a market. He had snakes, snapping turtles, and dead mice. He read all the books he could find to learn more about them.

No doctor seemed to be able to cure Theodore, whom everyone called Teedy. Finally Teedy's father had a talk with him. He told him that he would have to build up his body. Teedy started going to a gym to do strength training.

This book tells the story of how Teedy became a healthy young man, one so healthy he became the most powerful man in the United Sates.

Show the picture of Teedy with the seal and, on the two-page spread with it, the one of his parents looking worriedly at his animal collection.

St. George, Judith. *Take the Lead, George Washington.* Illustrated by Daniel Powers. Philomel Books, 2005. ISBN 0399238875. Unpaged. Grades 1–4.

George Washington was a farmer's son, and he loved farming. He was the first child of Gus Washington and his second wife, Mary. Gus's first wife had died, but he had two older sons and a daughter by her. When George was born, the boys were away at school in England.

George was born in 1732, and, when he was three years old, his family moved to a farm called Epsewasson on the Potomac River. His father had bought the farm years before, and it became very important to George.

But Epsewasson was to be inherited by George's older half-brother, Lawrence, who came back from England when George was six. George thought he was the best big brother ever—he was crazy about him.

George thought he, too, would go to school in England like his older brothers had, but when the time came, there was not enough money. George started studying hard. He especially loved arithmetic.

When George was eleven, his father died. George was going to have a small inheritance, so he knew he would always have to work. Lawrence inherited Epsewasson and changed its name to Mount Vernon. George still liked living there a lot.

When George was a teenager, he decided he knew what he wanted to do. He wanted to become a surveyor. There was a lot of work for surveyors those days, because there was a lot of American land that had never been surveyed.

His first surveying job on the frontier was the first adventure of his long life.

George, of course, became a great hero, but just like most of us, he was an ordinary kid. You'll enjoy reading about the kid that became the president.

Tanaka, Shelley. *Gettysburg: The Legendary Battle and the Address That Inspired a Nation* (A Day That Changed America). Paintings by David Craig. Historical consultation by John Y. Simon. Hyperion Books for Children. A Hyperion/Madison Press Book, 2003. ISBN 0786819227. 48 p. Grades 4–9.

Two major events happened in American history a few months apart in the sleepy little town of Gettysburg, Pennsylvania. It was not sleepy in 1863, however. Early in July, Robert E. Lee, the commander of the Confederate Army, started a great battle near the town. It became one of the bloodiest, most horrendous battles in American history. At the end of three horrible days of battle, the Confederates retreated, but thousands of men in both the Union Army and the Confederate Army died or were injured.

Then in November of that same year, President Abraham Lincoln came to the town and gave what is generally considered to be the greatest speech in American history. Only two minutes long, it said everything that needed to be said—and he wrote it himself. His speech was about that battle and about the Civil War. It begins "Four score and seven years ago, our fathers brought forth on this continent a new nation, conceived in liberty and dedicated to the proposition that all men are created equal."

This book has wonderful illustrations and photographs that tell some of the individual stories of the battle and the men who were in it. One man named John Burns came to join the fighting. He was a sixty-nine-year-old shoemaker, and he asked a wounded soldier for his musket—and got it. He was wounded himself, but recovered.

The dead body of a soldier who was clutching a photograph of his children was found. There was a lot of publicity about that, and the picture was published in magazines and newspapers all around the country. Eventually his body was identified, and his widow found out about his death when she saw that photo in the newspaper months later.

Jennie Wade was baking biscuits in her sister's house near the battlefield when a bullet came in the kitchen door and killed her.

You will learn the day-by-day story of the battle and a lot of other fascinating information.

NOT TO BE MISSED

Adler, David A. *A Picture Book of Dwight David Eisenhower*. Holiday House, 2002. ISBN 0823417026. Unpaged. Grades 1–3.

A lot of people called him "Ike," and the name stuck. Ike knew he did not have enough money to go to college, so he decided to try to get into a military academy, which was free. He made it into West Point. And that was just the beginning of a wonderful career, in which Ike became first a five-star general, and then president of the United States. David Adler's biographies are simple and interesting.

Allen, Thomas B. *Remember Pearl Harbor: American and Japanese Survivors Tell Their Stories*. National Geographic Society, 2001. ISBN 0792266900. 57 p. Grades 4–8. *Gotcha Covered.*

National Geographic Society does its usual superlative job with photographs, which only increases the quality of these compelling narratives told by people who planned the attack were there in Pearl Harbor on December 7, 1941.

Beeler, Sally B. *Throw Your Tooth on the Roof: Tooth Traditions from Around the World*. Illustrated by G. Brian Karas. Houghton Mifflin, 1998. ISBN 0395891086. Unpaged. Grades K–3. *Gotcha Again.*

Everyone on the planet has baby teeth, but what do they do with them when they fall out? In the United States, we have the tooth fairy, but it seems that she does not travel everywhere. This heavily illustrated book tells us what happens elsewhere on the globe and is a delight to share with children.

Bierman, Carol, with Barbara Hehner. *Journey to Ellis Island: How My Father Came to America*. Illustrated by Laurie McGaw. A Hyperion/Madison Press Book, 1999. ISBN 0786803770. 48 p. Grades 4–6. *Gotcha Again.*

Bierman tells the story of her father, Yehuda, who had his finger shot off in the middle of a Russian battle and who came to America with his arm in a sling. Getting in when you were in that shape was not easy, and this is a good, surprising story, well illustrated in color.

Bircher, William. *A Civil War Drummer Boy: The Diary of William Bircher 1861–1865*. Blue Earth Books, 2000. ISBN 0736803483. 32 p. Grades 4–up. *Gotcha Again.*

Military and Civil War aficionados with be drawn to this true account of service during the Civil War, written by an actual Minnesota drummer boy. Heavily illustrated with photographs.

Blumberg, Rhoda. *York's Adventures with Lewis and Clark: An African-American's Part in the Great Expedition*. HarperCollins, 2003. ISBN 0060091118. 88 p. Grades 4–9. *Gotcha Covered.*

He made history. He was the slave of William Clark, and he traveled with the Corps of Discovery on the Lewis and Clark Expedition. He was the first African

American ever to get a vote on an important issue during that trip. This heavily illustrated book tells his interesting story.

Carlson, Laurie. *Boss of the Plains: The Hat That Won the West*. Pictures by Holly Meade. DK Ink, 1999. ISBN 0789424797. 32 p. Grades 2–4. *Gotcha Again.*

This is the colorfully illustrated story of the most famous cowboy hat of all, the Stetson, and particularly of the most famous Stetson of them all, the "Boss of the Plains."

Chandra, Deborah, and Madeleine Comora. *George Washington's Teeth.* Pictures by Brock Cole. Farrar, Straus & Giroux, 2003. ISBN 0374325340. Unpaged. Grades 1–3. *Gotcha Covered.*

George Washington had perhaps the most famous set of false teeth of all time, and this is the story of what happened, told humorously in poem and prose. You'll never look at his portrait without checking out his mouth again.

Cline-Ransome, Lesa. *Major Tyler: Champion Cyclist.* Illustrated by James E. Ransome. An Anne Schwartz Book/Atheneum Books for Young Readers, 2004. ISBN 0689831595. Unpaged. Grades K–3. *Gotcha Covered.*

In 1891, Marshall Taylor was a thirteen-year-old African American who had few opportunities open to him. But he did something extraordinary. He made money and a career out of doing something he loved and was good at—bicycling and doing stunts on a bike.

Clinton, Catherine. *The Black Soldier: 1492 to the Present.* Houghton Mifflin, 2000. ISBN 039567722X. 117 p. Grades 4–8. *Gotcha Again.*

An African man arrived in the New World with Columbus in 1492. Black soldiers have fought in American wars ever since. But throughout most of our history, black soldiers were treated with appalling discrimination wherever they went. Only in 1946 did President Harry S. Truman desegregate the armed forces.

Cooper, Ilene. *Jack: The Early Years of John F. Kennedy.* Dutton Children's Books, 2002. ISBN 0525469230. 176 p. Grades 4–up. *Gotcha Covered.*

Jack Kennedy got in a lot of trouble when he was a kid, but he was always creative and never boring. Copiously illustrated with photographs, this is a good read.

Cooper, Michael L. *Fighting for Honor: The Japanese-Americans and World War II.* Clarion Books, 2000. ISBN 0395913756. 118 p. Grades 5–8. *Gotcha Again.*

After Japan attacked Pearl Harbor in 1941, Japanese Americans were in a horrible position. In fact, anyone who looked Asian was treated unfairly. This is the story of what happened to those people and how many of their young men joined the U.S. Armed Forces and proved their loyalty to their country.

Crowe, Chris. *Getting Away with Murder: The True Story of the Emmett Till Case.* Phyllis Fogelman Books, 2003. ISBN 0803728042. 128 p. Grades 5–8.

When fourteen-year-old Emmett Till was murdered by two racists, his mother decided not to go along with the cover-up—and the brutal crime shocked the nation.

Crutcher, Chris. *King of the Mild Frontier: An Ill-Advised Autobiography*. Greenwillow Books, an imprint of HarperCollins, 2003. ISBN 0060502509. 260 p. Grades 6–up. *Gotcha Covered.*

   Even the nerdiest kid in the class can turn out OK, as young adult author Chris Crutcher tells us in this hilarious story of his childhood and youth in a small Idaho town. It offers hope for us all!

Edwards, Judith. *The Great Expedition of Lewis and Clark by Private Reubin Field, Member of the Corps of Discovery*. Pictures by Sally Wern Comfort. Farrar, Straus & Giroux, 2003. ISBN 0374380392. Unpaged. Grades 2–5. *Gotcha Covered.*

   Not everyone who went on the Lewis and Clark expedition became famous. This tells the story from the point of view of one expedition member named Reubin Field, who, with his brother Joseph, joined the Corps of Discovery as an "able woodsman and hunter."

Fradin, Dennis. *Bound for the North Star: True Stories of Fugitive Slaves*. Clarion, 2000. ISBN 0395970172. Grades 5–8.

   Some slaves did escape, in spite of the terrible punishments that awaited them if they were recaptured. Creativity, intelligence, and imagination were required to come up with the plans that got them away from their hated masters. This tells the true stories of several slaves who managed, almost miraculously, to escape.

Fradin, Dennis. *My Family Shall Be Free: The Life of Peter Still*. HarperCollins, 2001. ISBN 0060295953. 190 p. Grades 4–up.

   This is an almost unbelievable true account of a slave who conquered all of the odds and bought his freedom—and then returned South to bring his family to freedom with him. It is a powerful and moving story.

Fradin, Dennis Brindell. *The Signers: The Fifty-Six Stories behind the Declaration of Independence*. Illustrations by Michael McCurdy. Walker, 2002. ISBN 0802788491. 160 p. Grades 4–9.

   The pictures of the signers of the Declaration of Independence, all based on actual historical portraits, and the biographies make for an irresistibly appealing read. Granted, only good readers will even try this, but ask them to read two biographies and see if they aren't immediately hooked.

Ganci, Chris. *Chief: The Life of Peter J. Ganci, A New York City Firefighter*. Orchard Books, 2003. ISBN 0439443865. Unpaged. Grades 3–5. *Gotcha Covered.*

   Peter Ganci was a Vietnam veteran who realized that he wanted to fight fires. He got a job as a firefighter and then studied hard and passed the test to become a lieutenant. He kept getting promoted until finally he became chief of the New York Fire Department. He was in charge of fifteen thousand firefighters. He worked hard and was a popular chief. And then, less than two years later, planes flew directly into the two towers of the World Trade Center. Peter rushed to the site to direct the operations there and became one of the 343 firefighters who died that day. This is his story, told by his son, with lots of wonderful photographs.

Gerstein, Mordicai. *The Man Who Walked between the Towers.* Roaring Brook Press, 2003. ISBN 0761328688. Unpaged. Grades K–4.

The dizzying illustrations, the almost perfect text, and the ultimate fate of the two towers Philippe Petit walked across combined to make this the 2004 Caldecott Medal Winner. It's an almost perfect book that's guaranteed to delight young readers.

Glass, Andrew. *Bad Guys: True Stories of Legendary Gunslingers, Sidewinders, Fourflushers, Drygulchers, Bushwhackers, Freebooters, and Downright Bad Guys and Gals of the Wild West.* Doubleday, 1998. ISBN 0385323107. 48 p. Grades 3–7.

Colorful illustrations and equally colorful true stories of legendary Wild West characters, such as Buffalo Bill, Calamity Jane, Wyatt Earp, Billy the Kid, and Wild Bill Hickock, combine to make a book with huge appeal.

Goodman, Susan E. *Ultimate Field Trip 4: A Week in the 1800s.* Photographs by Michael J. Doolittle. Atheneum Books for Young Readers, 2000. ISBN 0689830459. 50 p. Grades 4–7.

A group of modern kids spent a week living an 1800s life in the Kings Landing Historical Settlement in New Brunswick, Canada. Color photographs and the sometimes gross realities of living primitively make for a fun look at life in the past.

Greene, Meg. *Slave Young, Slave Long: The American Slave Experience.* Lerner, 1999. ISBN 0822517396. 88 p. Grades 4–8.

Full of photographs of slaves and descriptions of the horrors they endured in slavery, this is an excellent look at the lives of people who were not free.

Greenfield, Eloise. *How They Got Over: African Americans and the Call of the Sea.* Illustrated by Jan Spivey Gilchrist. HarperCollins/Amistad, 2002. ISBN 0060289910. 104 p. Grades 4–7.

Many African Americans love the sea so much that they make it a part of their lives, or in fact, their life's work. This interesting book profiles seven men and women at some length and gives us snapshots of a few others.

Hansen, Joyce, and Gary McGowan. *Freedom Roads: Searching for the Underground Railroad.* Illustrations by James Ransome. Cricket Books: A Marcato Book, 2003. ISBN 0812626737. 164 p. Grades 4–8.

The Underground Railroad was a secretive operation, and uncovering the secrets more than 135 years later is a difficult business. This is the story of how historians are searching for the real truth about the Underground Railroad.

Haskins, Jim. *Get on Board: The Story of the Underground Railroad.* Scholastic, 1993. ISBN 0590454196. 154 p. Grades 4–6.

Once you get into this compelling account of the lives of slaves and their courageous attempts to escape slavery, you'll find it hard to put down. The slaves took terrible risks and faced horrible punishments if caught, and their stories are immensely readable.

Heiligman, Deborah. *High Hopes: A Photobiography of John F. Kennedy.* National Geographic, 2003. ISBN 0792261410. 64 p. Grades 4–8.

  Filled with photographs, this is a biography of the youngest—and possibly most glamorous—man ever elected to the presidency. His appeal, his charisma, and the controversy his Catholic faith inspired in the American electorate make for a fine story.

Holzer, Harold. *The President Is Shot! The Assassination of Abraham Lincoln.* Boyds Mills Press, 2004. ISBN 1563979853. 181 p. Grades 5–up.

  This excellent account of the assassination of the president days after the end of the Civil War is written by one of the foremost experts on the topic.

Jones, Rebecca. *The President Has Been Shot! True Stories of the Attacks on Ten U.S. Presidents.* Dutton Children's Books, 1996. ISBN 0525453334. 134 p. Grades 5–8.

  Not every attempt to kill a president was successful, but all of those attempts make for incredibly interesting reading.

Krull, Kathleen. *Harvesting Hope: The Story of Cesar Chavez.* Illustrated by Yuyi Morales. Harcourt, 2003. ISBN 0152014373. Unpaged. Grades 1–4.

  A man who was poverty-stricken throughout most of his life, had few possessions, and worked for long hours under inhumane conditions, Cesar Chavez became a great American hero. He fought for the rights of the migrant workers like himself, who were housed in hovels and had little education. Wonderful color illustrations add appeal.

Krull, Kathleen. *The Night the Martians Landed: Just the Facts (Plus the Rumors) about Invaders from Mars.* Illustrations by Christopher Santoro. HarperCollins, 2003. ISBN 0688172474. 74 p. Grades 2–4.

  A lot of people believed the worst: Martians had invaded and attacked New Jersey. It was certainly one of the most famous radio broadcasts in American history, that night in 1938 when a dramatization of H. G. Wells's book *The War of the Worlds* went on the air. Many people, apparently unaware of or ignoring the commercial interruptions, tried to escape. It's easy to read and fun.

Lalicki, Tom. *Grierson's Raid: A Daring Cavalry Strike through the Heart of the Confederacy.* Original maps by David Cain. Farrar, Straus & Giroux, 2004. ISBN 0374327874. 200 p. Grades 5–up.

  Right in the middle of the Civil War, in 1863, Benjamin Grierson, a Union Army colonel who hated horses, rode one for six days. He led about 1,700 men through Mississippi and Alabama in an attempt to destroy Confederate supplies and create a diversion from the impending Yankee attack on Vicksburg. Unbelievable as it sounds, it worked, and good-reader military buffs will love this story.

Lanier, Shannon, & Jane Feldman. *Jefferson's Children: The Story of One American Family.* With photographs by Jane Feldman. Random House, 2000. ISBN 0375805974. 144 p. Grades 5–8.

  DNA evidence has made it virtually certain that Thomas Jefferson fathered children with his slave Sally Hemings. Today her descendants are stepping forth, with pride and pain, to claim their heritage and join the family reunions held at Monticello. But many of his other descendants are unhappy about this. Shannon Lanier is a young man descended from the president, and, accompanied by many photographs, he tells the story of his family and of himself.

Lourie, Peter. *Mississippi River: A Journey down the Father of Water.* Boyds Mills Press, 2000. ISBN 1563977567. 48 p. Grades 4–8.

Peter Lourie loves rivers and exploring, and this is the story of his journey down the Mississippi in a canoe. Particularly interesting are the descriptions of the way the river changes when it merges with the Missouri River and later with the Ohio River.

Lourie, Peter. *On the Trail of Lewis and Clark: A Journey up the Missouri River.* Boyds Mills Press, 2002. ISBN 1563979365. 48 p. Grades 4–8.

Peter Lourie and three of his friends decided to follow the Missouri River along the trail that the Lewis and Clark expedition followed about two hundred years ago. The landscape has changed, and comparison of their description and the way the land looks today is interesting—but a lot is much the same as well. This book contains lots of color photographs to pore over.

Lourie, Peter. *Rio Grande: From the Rocky Mountains to the Gulf of Mexico.* Boyds Mills Press, 1999. ISBN 1563977060. 48 p. Grades 4–6.

The Rio Grande is the third longest river in the United States, and for a thousand miles it creates the border between Texas and Mexico. Lourie traveled down the river from southern Colorado, in the Rocky Mountains, through Texas, taking many photographs and describing his adventures along the way.

Miller, Debbie S. *The Great Serum Race: Blazing the Iditarod Trail.* Illustrations by Jon Van Zyle. Walker, 2002. ISBN 0802788114. 32 p. Grades 1–5. *Gotcha Covered.*

In 1925, a disease called diphtheria broke out in Nome, Alaska, and there was no serum to vaccinate people against the disease. The nearest serum was a thousand miles away, and the only way to get through most of those miles was by dog sled. In temperatures as cold as fifty-six degrees below zero, with the wind blowing in their faces, the men and the dogs raced to save the people of Nome. They went over ice and through snow. Four dogs died because they got so cold, and several others became lame. They ran over seven hundred miles. Today, every year, that race is run again. It is now called the Iditarod, and this is its amazing story.

Murphy, Jim. *Gone A-Whaling: The Lure of the Sea and the Hunt for the Great Whale.* Clarion Books, 1998. ISBN 0395698472. 206 p. Grades 5–8.

What a glamorous life! You are a kid who wants to see the world, and you sign up to work on a whaling ship. That's the good news. You *do* get to see some of the world, although mostly the water part, but your life is hard, boring, filthy, and lonely—and usually you make very little money, if any. Trust author Jim Murphy to get good readers interested in this topic.

Murphy, Jim. *Inside the Alamo*. Delacorte Press, 2003. ISBN 0385900929. 122 p. Grades 4–8.

> There were between 192 and 257 people inside the Alamo (no one is certain exactly how many, and that figure included women and children), but there were *thousands* of Mexican soldiers outside waiting to attack them on March 6, 1836. Historians do know what happened before and after the attack, but it happened so fast and was over so quickly that no one is sure exactly what happened when the Alamo fell. What we *do* know, however, makes a great read from a wonderful writer.

Myers, Walter Dean. *Amistad: A Long Road to Freedom*. Dutton, 1998. ISBN 0525459707. 100 p. Grades 4–8.

> In 1839, an event unique in the history of American slavery took place. The captive slaves revolted on the filthy, cramped ship that was bringing them to America for sale as slaves. And the revolt was successful. They took over the ship and demanded that the navigator take them back to their home. He tricked them, they were brought to America, imprisoned—then they sued! And they won! This is one of the most incredible stories of slavery, and it is both inspiring and dramatic.

Myers, Walter Dean. *Malcolm X: A Fire Burning Brightly*. Illustrated by Leonard Jenkins. HarperCollins, 2000. ISBN 0060277076. Unpaged. Grades 3–5.

> This colorfully illustrated introduction to the life of one of the greatest African American leaders is an excellent read.

Nelson, Pete. *Left for Dead: A Young Man's Search for Justice for the USS* Indianapolis. With a preface by Hunter Scott. Delacorte Press, 2002. ISBN 0385729596. Grades 5–8.

> Hunter Scott researched the sinking of the USS *Indianapolis* when he was a sixth grader, and what he found out appalled him. After meeting many of the survivors of the disastrous sinking, he led the fight to restore the reputation of the ship's captain. Boys especially will relish the story of the disaster, including details about sharks attacking the capsized sailors.

Piven, Hanoch. *What Presidents Are Made of*. Atheneum Books for Young Readers, 2004. ISBN 0689868804. Unpaged. Grades 1–6.

> Creative portraits of the presidents made from all sorts of unusual objects inspire young artists and delight young viewers.

Schanzer, Rosalyn. *George vs. George: The American Revolution as Seen from Both Sides*. National Geographic, 2004. ISBN 0792273494. 60 p. Grades 3–5.

> Two leaders, who looked vaguely alike and shared many of the same interests, could not have disagreed more on what the future of the American colonies should be. Who was right? It all depends on your point of view. This is a wonderful introduction to the American Revolution.

Schanzer, Rosalyn. *How Ben Franklin Stole the Lightning*. HarperCollins, 2003. ISBN 0688169937. Unpaged. Grades 1–4.

> Ben Franklin is one of the most beloved, not to mention among the most interesting, people in all of American history. Here we learn a little bit about his life and a lot about his scientific experiments, all delightfully illustrated in color.

Schanzer, Rosalyn. *How We Crossed the West: The Adventures of Lewis and Clark.* National Geographic Society, 1997. ISBN 0792237382. Unpaged. Grades 1–4.

This is a fine introduction to the most famous journey of discovery in American history—Lewis and Clark's expedition to explore the newly purchased Louisiana Territory and their attempt to find a water passage to the west coast. Including some journal entries, this is a fine, colorfully illustrated introduction for young readers.

St. George, Judith. *In the Line of Fire: Presidents' Lives at Stake.* Holiday House, 1999. ISBN 0823414280. 144 p. Grades 4–8.

Although this is not an easy read, it commands the interest of anyone who starts browsing. Here are the stories of the attempts made on the lives of U.S. presidents, four of which were successful: the assassinations of Lincoln, Garfield, McKinley, and Kennedy. Other, less successful attempts have been made on other presidents, and Garfield and McKinley might have survived their shootings if they lived today with modern medicine and knowledge of basic hygiene. An excellent read.

St. George, Judith. *So You Want to Be President?* Illustrated by David Small. Philomel Books, 2000. ISBN 0399234071. 54 p. Grades 1–4.

Filled with unusual facts and great information, this picture book is humorous and delightful and was the winner of the Caldecott Medal in 2001.

Stanley, Jerry. *Hurry Freedom: African Americans in Gold Rush California.* Crown, 2000. ISBN 0517800942. 86 p. Grades 5–8.

Most of them never struck gold, and a lot of them came because they were slaves and their masters brought them, but there were many African Americans in California during the Gold Rush, some with extraordinary stories to tell.

Stier, Catherine. *If I Were President.* Illustrated by DyAnne DiSalvo-Ryan. Albert Whitman, 1999. ISBN 0807535419. Unpaged. Grades K–3.

Exactly what do you have to do to get the job many people believe is the most important in the world? How old must you be? What are some of the fun things that come with the job, and what are the downsides? How would you get elected anyway? These are all good questions presented here in an interesting way.

Swain, Gwenyth. *President of the Underground Railroad: A Story about Levi Coffin.* Illustrations by Ralph L. Ramstad. Carolrhoda Books, 2001. ISBN 1575055511. 64 p. Grades 4–6.

Some called him the president of the Underground Railroad because he helped so many slaves to escape to the north and to Canada. Levi Coffin, born in North Carolina, was a Quaker who detested slavery and moved to Indiana simply because he did not want to live in a slave state. Then he fought for what he believed, helping more than three thousand enslaved people to escape to freedom.

Tanaka, Shelley. *The Alamo: Surrounded and Outnumbered, They Chose to Make a Defiant Last Stand* (A Day That Changed America). Paintings by David Craig. Historical Consultation by Dr. Bruce Winders. Hyperion Books for Children/A Hyperion/Madison Press Book, 2003. ISBN 0786819235. 48 p. Grades 4–8.

Although this book is not as good as Jim Murphy's *Inside the Alamo,* it contains paintings of the battle with a lot of kid appeal, as well as some interesting information.

Tanaka, Shelley. *Attack on Pearl Harbor: The True Story of the Day America Entered World War II.* Paintings by David Craig. A Hyperion/Madison Press Book, 2001. ISBN 0786807369. 64 p. Grades 4–8.

True stories of a Japanese submarine pilot (who did not expect he would survive), an American seaman, and children living in Hawaii make this account of the attack especially interesting.

Warren, Andrea. *We Rode the Orphan Trains.* Houghton Mifflin, 2001. ISBN 0618117121. 144 p. Grades 4–6.

Seven survivors tell their stories of how they, as homeless or orphaned (at least by one parent) children in New York City were sent west on trains, put out on display at depots—rather like slaves, said one—and given new homes by good, bad, and all other kinds of people.

WORTH READING

Nonfiction books with "boy appeal" that have received positive reviews in *Booklist, Horn Book Guide,* and/or *School Library Journal.*

Anderson, Dale. *Lexington and Concord: April 19, 1775* (American Battlefields). Enchanted Lion, 2004. ISBN 1592700276. 32 p. Grades 4–7.

Ashby, Ruth. *Fury on Horseback* (Civil War Chronicles). Creative/Smart Apple, 2002. ISBN 1583401857. 48 p. Grades 4–8.

Ashby, Ruth. *Gettysburg* (Civil War Chronicles). Creative/Smart Apple, 2002. ISBN 1583401865. 48 p. Grades 4–8.

Dolan, Edward F. *The Battle of Little Bighorn* (Kaleidoscope). Benchmark Books, 2002. ISBN 0761414576. 48 p. Grades 2–4.

Dowswell, Paul. *Pearl Harbor: December 7, 1941* (Days That Shook the World). Raintree, 2003. ISBN 0739860518. 48 p. Grades 4–8.

***Read about Crazy Horse* by Stephen Feinstein.**

Feinstein, Stephen. *Read about Crazy Horse* (I Like Biographies!). Enslow, 2005. ISBN 076602590x. 24 p. Grades K–3.

Hoena, B. A. *Matthew Henson: Arctic Adventurer* (Graphic Library). Illustrated by Phil Miller. Capstone Press, 2005. ISBN 0736846344. 32 p. Grades 4–7.

January, Brendan. *Gettysburg: July 1–3, 1863* (American Battlefields). Enchanted Lion, 2004. ISBN 159270025x. 32 p. Grades 4–7.

January, Brendan. *Little Bighorn: June 25, 1876* (American Battlefields). Enchanted Lion, 2004. ISBN 1592700284. 32 p. Grades 4–7.

Koehler-Pentacoff, Elizabeth. *John Muir and Stickeen: An Alaskan Adventure.* Illustrated by Karl Swanson. Millbrook Press, 2003. ISBN 0761319972. 32 p. Grades K–3.

Landau, Elaine. *Bill Pickett: Wild West Cowboy* (Best of the West Biographies). Enslow, 2004. ISBN 0766022153. 48 p. Grades 3–6.

Landau, Elaine. *Billy the Kid: Wild West Outlaw* (Best of the West Biographies). Enslow, 2004. ISBN 0766022072. 48 p. Grades 3–6.

Landau, Elaine. *Crazy Horse: American Indian Leader* (Best of the West Biographies). Enslow, 2005. ISBN 0766022161. 48 p. Grades 4–6.

Landau, Elaine. *Jesse James: Wild West Train Robber* (Best of the West Biographies). Enslow, 2004. ISBN 0766022080. 48 p. Grades 3–6.

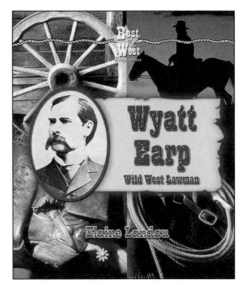

Wyatt Earp: Wild West Lawman
by Elaine Landau.

Landau, Elaine. *Wyatt Earp: Wild West Lawman* (Best of the West Biographies). Enslow, 2004. ISBN 076602217x. 48 p. Grades 3–6.

Levy, Pat. *The Home Front in World War II* (World Wars). Raintree, 2003. ISBN 0739860658. 64 p. Grades 5–up.

Pringle, Laurence. *Dog of Discovery: A Newfoundland's Adventures with Lewis and Clark*. Illustrated by Meryl Henderson. Boyds Mills Press, 2002. ISBN 1590780280. 149 p. Grades 3–6.

Stewart, Mark. *The Alamo: February 23–March 6, 1836* (American Battlefields). Enchanted Lion, 2004. ISBN 1592700268. 32 p. Grades 4–7.

True Tales of the Wild West by Paul Walker.

Walker, Paul. *True Tales of the Wild West*. National Geographic Children's Books, 2002. ISBN 0792282183. 128 p. Grades 4–8.

Chapter 3

Prehistoric Creatures

Many kids (and grown-ups too) are fascinated by dinosaurs. They are scary, mysterious, and exotic, and there is much to learn about them. Lucky for us, scientists are hard at work studying and learning about all kinds of prehistoric animals, and new children's books are written about them every year. Scientific thought is rapidly changing in this field, so make sure you give young readers recent information (for a dinosaur book, even five years is too old). In this chapter, you will find a wide range of creatures—from feathered dinosaurs to supercrocs to wooly mammoths.

NEW AND NOTABLE

Arnold, Caroline. *Pterosaurs: Rulers of the Skies in the Dinosaur Age.* Illustrated by Laurie Caple. Clarion Books, 2005 ISBN 0618313540. 40 p. Grades 3–5.

 Millions of years ago, as we all know, there were dinosaurs. But there were also animals perhaps even more amazing—reptiles that flew! Some of the reptiles had wingspans as wide as forty feet.

 The name *pterosaurs* comes from Greek words that mean "wing lizards." And these were incredible creatures. They were related to dinosaurs, and the oldest one that has been found (in northern Italy) lived about 215 million years ago. Its name, *Eudimorphodon,* means "true two form tooth." It had fangs and teeth, perfect for catching and holding fish. Another early pterosaur was the *Dimorphodon.* The first fossil ever found of this animal was found by Mary Anning, who is one of the most famous fossil hunters and who started out looking for them when she was a child.

Later pterosaurs are called pterodactyloids, which means "wing fingers." Their fourth fingers became wings. The pictures show clearly how it all worked.

Pterosaurs were spectacular-looking animals. Some of them had crests—take a look at the picture on page 15. One, called the *Pterodaustro,* had hundreds of teeth, rather like wires. Paleontologists believe they lived near ponds and streams and swept up water with their teeth, much as fishermen use nets. Show the picture on page 17.

Pterosaur fossils have been found on every continent, and scientists regularly find new fossils and are learning more and more.

This book has great pictures to go along with lots of fascinating information.

Chin, Dr. Karen, and Thom Holmes. *Dino Dung: The Scoop on Fossil Feces* (Step into Reading Step Five). Illustrated by Karen Carr. Random House, 2005. ISBN 0375927026. 48 p. Grades 1–3.

Karen Chin has a unique job. She is an expert on dinosaur poop. Properly, it is called fossil feces and is the fossilized remains of dinosaur dung.

In 1820, a scientist named William Buckland was looking for fossils in a cave in England when he came across some white, rocklike blobs. He started wondering if they were fossilized feces. He did some research by studying modern living animals and found that indeed they were feces. He even named them. He called fossil dung "coprolite," which means "dung stone," combining two Greek words.

Paleontologists love to study fossil feces, for they can learn a lot about ancient animals from them. Coprolites are a rare find. The dung usually has to be buried in a place that will help it to fossilize, and that did not happen often. Also, when a scientist—or anyone else—finds one, it is not always easy to be sure that the rock is, in fact, a coprolite. But Dr. Chin tells us about how the testing is done and also about what to look for if you decide to go hunting.

Readers will want to start looking for dino dung immediately after reading this book.

Diffily, Deborah. *Jurassic Shark.* Paintings by Karen Carr. A Byron Preiss Book/HarperCollins, 2004. ISBN 0060082496. Unpaged. Grades K–3.

This is a beautiful picture book about a shark, one called *Hybodus,* an ancestor of the great white sharks we have in our oceans now. *Hybodus* was not afraid of anything, ever, and she would attack anything as well. This tells the story of how a *Hybodus* protects herself and her baby that is about to be born.

There are some great pictures here to show to your audience. Show the one of the *Liopleurodon* stealing the ichthyosaur that *Hybodus* killed.

French, Vivian. *T. Rex*. Illustrated by Alison Bartlett. Candlewick Press, 2004. ISBN 0763621846. 29 p. Grades K–3.

This is the story of a boy who sees a real *Tyrannosaurus rex* with his grandfather and asks a lot of questions. Many of these his grandpa cannot answer—because no one can answer them. Someday, someone may be able to find out the answers. Tell your students that maybe it will be one of them.

Hort, Lenny. *Did Dinosaurs Eat Pizza? Mysteries Science Hasn't Solved*. Illustrated by John O'Brien. Henry Holt, 2006. ISBN 0805067574. Unpaged. Grades K–3.

Although scientists have learned a ton of stuff about dinosaurs over the last few years, they still have a great many mysteries to solve about them. Some of those mysteries are almost certainly going to remain so forever.

- What color were they?

- How did the giant plant-eating dinosaurs eat enough food to stay alive?

- What did dinosaurs sound like?

- How did huge dinosaurs lay eggs without breaking them?

Show your audience any of these double spreads and read—they will laugh along with you.

Jenkins, Steve. *Prehistoric Actual Size*. Houghton Mifflin, 2005. ISBN 0618535780. Unpaged. All ages.

Exactly how big was the head of an actual velociraptor? It was six feet long, but exactly what does that mean?

With this book, you can tell. Put your hand up next to the picture of the velociraptor's head, and you will have a great way to compare the actual size with the actual size of your own hand.

How about an ancient dragonfly, with a wingspread of more than two feet? Or the head of a six-foot-long giant millipede, a bug that would give anybody nightmares? Or the teeth of giganotosaurus, which may have been the largest predator on land ever?

Boys (and girls) will have a lot of fun comparing these ancient animals to themselves—and they'll learn a lot more interesting facts in the extra information at the back of the book.

Boy, Were We Wrong about Dinosaurs
by Kathleen Kudlinski.

Kudlinski, Kathleen V. *Boy, Were We Wrong about Dinosaurs.* Illustrated by S.D. Schindler. Dutton Children's Books, 2005. ISBN 0525469788. Unpaged. Grades K–4.

Long ago, when people in China found huge bones, they decided they must have come from dragons. They were badly mistaken.

Because no one had ever seen a living dinosaur, people had to guess what dinosaurs looked like, what they ate, and how they behaved. But now scientists are discovering more and more about dinosaurs—and learning that much of the information they previously believed is wrong.

The first time anyone found an Iguanadon fossil, they thought the bone that looked like a rhinoceros horn fit on his head. *Wrong.* It was part of his hand.

People believed that all dinosaurs dragged their tails behind them. *Wrong.* Many dinosaurs had heavy tails with stiff tendons that held the tails straight out behind their bodies.

Most people thought dinosaurs were scaly, like lizards. *Wrong.* Now they think that at least some dinosaurs had feathers!

This is a fun and interesting look at what we now know about dinosaurs. At the rate discoveries are made, it could all change tomorrow.

How Dinosaurs Took Flight: The Fossils, the Science, What We Think We Know, and the Mysteries Yet Unsolved **by Christopher Sloan.**

Sloan, Christopher. *How Dinosaurs Took Flight: The Fossils, the Science, What We Think We Know, and the Mysteries Yet Unsolved.* Foreword by Dr. Xu Xing. National Geographic, 2005. ISBN 0792272986. 64 p. Grades 4–up.

It seems unbelievable, but it is a fact. Modern birds are descended from dinosaurs. Some scientists suspected this long ago, but proof started arriving in 1996, when fossils were found in the Liaoning Province of China. They were fossils of dinosaurs, and those fossils had feathers.

Scientists have learned a lot since this discovery, but they have a lot left to figure out. This book explains the evidence that has been found, and the hypotheses (or temporary conclusions) scientists have developed to explain the facts. Hypotheses are often wrong, and sometimes several hypotheses explain the facts. When that is the case, we learn what the different hypotheses are.

Here are some of the questions that are explored:

- If the dinosaurs had feathers, what kind of feathers did they have?

- What kind of dinosaurs are birds?

- Which dinosaurs are the most likely ancestors of birds?

- How did feathers evolve from bits of fuzz into their present form?

- What are the different types of feathers?

- Did *Tyrannosaurus rex* have feathers?

- How did dinosaurs develop the ability to fly?

- What happened to the dinosaurs? Why did so many of them become extinct?

The pictures are amazing. Kids who like dinosaurs will love this book.

**Feathered Dinosaurs of China
by Gregory Wenzel.**

Wenzel, Gregory. *Feathered Dinosaurs of China.* Charlesbridge, 2004. ISBN
157091561x. 32 p. Grades 4–7.

In the Liaoning Province in China, there are ancient lakebeds containing some of
the best fossils ever found. These fossils show animals and plants in amazing detail.
They show "the delicate wings of insects, veins of leaves, fragile skin, feathers and
soft anatomy, such as internal organs. Many animals are fossilized as complete skeletons, with all of the bones in their proper positions" (page 3). Most of these fossils are
about 124 million years old.

Because of these fossils, we have learned a lot about what life was like in the region so long ago, and the author of this book describes the kind of animals and plants
you would see on a typical day. There are frogs, dragonflies, beetles, turtles, and many
more—including dinosaurs.

The biggest dinosaurs there are called *Jinzhousaurus.* They grew to be up to
twenty feet long. They were plant eaters, but the *Sinornithosaurus* was a meat eater, or
carnivore. It was about five feet long and covered with hairlike feathers.

There are wonderful pictures of the different animals. If you like dinosaurs, take a
look at this book.

Show the picture of *Jinzhousaurus* on page 8.

Williams, Judith. *Discovering Dinosaurs with a Fossil Hunter* (I Like Science!). Illustrations by Michael W. Skrepnick. Enslow, 2004. ISBN 0766022676. 24 p. Grades K–3.

Phil Currie has liked dinosaurs since he was a kid. Today he is a paleontologist, a
scientist who researches and looks for dinosaur fossils. When they find fossils, they
cover them in plaster that turns hard when it dries. This preserves the fossils so it is
safe to move them.

This book tells us some of the things that paleontologists learn from dinosaur fossils. Here are a few:

• Dinosaurs laid eggs, just like birds do.

• Meat-eating dinosaurs would eat any animal they could catch.

• Meat-eating dinosaurs lived in groups.

The book tells us how fossils are formed and how readers can create their own copy of a fossil.

NOT TO BE MISSED

Arnold, Caroline. *When Mammoths Walked the Earth.* Illustrated by Laurie Caple. Clarion Books, 2002. ISBN 0618096337. 40 p. Grades 3–5.

 The Ice Age began 1.8 million years ago and ended only 10,000 years ago. One of the animals that thrived during this period was the mammoth. It was a huge animal resembling an elephant that originally lived in Africa but then spread throughout much of the world, even crossing the Bering Strait into North America. The biggest ones were in what is now Siberia. This is their amazing story, with fine color illustrations.

Barner, Bob. *Dinosaur Bones!* Chronicle, 2001. ISBN 0811831582. 32 p. Grades K–3.

 Colorful pictures illustrate the rhyming, fun-to-read-aloud text. Scientific facts are included on each page.

Bonner, Hannah. *When Bugs Were Big, Plants Were Strange, and Tetrapods Stalked the Earth: A Cartoon Prehistory of Life before the Dinosaurs.* Written and illustrated by Hannah Bonner. National Geographic, 2004. ISBN 079226326x. 45 p. Grades 2–5. *Gotcha Covered.*

 You just plain won't believe the size of the bugs during the Permian age. You will be happy to know they all died out before humans came along. Lots of neat information here.

Camper, Cathy. *Bugs before Time: Prehistoric Insects and Their Relatives.* Illustrated by Steve Kirk. Simon & Schuster Books for Young Readers, 2002. ISBN 0689820925. Unpaged. Grades 3–6. *Gotcha Covered.*

 Did you know that for every pound in your body, there are three hundred pounds of insects on are planet? They've been around since before the dinosaurs, and this book tells about many interesting prehistoric bugs.

Carr, Karen. *Dinosaur Hunt: Texas 115 Million Years Ago.* HarperCollins, 2002. ISBN 0060297034. 48 p. Grades K–3.

 Big color spreads show the life of the *Arocanthosaurus,* a meat eater living in Texas 115 million years ago, and her victorious attack on a plant-eating *Pleurocoelus.* The footprints of the two dinosaurs were discovered in 1938, and this is a depiction of the struggle that might have taken place between them.

Chorlton, Windsor. *Woolly Mammoth: Life, Death and Rediscovery.* Scholastic, 2001 ISBN 0439241340. 40 p. Grades 3–6. *Gotcha Covered.*

 Two Siberian boys saw two tusks sticking out of the snow. They broke them off, took them to market, and discovered they had made one of the greatest scientific finds ever! This is the story of the Jarkov mammoth, frozen solid and perfectly preserved.

Marrin, Albert. *Secrets from the Rocks: Dinosaur Hunting with Roy Chapman Andrews.*
Dutton Children's Books, 2002. ISBN 0525467432. 80 p. Grades 4–up.

Some people say Roy Chapman Andrews was the original Indiana Jones, and like
the fictional character, he hated snakes and he had a lot of adventures. When he graduated from college in 1906, he took the only job he could get at the Museum of Natural
History in New York—working as a janitor. But eventually he became the museum's
director and led several expeditions to the Gobi Desert in Mongolia. What his expeditions found was staggering and greatly increased our knowledge of the prehistoric
world.

Sloan, Christopher. *Feathered Dinosaurs.* Introduction by Dr. Philip J. Currie. National
Geographic Society, 2000. ISBN 0792272196. 64 p. Grades 4–7.

Many scientists believe that there is a dinosaur in your backyard. They also believe that you see dinosaurs every day. Sound unbelievable? A few years ago, they
would have had a hard time believing it too, but now fossils have been found and research done, and a lot of experts agree that dinosaurs were the ancestors of birds. Read
all about it in this beautiful book.

Sloan, Christopher. *Supercroc and the Origin of Crocodiles.* Introduction by Dr. Paul
Sereno. National Geographic, 2002. ISBN 0792266919. 56 p. Grades 2–6. *Gotcha
Covered.*

Crocodiles have been around so long that scientists sometimes call them "living
fossils." Millions of years ago, they fought and often defeated dinosaurs. Visual learn-
ers will love the wonderful illustrations.

Tanaka, Shelley. *New Dinos: The Latest Finds! Coolest Dinosaur Discoveries!* Illustrated
by Alan Bernard. Paleontological consultation by Dr. Philip J. Currie. An Atheneum
Book for Young Readers/Madison Press Book, 2003. ISBN 0689851839. 48 p.
Grades 4–8. *Gotcha Covered.*

Dinosaur information is changing so rapidly that we can barely keep up with it.
Current thinking undergoes constant transformation. Scientists are continuing to discover amazing things. This book brings us up to date as of 2002. The great facts here
often are at odds with what we used to believe.

Walker, Sally M. *Fossil Fish Found Alive: Discovering the Coelacanth.* Carolrhoda
Books, 2002 ISBN 1575055368. 72 p. Grades 4–8. *Gotcha Covered.*

Imagine discovering a fish that everyone thought had become extinct seventy
million years ago! That's what happened with the coelacanth, but it took years to
prove that the fish was still alive and living somewhere in an ocean. Sally Walker tells
an incredible story.

WORTH READING

Nonfiction books with "boy appeal" that have received positive reviews in *Booklist, Horn Book Guide,* and/or *School Library Journal.*

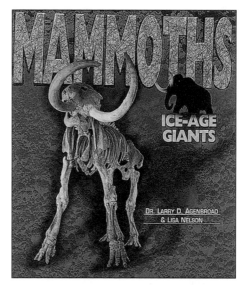

Mammoths: Ice-Age Giants
by Larry D. Agenbroad and Lisa Nelson.

Agenbroad, Larry D., and Lisa Nelson. *Mammoths: Ice-Age Giants* (Discovery!). Lerner, 2002. ISBN 0822528622. 120 p. Grades 5–up.

Arnold, Caroline. *Dinosaurs with Feathers: The Ancestors of Modern Birds*. Illustrated by Laurie Caple. Clarion Books, 2002. ISBN 0618003983. 32 p. Grades 3–6.

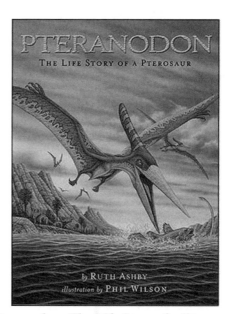

Pteranodon: The Life Story of a Pterosaur
by Ruth Ashby.

Ashby, Ruth. *Pteranodon: The Life Story of a Pterosaur*. Illustrated by Phil Wilson. Abrams, 2005. ISBN 0810957787. 32 p. Grades K–3.

Bergen, David. *Life-Size Dinosaurs*. Sterling, 2004. ISBN 140271755x. 48 p. Grades K–3.

Burnie, David. *The Kingfisher Illustrated Dinosaur Encyclopedia.* Illustrated by John Sibbick. Kingfisher, 2002. ISBN 0753452871. 224 p. Grades 5–up.

Cohen, Daniel. *Allosaurus* (Discovering Dinosaurs). Bridgestone Books, 2003. ISBN 0736816186. 24 p. Grades K–3.

Cohen, Daniel. *Ankylosaurus* (Discovering Dinosaurs). Bridgestone Books, 2003. ISBN 0736816194. 24 p. Grades K–3.

Cohen, Daniel. *Brachiosaurus* (Discovering Dinosaurs). Bridgestone Books, 2003. ISBN 0736816208. 24 p. Grades K–3.

Davis, Kenneth C. *Don't Know Much about Dinosaurs* (Don't Know Much About). HarperCollins, 2004. ISBN 0060286199. 48 p. Grades K–3.

Dixon, Dougal. *Herbivores* (Dinosaurs). Gareth Stevens, 2001. ISBN 0836829166. 36 p. Grades 3–7.

Dixon, Dougal. *In the Sky* (Dinosaurs). Gareth Stevens, 2001. ISBN 0836829182. 36 p. Grades 3–7.

Dixon, Dougal. *Stegosaurus and Other Plains Dinosaurs* (Dinosaur Find). Picture Window Books, 2004. ISBN 1404806687. 24 p. Grades K–3.

Dixon, Dougal. *Triceratops and Other Forest Dinosaurs* (Dinosaur Find). Picture Window Books, 2004. ISBN 1404806717. 24 p. Grades K–3.

***Dinosaur Discoveries* by Gail Gibbons.**

Gibbons, Gail. *Dinosaur Discoveries.* Holiday House, 2005. ISBN 0823419711. 32 p. Grades K–3.

Goecke, Michael P. *American Mastodon* (Buddy Books: Prehistoric Animals). ABDO, 2003. ISBN 1577659732. 24 p. Grades K–3.

Goecke, Michael P. *Giant Armadillo* (Buddy Books: Prehistoric Animals). ABDO, 2003. ISBN 1577659740. 24 p. Grades K–3.

Goecke, Michael P. *Irish Elk* (Buddy Books: Prehistoric Animals). ABDO, 2003. ISBN 1577659759. 24 p. Grades K–3.

Goecke, Michael P. *Scimitar Cat* (Buddy Books: Prehistoric Animals). ABDO, 2003. ISBN 1577659775. 24 p. Grades K–3.

Goecke, Michael P. *Short-Faced Bear* (Buddy Books: Prehistoric Animals). ABDO, 2003. ISBN 1577659767. 24 p. Grades K–3.

Goecke, Michael P. *Woolly Rhinoceros* (Buddy Books: Prehistoric Animals). ABDO, 2003. ISBN 1577659783. 24 p. Grades K–3.

Gray, Susan H. *Apatosaurus* (Exploring Dinosaurs). The Child's World, 2004. ISBN 159296043X. 32 p. Grades 3–8.

Kathy's Favorite Prehistoric Animal Books to Booktalk

Talk about an area in which the information is changing almost constantly! I have to make sure that the information I am sharing is not inaccurate or outdated.

- Sloan, Christopher. *How Dinosaurs Took Flight: The Fossils, the Science, What We Think We Know, and the Mysteries Yet Unsolved.*

- Bonner, Hannah. *When Bugs Were Big, Plants Were Strange, and Tetrapods Stalked the Earth: A Cartoon Prehistory of Life before the Dinosaurs.*

- Chin, Dr. Karen, and Thom Holmes. *Dino Dung: The Scoop on Fossil Feces* (Step into Reading Step Five).

- Chorlton, Windsor. *Woolly Mammoth: Life, Death and Rediscovery.*

- Arnold, Caroline. *Pterosaurs: Rulers of the Skies in the Dinosaur Age.*

- Jenkins, Steve. *Prehistoric Actual Size.* Houghton Mifflin, 2005.

- Walker, Sally M. *Fossil Fish Found Alive: Discovering the Coelacanth.*

From *Gotcha for Guys! Nonfiction Books to Get Boys Excited About Reading* by Kathleen A. Baxter and Marcia Agness Kochel. Westport, CT: Libraries Unlimited. Copyright © 2007.

Gray, Susan H. *Coelophysis* (Exploring Dinosaurs). The Child's World, 2004. ISBN 1592961851. 32 p. Grades 3–8.

Gray, Susan H. *Iguanadon* (Exploring Dinosaurs). The Child's World, 2004. ISBN 1592961878. 32 p. Grades 3–8.

Gray, Susan H. *Maiasaura* (Exploring Dinosaurs). The Child's World, 2004. ISBN 1592961886. 32 p. Grades 3–8.

Gray, Susan H. *Megalosaurus* (Exploring Dinosaurs). The Child's World, 2004. ISBN 159296236X. 32 p. Grades 3–8.

Gray, Susan H. *Oviraptor* (Exploring Dinosaurs). The Child's World, 2004. ISBN 1592961894. 32 p. Grades 3–8.

Gray, Susan H. *Psittacosaurus* (Exploring Dinosaurs). The Child's World, 2004. ISBN 1592962378. 32 p. Grades 3–8.

Gray, Susan H. *Spinosaurus* (Exploring Dinosaurs). The Child's World, 2004. ISBN 1592962343. 32 p. Grades 3–8.

Hall, Katy, and Lisa Eisenberg. *Dino Riddles.* Illustrated by Nicole Rubel. Dial Books for Young Readers, 2002. ISBN 0803722397. 40 p. Grades K–3.

Hehner, Barbara. *Ice Age Cave Bear: The Giant Beast That Terrified Ancient Humans.* Illustrated by Mark Hallett. Crown, 2002. ISBN 0779113470. 32 p. Grades 4–8.

Hehner, Barbara. *Ice Age Sabertooth: The Most Ferocious Cat That Ever Lived.* Illustrated by Mark Hallett. Crown, 2002. ISBN 0375813284. 32 p. Grades 5–up.

Horsfall, Jacqueline. *Dinosaur Jokes* (Giggle Fit). Illustrated by Steve Harpster. Sterling, 2003. ISBN 1402704410. 48 p. Grades K–3.

Lessem, Don. *Armored Dinosaurs* (Meet the Dinosaurs). Carolrhoda Books, 2004. ISBN 0822525704. 48 p. Grades 2–4.

Lessem, Don. *The Deadliest Dinosaurs* (Meet the Dinosaurs). Illustrated by John Bindon. Lerner, 2005. ISBN 0822514214. 32 p. Grades K–3.

Lessem, Don. *The Fastest Dinosaurs* (Meet the Dinosaurs). Illustrated by John Bindon. Lerner, 2005. ISBN 0822514222. 32 p. Grades K–3.

Flying Giants of Dinosaur Time
by Don Lessem.

Lessem, Don. *Flying Giants of Dinosaur Time* (Meet the Dinosaurs). Illustrated by John Bindon. Lerner, 2005. ISBN 0822514249. 32 p. Grades K–3.

Lessem, Don. *Giant Meat-Eating Dinosaurs* (Meet the Dinosaurs). Carolrhoda Books, 2004. ISBN 082253925X. 48 p. Grades 2–4.

Lessem, Don. *Horned Dinosaurs* (Meet the Dinosaurs). Carolrhoda Books, 2004. ISBN 0822513706. 48 p. Grades 2–4.

Lessem, Don. *Scholastic Dinosaurs A to Z: The Ultimate Dinosaur Encyclopedia.* Illustrated by Jan Slovak. Scholastic, 2003. ISBN 0439165911. 223 p. Grades 4–8.

Lessem, Don. *Sea Giants of Dinosaur Time* (Meet the Dinosaurs). Illustrated by John Bindon. Lerner, 2005. ISBN 0822514257. 32 p. Grades K–3.

Lessem, Don. *The Smartest Dinosaurs* (Meet the Dinosaurs). Illustrated by John Bindon. Lerner, 2005. ISBN 0822513730. 32 p. Grades K–3.

Matthews, Rupert. *Ankylosaurus* (Gone Forever). Heinemann Library, 2004. ISBN 1403449090. 32 p. Grades K–3.

Matthews, Rupert. *Apatosaurus* (Gone Forever). Heinemann Library, 2004. ISBN 1403449104. 32 p. Grades K–3.

McMullan, Kate. *Dinosaur Hunters* (Step into Reading). Illustrated by John R. Jones. Random House Children's Books, 2005. ISBN 0375924507. 48 p. Grades 2–4.

Nye, Bill, and Ian G. Saunders. *Bill Nye the Science Guy's Great Big Dinosaur Dig.* Illustrated by Michael Koelsch. Hyperion Books for Children, 2002. ISBN 0786824727. 48 p. Grades 2–5.

Osborne, Mary Pope, and Natalie Pope Boyce. *Sabertooths and the Ice Age: A Nonfiction Companion to Sunset of the Sabertooth* (Magic Tree House Research Guide). Illustrated by Sal Murdocca. Random House Children's Books, 2005. ISBN 0375923802. 128 p. Grades K–3.

Schomp, Victoria. *Ankylosaurus and Other Armored Plant-Eaters* (Prehistoric World). Benchmark, 2002. ISBN 0761410236. 32 p. Grades 1–4.

Schomp, Victoria. *Apatosaurus and Other Giant, Long-Necked Plant-Eaters* (Prehistoric World). Benchmark, 2002. ISBN 0761410228. 32 p. Grades 1–4.

Schomp, Victoria. *Triceratops and Other Horned Plant-Eaters* (Prehistoric World). Benchmark, 2002. ISBN 0761410244. 32 p. Grades 1–4.

Schomp, Victoria. *Tyrannosaurus and Other Giant Meat-Eaters* (Prehistoric World). Benchmark, 2002. ISBN 0761410201. 32 p. Grades 1–4.

Schomp, Victoria. *Velociraptor and Other Small, Speedy Meat-Eaters* (Prehistoric World). Benchmark, 2002. ISBN 0761410252. 32 p. Grades 1–4.

Skrepnick, Michael W. *Diplodocus: Gigantic Long-Necked Dinosaur* (I Like Dinosaurs).
    Enslow, 2005. ISBN 0766026221. 24 p. Grades K–3.

Triceratops: Mighty Three-Horned Dinosaur
by Michael W. Skrepnick.

Skrepnick, Michael W. *Triceratops: Mighty Three-Horned Dinosaur* (I Like Dinosaurs).
    Enslow, 2005. ISBN 0766026205. 24 p. Grades K–3.

Skrepnick, Michael W. *Tyrannosaurus Rex: Fierce King of the Dinosaurs* (I Like Dino-
    saurs). Enslow, 2005. ISBN 0766026213. 24 p. Grades K–3.

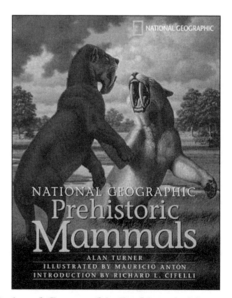

National Geographic Prehistoric Mammals
by Alan Turner.

Turner, Alan. *National Geographic Prehistoric Mammals*. Illustrated by Mauricio Anton.
    National Geographic Children's Books, 2004. ISBN 0792271343. 192 p. Grades 4–up.

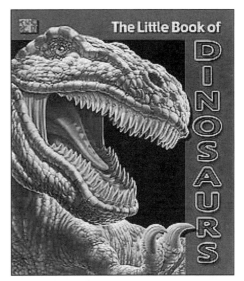

Little Book of Dinosaurs **by Cherie Winner.**

Winner, Cherie. *Little Book of Dinosaurs.* Two-Can, 2005. ISBN 1587284847. 24 p. Grades K–3.

Zoehfeld, Kathleen Weidner. *Did Dinosaurs Have Feathers?* (Let's-Read-and-Find-Out Science). HarperCollins, 2004. ISBN 0060290277. 40 p. Grades K–3.

Chapter

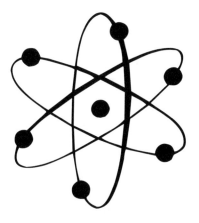

Science

4

Science is everywhere, and that fact is reflected in the variety of books listed here—from coral reefs to space travel to poetry to solving crimes with forensic science. Adults will learn just as much as kids from reading these colorful, appealing, boy-friendly science titles.

NEW AND NOTABLE

Aldrin, Buzz. *Reaching for the Moon.* Paintings by Wendell Minor. HarperCollins, 2005. ISBN 0060554460. Unpaged. Grades 2–5.

Buzz Aldrin's real name was Edwin Eugene, but his big sister Fay Ann could not say "Brother," which was what everyone called him. She said "Buzzer." That got shortened to "Buzz," and it has been his name ever since.

Buzz's father was an airplane pilot who flew all over the country. Buzz loved to fly too, and Buzz was clearly a high achiever. He tells us of the time when he was seven years old and collected rocks (show the wonderful picture). A friend pushed him and his bucket of rocks into a lake, and Buzz would not let go. His father had to pull him out because the rocks were so heavy they were holding him down!

He graduated first in his class at West Point and then joined the U.S. Air Force and flew fifty-six missions in combat during the Korean War. But Buzz became world famous when he was chosen to be an astronaut—and especially when he was, with Neil Armstrong, one of the first two men to land on the moon. He tells us what *that* was like, too.

Buzz has had an amazing life. You will enjoy reading about it.

Branley, Franklyn M. *Earthquakes* (Let's-Read-and-Find-Out Science Books Stage 2). Illustrated by Megan Lloyd. HarperCollins, 2005. ISBN 0060280093. 33 p. Grades 1–3.

Earth is constantly moving, even though it is so slow that human beings cannot feel it. When the earth beneath our feet moves quickly, it may mean an earthquake. Most earthquakes are small, but some are big—so big that they can make tall buildings collapse.

"We live on the outer part of Earth. It is called Earth's crust. In some places the crust is 30 or 40 miles thick. If Earth were an apple, the crust would be only as thick as the skin of the apple. Most earthquakes occur in the crust" (page 12).

And most earthquakes occur along the shores of the Pacific Ocean. Japan has about seven thousand earthquakes every year, but most of them are very small.

There is a great fact at the end of the book: between 1975 and 1995, only four states did not have earthquakes. Guess which they were. (Answer: Florida, Iowa, North Dakota, and Wisconsin.)

Read this interesting book to find out more!

***Fireworks* by Vicki Cobb.**

Cobb, Vicki. *Fireworks* (Where's the Science Here?). Photographs by Michael Gold. Millbrook Press, 2006. ISBN 0761327711. 48 p. Grades 3–6.

Have you ever wondered how in the world fireworks are made? This tells us exactly how, and they are made with fire, just as their name says. Fireworks are very dangerous, and the people who make them can be killed during the manufacturing process.

Vicki Cobb tells us and the photographs show us exactly what happens during the manufacturing process. It is great fun to find out how it all works.

Show your audience the picture of the fireworks display on page 29.

Collard, Sneed B. *The Prairie Builders: Reconstructing America's Lost Grasslands*. Photographed by Sneed B. Collard III. Houghton Mifflin, 2005. ISBN 061839687x. 72 p. Grades 3–up.

In the middle of the 1800s, "tallgrass prairie once dominated the central part of our nation. According to the National Park Service, it covered 400,000 square miles from Ohio to North Dakota and Minnesota to Texas. An explosion of plant and animal species thrived on this expanse. Grasses up to twelve feet tall fed elk, deer, pronghorn, and between 30 and 75 *million* bison, or buffalo." Wolves, grizzly bears, coyotes, birds, insects, and hundreds of kinds of butterflies lived there.

It did not take the pioneers and settlers long to destroy that prairie almost completely. They plowed the soil and planted crops. The land that had supported so many kinds of life was changed forever.

Or was it?

Today, in Iowa, there is a huge prairie restoration area, where many scientists and volunteers are trying to bring back the prairie as it was so long ago. It will never be exactly the same, but the story of what they are doing and the wonderful photographs of the prairie coming back (they had to burn the land and continue to burn the land regularly) make this a book that will make you want to get to the Neal Smith National Wildlife Refuge as quickly as you can.

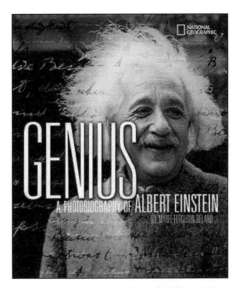

***Genius: A Photobiography of Albert Einstein*
by Marfé Ferguson Delano.**

Delano, Marfé Ferguson. *Genius: A Photobiography of Albert Einstein*. National Geographic, 2005. ISBN 0792295447. 64 p. Grades 4–8.

Albert Einstein was a fairly ordinary little boy, although he was very bright. When he was about two and a half years old, his little sister Maja was born. When his parents first showed her to him, he said, "Where are the wheels?" He had apparently been expecting a toy, not a baby! But Albert got used to her, and she was his closest friend throughout his life.

Albert didn't like school much, especially as he became a teenager. He was very good at math and science but did not get good grades in anything else. When his parents moved to Italy without him (they wanted him to finish school in Germany), he became very unhappy indeed. He dropped out of school and not only went to Italy to be with them but also decided to renounce his German citizenship. Later, he went to school in Switzerland.

When Albert finished school, he started working in a patent office. In his spare time, he wrote some articles that completely changed scientific thinking. Four of them were published, the first was on the nature of light. The second was on atoms and molecules, and the third and fourth launched his amazing theory of relativity. Albert became world famous.

Albert was working in Germany when the Nazis took over. He was Jewish, and he hated their regime. When he was in California, he learned that the Nazis had frozen his bank account, seized his property, and burned copies of his books. He never went back. Eventually he became a citizen of the United States.

Albert was a truly amazing man who loved music and sailing and who worked for peace. You'll enjoy learning about him.

Show the picture on the back cover of the book of Einstein with his tongue out.

Guinea Pig Scientists: Bold Self-Experimenters in Science and Medicine **by Leslie Dendy and Mel Boring. Used by permission of Henry Holt & Co.**

Dendy, Leslie, and Mel Boring. *Guinea Pig Scientists: Bold Self-Experimenters in Science and Medicine.* With illustrations by C. B. Mordan. Henry Holt, 2005. ISBN 0805073167. 213 p. Grades 5–up.

Everyone knows what happens to guinea pigs in science labs—scientists experiment on them. But what if a guinea pig isn't enough for the experiment? What if a scientist needs a human being? Who will volunteer to be a human science experiment?

Many times throughout history, the scientist who thinks of the experiment in the first place decides that he himself or she herself will be the "human guinea pig." After all, many experiments are risky. If something goes wrong, only one person will suffer —the person on whom the experiment was performed. So why not take the risk yourself? Who better than you understands what is going on? And, in many cases, the scientist who thought of the experiment believes that the experiment will come out all right—or else he or she would not want to try it in the first place.

This is the story of several human guinea pigs, and you won't believe all of the experiments they tried—and all of the things that *did* go wrong. In Italy in the 1770s, Lazzaro Spallanzani wanted to find out what happens inside a person's digestive tract. He filled linen bags with food, ate them, and then watched them come out the other end, usually the next day. Then he tested the contents of those bags to see what had happened. Then he started swallowing wooden tubes filled with food. What difference did that make to the food inside them?

William Morton and Horace Wells were among the first ever to use anesthesia on patients so that they could experience relatively pain-free surgery and tooth pulling. But they suffered some bad consequences.

Daniel Carrion and Jesse Lazear infected themselves with deadly diseases—and died. Marie Curie suffered from radiation disease. The fascinating John Paul Stapp made life much safer for pilots and drivers. And Jack Haldane, who did many experiments with air and breathing and whose family motto was "Suffer," explained why human beings make better subjects than animals for experimentation. "It is difficult to be sure how a rabbit feels at any time. Indeed, many rabbits make no serious attempt to co-operate with one" (page 109).

Young readers will be delighted by the incredible stories of these brave human beings.

***Investigating Murders* by Paul Dowswell.**

Dowswell, Paul. *Investigating Murders* (Forensic Files). Heinemann Library, 2004. ISBN 1403448310. 48 p. Grades 4–8.

It seems like everyone is interested in forensic science. The name tells us a lot—"forensic science" is any kind of science used in a criminal investigation. But what it can do is absolutely staggering. The clues that are considered evidence at a crime scene can point to the perpetrator of that crime in a truly astonishing way.

Dr. Edmund Locard, working in the 1880s, told us that "Every contact leaves a trace" (page 8), and today this is called the "two-way-transfer." It is the basic foundation of forensic science. In his time, forensic science made great advances—microscopes became much more powerful than ever before, and there were great strides in chemical analysis, fingerprints, ballistics, and photography.

Paul Dowswell tells us about a few cases in which forensic scientists caught the criminal. The first he discusses was called the Last Great Train Robbery, and it happened in 1923 in Oregon. Three brothers hijacked a train and blew up the mail car, which they thought held a lot of gold and money. The problem was that the explosive they used to open the mail car was too strong—and it blew it up and killed the mail clerk inside. They destroyed completely the treasure they were trying to steal, and then killed some other people. At first, no one knew who committed the crime, but then forensic scientists stepped in and solved the case.

In another case, a Bulgarian immigrant in London was murdered while walking across a bridge. Who did it and what was used to poison him?

There are lots of case studies and many photographs here. This book may inspire kids to pursue a career in forensic science.

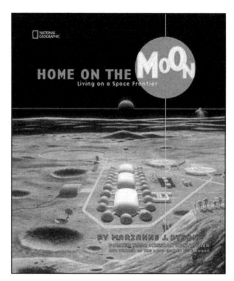

***Home on the Moon: Living on the Space Frontier* by Marianne J. Dyson.**

Dyson, Marianne J. *Home on the Moon: Living on the Space Frontier*. National Geographic, 2003. ISBN 0792271939. 64 p. Grades 4–8.

This book tells what it would be like to live on the moon and how scientists would create a place for people to live there.

We know what kind of rocks make up the moon. Many of them are rocks shared with earth. Scientists believe that the moon and Earth were once united, and an impact from outer space caused the moon to float away and become separate. Some scientists believe that there is frozen water on the moon as well, but not a lot of it. What is there would have to be recycled constantly.

The moon does not have a global magnetic field. A compass would not work there. But people could see Earth from the near side of the moon, where any colonies would be set up, and that could tell them which direction they were going. And earthlight, even at night, would be bright enough to read by.

Any moon colonies would almost certainly be created underground. People need air, and that is easier to create in an enclosed environment. Also, the temperature outside would be deadly. The average dayspan temperature is 225 degrees Fahrenheit, and the average nightspan temperature is negative 243 degrees Fahrenheit. That is a huge span, and either of those would kill any human being.

This book is loaded with photographs and great information.

Farrell, Jeanette. *Invisible Allies: Microbes That Shape Our Lives.* Farrar, Straus & Giroux, 2005. ISBN 0374336083. 165 p. Grades 4–up.

If you are like most people, you have probably never thought much about microbes. But maybe it is time that you do. After all, 90 percent of your body is made up of them. In fact, more than one hundred trillion of them live on and in your body.

Kathy's Favorite Science Books to Booktalk

- Jackson, Donna M. *The Wildlife Detectives: How Forensic Scientists Fight Crimes against Nature.*

- Dendy, Leslie, and Mel Boring. *Guinea Pig Scientists: Bold Self-Experimenters in Science and Medicine.*

- Fradin, Dennis Brindell. *With a Little Luck: Surprising Stories of Amazing Discoveries.*

- Editors of YES Magazine. *Fantastic Feats and Failures.*

- Wulffson, Don. *Toys! Amazing Stories behind Some Great Inventions.*

- Seuling, Barbara. *From Head to Toe: The Amazing Human Body and How It Works.*

- Cobb, Vicki. *Fireworks* (Where's the Science Here?).

- Tomecek, Stephen M. *What a Great Idea: Inventions That Changed the World.*

- Delano, Marfé Ferguson. *Genius: A Photobiography of Albert Einstein.*

- Swanson, Diane. *Burp! The Most Interesting Book You'll Ever Read about Eating* (Mysterious You).

From *Gotcha for Guys! Nonfiction Books to Get Boys Excited About Reading* by Kathleen A. Baxter and Marcia Agness Kochel. Westport, CT: Libraries Unlimited. Copyright © 2007.

And we probably couldn't live very well without them, for they do all sorts of wonderful things for us. One microbiologist figured that about 29,999 out of every 30,000 bacteria do good things.

Many popular foods are made by microbes. Cheese. Bread. Sausage. Chocolate. Many ethnic foods, such as soy sauce, cassava, and the Korean kimchi, are also created by microbes. Without them, none of these good tasting things would exist.

Without microbes to eat up our waste, the world would be a much dirtier place, probably too dirty to live in. And without microbes to eat up the dead bodies of humans and other animals, we would not have space to live. Dead bodies three bodies deep would cover the entire earth—and that is not even counting the bodies of dead animals, including really big ones, such as dinosaurs and mammoths.

Microbes clean our water. We can pour raw sewage into sewage treatment plants, and within a fairly short time, it emerges as clean water once more.

You will not believe all the things that microbes can do. The story of how they were discovered is a fascinating one as well. The first man to see them, Antony van Leeuwenhoek, was astounded. When he realized they were living in his own mouth, he did everything he could to get rid of them.

Kids will have a great time reading this book.

Read your audience the song lyric by Lee Hays on page 124.

In Your Face: The Facts about Your Features
by Donna M. Jackson.

Jackson, Donna M. *In Your Face: The Facts about Your Features.* Viking, 2004. ISBN 0670036579. 42 p. Grades 4–8.

It seems that humans all began with fish faces. Maybe five hundred million years ago, the first creatures existed with an opening on one end that enabled them to sift food from the water they took in. After that first primitive mouth, later animals developed primitive eyes, noses, and jaws—jaws that could close that mouth and keep in food.

Then "nature handed down a facial pattern to ensure success: two eyes, a nose, and a mouth, shaped in a t formation. While variations within species exist, these features are strategically placed for survival in most animals so that as the mouth consumes food, the eyes and nose above it can watch for and sniff out danger" (page 2).

Faces can reveal many things. Our eyes can tell whether we are paying attention to something. If they drift away, we are not. Teachers definitely know this! People spend about twenty-three minutes a day blinking, trying to keep their eyes moist. And eyelids are covered by the thinnest skin on the human body.

Ears are unique to each person, almost as unique as a fingerprint. Everyone's ears look just like theirs, not like anyone else's.

Here are some more facts about faces:

- Human babies recognize their own reflections at about eighteen months of age. Most animals never do.

- Studies show that we find people attractive who look a lot like we do.

- Scientists have determined ways to predict what children will look like as they grow up. This helps when children are kidnapped or go missing—searchers can recognize that person even though he or she has gotten older.

- It takes a three-dimensional view of a face to show what someone really looks like it, which is why line drawings of people do not work very well.

- Some people cannot see faces. They have a condition called face blindness and are unable to recognize people just from looking at their faces.

This is a fascinating book and will give kids a lot of information they'll want to share with their friends.

Katz, Susan. *Looking for Jaguar and Other Rain Forest Poems.* Pictures by Lee Christiansen. Greenwillow Books, an imprint of HarperCollins, 2005. ISBN 006029793x. 40 p. Grades K–5.

Most people who live in North America don't get to see many tropical rain forests. But readers can take an imaginary journey through some of the world's most famous ones in this colorful book of poems about the animals and plants you would see on your trip. At the back of the book are some fascinating facts about them all, such as the following:

- Giant armadillos in South America weigh up to 130 pounds and are four to five feet long. Read the poem on page 9.

- In the Amazon rain forest, the walking tree is rooted by thin, tall stilt roots. When the roots die, new ones take their place—but they always root toward sunlight, so these trees can move as much as ten feet in a decade! Read the poem on page 13.

- Europeans did not believe in the okapi, an African rain forest animal, until the early 1900s when Sir Harry Johnston "discovered" one. Of course, the native people had always known about them. Read the poem on page 22.

***Leonardo da Vinci* by Kathleen Krull.**

Krull, Kathleen. *Leonardo da Vinci* (Giants of Science). Illustrated by Boris Kulikov. Viking, 2005. ISBN 067005920x. 124 p. Grades 6–8.

"Europe in the Middle Ages—first of all, there were no books. No printed books, that is. Just manuscripts in Latin, tediously copied by hand for the rich. Peasants had never seen one. Most people couldn't read or write anyway.

"There were no bathrooms. Hardly anyone knew what soap or underwear was. The poor ate with their fingers; utensils were for the rich. Most adults had no more than a few teeth in their head" (page 11).

When you read the first two paragraphs of this book, you know you are in for a treat. Would you want to have lived at a time like that?

One man who did, Leonardo da Vinci, was one of the greatest geniuses of all time. The thoughts he thought and the ideas he came up with have never, to anyone's knowledge, been equaled.

What was his life like? How did he live? How did he make money? What got him into trouble? Krull writes about da Vinci the scientist, da Vinci the man, and life in the Renaissance in this chatty, eye-opening book. It's a compelling read about an amazing human being.

McNulty, Faith. *If You Decide to Go to the Moon.* Illustrated by Steven Kellogg. Scholastic Press, 2005. ISBN 0590483595. Unpaged. Grades 1–4.

Kids are fascinated by the moon. Ask your audience these questions: What would you need to pack for a trip to the moon? How would you get there? What would it be like when you land? Could you breathe? Could you take off your space suit and run around? How long would it take to get there? What would it *feel* like to travel in space and be weightless?

This is a beautiful look at what it would be like to travel to a place 240,000 miles away from Earth. A boy astronaut leaves home and goes on a lonely but glorious adventure—and returns safely.

Show any of the wonderful illustrations in the book. A nice one to show is the foldout spread of life on Earth.

Pitkin, Linda. *Journey Under the Sea*. Oxford University Press, 2003. ISBN 0195219716. 48 p. Grades 4–8.

Imagine that you have learned how to dive and are about to go on an expedition off the coast of Indonesia. This book, by an expert diver and photographer, tells us what it is like. First of all, you will go on a dive boat, led by a dive guide, whose name is Dedi. He will take care of you and make sure you do not make dangerous mistakes when you dive.

In the water you will see colorful and beautiful coral formations and unimaginable sea animals. These are incredible creatures: look at the photos of the leafy nose moray eel, the porcupinefish, the lionfish, the sea slug, the mimic octopus (which camouflages itself as other sea animals), the scorpionfish, and the ghost pipefish—even their names are astonishing.

The book is filled with fun facts such as the fact that octopuses are very intelligent. In captivity, they have even been known to learn how to screw the lids off of jars! And a big manta ray can weigh more than 2,200 pounds and be more than six yards wide.

But all of the extraordinary sea life you see is in serious danger. Its worst enemy is human beings—people who take too many fish out of the water, damage coral reefs, and litter the oceans.

Take a look at the picture of the scorpionfish on page 25.

Platt, Richard. *Forensics* (Kingfisher Knowledge). Foreword by Kathy Reichs. Kingfisher, 2005. ISBN 0753458624. 65 p. Grades 4–up.

What happens at a crime scene? How do the detectives decide which evidence is important? Is some evidence invisible to the human eye? How can the police be certain they have arrested the right suspect?

Readers will discover the following:

- Why detectives and observers must be very careful never to touch anything at a crime site.

- How the "mug shot" was developed and why police photos are always taken showing the same areas of the subject's face.

- How detectives lift fingerprints and how they make invisible ones become visible.

- How DNA testing, which is still a fairly new technology, helps catch criminals.

- How scientists can tell whether a skeleton belonged to a man or to a woman.

- Why trace evidence—tiny specks of material—is so important.

- How dirt helps catch criminals (you may be surprised!)

And much, much more in this colorful book.

Show the frontispiece photograph of all the detectives lined up, searching for evidence at a crime scene.

Prelutsky, Jack. *It's Snowing! It's Snowing! Winter Poems* (An I Can Read Book). Pictures by Yossi Abolafia. HarperCollins, 2006. ISBN 006537167. 48 p. Grades K–4.

Jack Prelutsky's poems are always a blast. These are in the easy reader format, some recycled from an earlier book, but they are all winners. Some favorites are "December Days are So Short" on page 12, "Winter Signs" on page 17, "My Mother Took Me Skating" on page 22, "My Snowman Has a Noble Head" on page 24, "I am Freezing" on page 27, and "My Mother's Got Me Bundled Up" on page 30.

Romanek, Trudee. *Aha! The Most Interesting Book You'll Ever Read about Intelligence* (Mysterious You). Illustrated by Rose Cowles. Kids Can Press, 2004. ISBN 1553374851. 40 p. Grades 3–8.

Did you know that a person may be extremely intelligent and not have a high IQ? On page 5 of this book, it says, "many experts agree that intelligence is not just the information you know or the activities you've learned to do. Instead, it's your ability to use what you know to solve problems, learn new things or change when a situation changes. Intelligence is really about how well you cope in the world."

People learn in all sorts of ways, and on page 13 there is a quiz to help young people figure out which ways they learn. There are different ways to be a genius. Tiger Woods is a genius at golf; Mozart was a musical genius; Maria Gaetana Agnesi was a genius at math (read about her on page 26).

On page 27 is a quiz to help readers figure out what kind of intelligences are their strongest. Are they musically intelligent? Logically/mathematically intelligent? Bodily/kinesthetic intelligent? Spatially? Linguistically? Interpersonally or intrapersonally?

The experts all agree that human brains need to be exercised just as human bodies do. Read the book to learn more.

Sayre, April Pulley. *Stars Beneath Your Bed: The Surprising Story of Dust*. Pictures by Ann Jonas. Greenwillow Books, an imprint of HarperCollins, 2005. ISBN 0060571896. Unpaged. Grades K–4.

You can see it. You can feel it. But do you really know what it is or where it comes from?

That's dust, and in all sorts of ways, it shows up in our lives. Some of it is almost ancient, and some of it is brand new, but it is all around us.

April Pulley Sayre tells us what it really is and how it got here.

Science Verse **by Jon Scieszka.**

Scieszka, Jon. *Science Verse.* Illustrated by Lane Smith. Viking, 2004. ISBN 0670910570. Unpaged. Grades 3–up.

On Wednesday in science class, Mr. Newton tells his class that they can hear the poetry of science in everything if they just listen close enough.

It drives our hero crazy, but Mr. Newton is right. Boys love books by Jon Scieszka (author of *The True Story of the Three Little Pigs*, *The Stinky Cheese Man*, and *The Time Warp Trio* series to name a few), and they will love reading the silly poems in this funny book. They can even sing a lot of them.

Simon, Seymour. *Guts: Our Digestive System.* HarperCollins, 2005. ISBN 00602546522. Unpaged. Grades 1–5.

This is a great way to find out what happens to your food after you eat it. Seymour Simon has picked out some wonderful photographs of the insides of the body—and some of those insides aren't very pretty.

Although they may look more than a little gross, they do some amazing work. Take a look at the esophagus, covered with mucus. Everything you eat goes through that. And on the next page, take a look at what the inside of the stomach looks like.

It's a fun way to learn about what happens inside us.

NOT TO BE MISSED

Berger, Melvin. *Why I Sneeze, Shiver, Hiccup and Yawn* (Let's Read-and-Find-Out Science Stage 2). Illustrated by Paul Meisel. HarperCollins, 2000. ISBN 0060281448. 33 p. Grades 1–3. *Gotcha Again.*

Reflex actions are what this book is about. Humans cannot physically stop their bodies from doing them, and they are incredibly interesting to read about in this well-written book.

Bradley, Kimberly Brubaker. *Energy Makes Things Happen.* Illustrated by Paul Meisel. HarperCollins, 2003. ISBN 0060289082. 33 p. Grades K–3.

Energy is a wonderful thing. Unless they are not feeling well, kids usually have a lot of it. The food we eat contributes a lot to human energy levels. Heat, light, and all sorts of movement come from energy. This is an exciting introduction to the subject.

Branley, Franklyn M. *Flash, Crash, Rumble, and Roll* (Let's-Read-and-Find-Out Science). Illustrated by True Kelley. HarperCollins, 1964, 1985, 1999 (revised edition, newly illustrated). ISBN 0060278587. 32 p. Grades 2–3. *Gotcha Again.*

Thunder and lightning are some of the scariest natural phenomena that kids experience, more often than they would like. What makes it happen? What causes these outbursts? This offers great information and safety advice for younger kids.

Charlip, Remy. *Peanut Butter Party: Including the History, Uses, and Future of Peanut Butter.* Tricycle Press, 1999. ISBN 1883672694. Unpaged. Grades 1–4. *Gotcha Again.*

The title tells it all: here you will find out a great deal of information about one of those foods almost everyone loves. Americans who leave the country go crazy without it and have to ask their friends and relatives to send it to them. There are recipes, games, and stories galore.

Cobb, Vicki. *Magic ... Naturally! Science Entertainments and Amusements.* Illustrated by Lionel Kalish. HarperCollins, 1993. ISBN 0060224746. 150 p. Grades 4–6. *Gotcha.*

This has several tricks that the reader can do in front of an audience—or for friends. Try "The Clinging Cup," "Drag Race," or "Intelligent Eggs."

Dahl, Michael. *Computer Evidence* (Edge Books: Forensic Crime Solvers). Capstone Press, 2004. ISBN 073682698x. 32 p. Grades 3–9. *Gotcha Covered.*

Most of us love computers, and this describes an interesting way in which they are now used—to solve crimes. Computer evidence can be helpful in all sorts of criminal acts, and this is high interest at a fairly low reading level.

Dunphy, Madeleine. *Here Is the Coral Reef.* Illustrated by Tom Leonard. Hyperion Books for Children, 1998. ISBN 0786821353. Unpaged. Grades K–2. *Gotcha Again.*

Younger boys will be drawn to the stunning illustrations in this simple description of the ecosystem of a coral reef. Even the beloved sharks live here.

Dussling, Jennifer. *Pink Snow and Other Weird Weather* (All Aboard Reading). Illustrated by Hedi Petach. Grosset & Dunlap, 1998. ISBN 0448418584. 48 p. Grades 1–3. *Gotcha Again.*

Pink snow has fallen: it had red dust in it. Toads have really rained from the sky! Fun facts that easily lend themselves to conversation (you won't be able to help yourself) fill this interesting book. Can you believe that one park ranger has been struck by lightning *seven* times?

Farmer, Jacqueline. *Bananas!* Illustrated by Page Eastburn O'Rourke. Charlesbridge, 1999. ISBN 088106114X. Unpaged. Grades 2–4.

> Bananas definitely win first prize in the contest for the easiest fruit to eat. This is filled with intriguing facts and fun information. Did you know that there were no yellow bananas before 1836?

Hauser, Jill. *Super Science Concoctions: 50 Mysterious Mixtures for Fabulous Fun.* Illustrated by Michael Kline. Williamson, 1997. ISBN 1885593023. 160 p. Grades 4–6. *Gotcha.*

> There are a lot of fun experiments and activities here, such as making your own watercolors, gelatin worms, lava, and bubble brew.

Hopping, Lorraine Jean. *Blizzards!* (Wild Weather). Illustrated by Jody Wheeler. Scholastic, 1998. ISBN 0590397303. Unpaged. Grades 2–3. *Gotcha Again.*

> Blizzards are not just bad snowstorms. They are also bad windstorms, and the combination can be deadly. There are some amazing true stories here that are just the thing for a cold, stormy day.

Jackson, Donna M. *The Wildlife Detectives: How Forensic Scientists Fight Crimes against Nature.* Photographs by Wendy Shattil and Bob Rozinski. Houghton Mifflin, 2000. ISBN 0395869765. 48 p. Grades 3–7. *Gotcha Again.*

> Charger, an elk in Yellowstone Park, was found dead by park rangers one morning. The killer had taken his antlers, which were worth a lot of money. This is the true story of how forensic scientists track the people who commit crimes against nature.

Jenkins, Steve. *Hottest Coldest Highest Deepest.* Houghton Mifflin, 1998. ISBN 0395899990. 32 p. Grades 1–3. *Gotcha Again.*

> What's the hottest spot in the world? The windiest? The longest river? It's a fun guessing game that includes information about the United States as well as the entire world.

Kent, Peter. *Hidden under the Ground: The World Beneath Your Feet.* Dutton Children's Books, 1998. ISBN 0525675523. 33 p. Grades 3–6.

> When kids read this book, they'll start wondering what is going on underneath the ground they walk on. They may be surprised! Many animals live there, and prisoners are frequently kept there, too. This is a fun book.

Muller, Eric. *While You're Waiting for the Food to Come: A Tabletop Science Activity Book: Experiments and Tricks That Can Be Done at a Restaurant, the Dining Room Table, or Wherever Food Is Served.* Illustrated by Eldon Doty. Orchard Books, 1999. ISBN 0531301990. 83 p. Grades 4–6. *Gotcha Again.*

> It may not always please the parents at the table, but there are all sorts of interesting things to do in a restaurant while waiting for the food to come. Try, for instance, looking through the top of a salt shaker. You may be surprised. Full of interesting ideas.

Nurosi, Aki. *Colorful Illusions: Tricks to Fool Your Eyes.* With Mark Shulman. Sterling, 2000. ISBN 0806929979. 80 p. Grades 4–up.

> The illustrations and the questions asked about them provide a surefire hit. These optical illusions deal with the way the eye sees color.

Nye, Bill. *Bill Nye the Science Guy's Big Blue Ocean.* Illustrated by John Dykes. Hyperion Books for Children, 1999. ISBN 0786842210. 48 p. Grades 3–5. *Gotcha Again.*

> Can you name all four oceans? How about the seven seas? Bill Nye, the famous science guy, gives us a lot of fun information about the oceans on our planet. They use the exact same water that was on our planet four billion years ago!

Pfeffer, Wendy. *Sounds All Around* (Let's-Read-and-Find-Out Science, Stage 1). Illustrated by Holly Keller. HarperCollins, 1999. ISBN 0060277122. 32 p. Grades 1–3. *Gotcha Again.*

> How many sounds can you make using your mouth? Your hands? Your feet? They are all made from vibrations, and we can use them to send all sorts of messages. This is a great introduction to the subject, one that even makes an adult think.

Rowan, Dr. Pete. *Big Head!* Illustrated by John Temperton. Knopf, 1998. ISBN 0679890181. 44 p. Grades 5–up. *Gotcha Again.*

> Our heads are miraculous. Amazing things go on in them all of the time. There are a lot of overlays in this colorful book to attract browsers who start reading to learn more.

Schyffert, Bea Uusma. *The Man Who Went to the Far Side of the Moon: The Story of* Apollo 11 *Astronaut Michael Collins.* Chronicle Books, 2003. ISBN 0811840077. 78 p. Grades 5–9. *Gotcha Covered.*

> Can you imagine what it would be like to get nearer to the moon than anyone had ever gotten to it before, then to have to sit in your space capsule while two other men made the actual landing? Michael Collins did get the consolation of seeing a view that no naked human eye had seen before—the far side of the moon. Of course, it was so black that he couldn't see it, he could only see a place where no stars shone through it. This strikingly designed book tells an amazing story.

Seuling, Barbara. *From Head to Toe: The Amazing Human Body and How It Works.* Illustrated by Edward Miller. Holiday House, 2002. ISBN 0823416992. 32 p. Grades 2–5. *Gotcha Covered.*

> Did you know that every single part of your body has a purpose except one? The appendix seems to be useless. This book is jam-packed with information about our bodies and full of colorful illustrations.

Simon, Seymour. *Danger! Volcanoes.* SeaStar Books, 2002. ISBN 1587171821. Unpaged. Grades K–3. *Gotcha Covered.*

> Did you know that there are more than five hundred active volcanoes around the world—and that more than half of them are around the Pacific Ocean in a region called the Ring of Fire? The fine color photographs are compelling.

Skurzynski, Gloria. *Are We Alone? Scientists Search for Life in Space.* National Geographic, 2004. ISBN 079226567x. 92 p. Grades 4–8. *Gotcha Covered.*

    Are we all alone in the universe, or are there other intelligent beings out there, on other planets, in other solar systems? No one really knows for sure, but scientists are experimenting in all sorts of ways to try to discover the answer to this bewildering question. Excellent photographs highlight the text.

Skurzynski, Gloria. *Zero Gravity.* Simon & Schuster Books for Young Readers, 1994. ISBN 0027829251. 32 p. Grades 4–6. *Gotcha Again.*

    In zero gravity, a human can float weightless in the air. Astronauts who orbit around Earth know what this is like, and they have to take special precautions whenever they do just about anything—to keep from floating away themselves or to keep the things they are using from floating away. You'll find excellent information well presented in this book.

Sullivan, George. *To the Bottom of the Sea: The Exploration of Exotic Life, the* Titanic, *and Other Secrets of the Oceans.* Twenty-First Century Books, 1999. ISBN 0761303529. 80 p. Grades 4–6. *Gotcha Again.*

    For most of human history, people could not explore the ocean floor. Human beings cannot dive on their own more than thirty to forty feet beneath the surface because of the pressure, so a vehicle had to be invented in which they could safely stay way below the water surface and take a good look around without hurting themselves.

    This tells us how we are exploring the ocean floor and what we are learning down there.

Swanson, Diane. *Hmm? The Most Interesting Book You'll Ever Read about Memory* (Mysterious You). Illustrated by Rose Cowles. Kids Can Press, 2001. ISBN 1550745956. 40 p. Grades 4–7. *Gotcha Again.*

    Did you know that the human brain can send and receive millions of signals in a second? There are some great fast facts here, and a lot of "You Try It" fun activities. You will be astounded at what that brain in your head can do—and by exactly how it does it.

Wells, Robert E. *What's Faster than a Speeding Cheetah?* Albert Whitman, 1997. ISBN 0807522805. Unpaged. Grades 1–3. *Gotcha Again.*

    This book has some fine facts about speed. The fastest human being can go, sometimes, as fast as fifteen miles an hour. But a cheetah can go up to seventy miles an hour, an ostrich up to forty-five miles per hour. This is full of good information to share with friends.

Wolf, Alan. *The Blood-Hungry Spleen and Other Poems about Our Parts.* Illustrated by Greg Clark. Candlewick Press, 2003. ISBN 076361565x. 53 p. Grades 4–7. *Gotcha Covered.*

    These poems about various body parts written by a science teacher are both funny and dead on.

Zubrowski, Bernie. *Soda Science: Designing and Testing Soft Drinks.* Illustrated by Roy Doty. Morrow Junior Books, 1997. ISBN 0688139175. 92 p. Grades 4–6. *Gotcha.*
What do *you* call it? Soda or pop? There are directions here for kids to make their own new soft drink sensations.

WORTH READING

Nonfiction books with "boy appeal" that have received positive reviews in *Booklist, Horn Book Guide,* and/or *School Library Journal.*

Aldrich, Lisa. *Nikola Tesla and the Taming of Electricity.* Morgan Reynolds, 2005. ISBN 193179846x. 160 p. Grades 5–up.

Allan, Tony. *Wild Water: Floods* (Turbulent Planet). Raintree, 2004. ISBN 1410911020. 48 p. Grades 4–6.

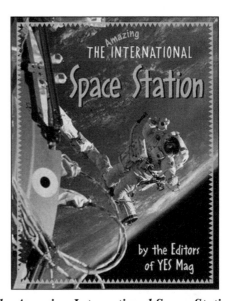

The Amazing International Space Station.

The Amazing International Space Station. Kids Can Press, 2003. ISBN 1553373804. 48 p. Grades 4–6.

Arnosky, Jim. *Under the Wild Western Sky.* HarperCollins, 2005. ISBN 0688171214. 32 p. Grades K–3.

Branley, Franklyn M. *Mission to Mars* (Let's-Read-and-Find-Out Science). Illustrated by True Kelley. HarperCollins, 2002. ISBN 0060298081. 40 p. Grades K–3.

Buttitta, Hope. *It's Not Magic, It's Science! 50 Science Tricks That Mystify, Dazzle & Astound!* Lark Books, 2005. ISBN 1579906222. 80 p. Grades 4–6.

Tornadoes: Disaster and Survival
by Bonnie Ceban.

Ceban, Bonnie J. *Tornadoes: Disaster and Survival* (Deadly Disasters). Enslow, 2005. ISBN 0766023834. 48 p. Grades 4–6.

Colson, Mary. *Shaky Ground: Earthquakes* (Turbulent Planet). Raintree, 2004. ISBN 1410919110. 48 p. Grades 4–6.

Coral Reef (24 Hours). DK, 2005. ISBN 0756611253. 48 p. Grades K–3.

DiSpezio, Michael A. *How Bright Is Your Brain? Amazing Games to Play with Your Mind.* Illustrated by Catherine Leary. Sterling, 2005. ISBN 1402706510. 80 p. Grades 4–6.

DiSpezio, Michael. *Space Mania: Discovering Distant Worlds without Leaving Your Own.* Sterling, 2003. ISBN 0806972874. 80 p. Grades 4–6.

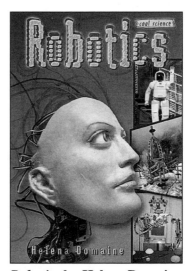

Robotics **by Helena Domaine.**

Domaine, Helena. *Robotics* (Cool Science!). Lerner, 2005. ISBN 0822521121. 48 p. Grades 4–6.

Electricity and Magnetism Science Fair Projects: Using Batteries, Balloons, and Other Hair-Raising Stuff **by Robert Gardner.**

Gardner, Robert. *Electricity and Magnetism Science Fair Projects: Using Batteries, Balloons, and Other Hair-Raising Stuff* (Physics! Best Science Projects). Enslow, 2004. ISBN 0766021270. 128 p. Grades 5–up.

Gardner, Robert. *Far-Out Science Projects with Height and Depth: How High Is Up? How Low Is Down?* (Sensational Science Experiments Series). Enslow, 2003. ISBN 0766020169. 48 p. Grades 1–4.

Gardner, Robert. *Heavy-Duty Science Projects with Weight: How Much Does It Weigh?* (Sensational Science Experiments Series). Enslow, 2003. ISBN 0766020134. 48 p. Grades 1–4.

Gardner, Robert. *It's about Time! Science Projects: How Long Does It Take?* (Sensational Science Experiments Series). Enslow, 2003. ISBN 0766020126. 48 p. Grades 1–4.

Gardner, Robert. *Split-Second Science Projects with Speed: How Fast Does It Go?* (Sensational Science Experiments Series). Enslow, 2003. ISBN 0766020177. 48 p. Grades 1–4.

Goldish, Meish. *Fossil Tales* (On the Job). Chelsea Clubhouse, 2003. ISBN 0791074110 32 p. Grades 3–6.

Goodman, Susan E. *Choppers!* Photographs by Michael J. Doolittle. Random House Children's Books, 2005. ISBN 0375925171. 48 p. Grades K–3.

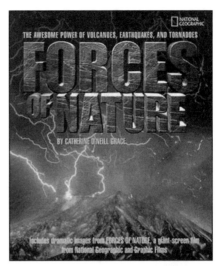

**Forces of Nature: The Awesome Power of
Volcanoes, Earthquakes, and Tornadoes
by Catherine Grace.**

Grace, Catherine. *Forces of Nature: The Awesome Power of Volcanoes, Earthquakes, and
Tornadoes.* National Geographic, 2005. ISBN 0792263286. 62 p. Grades 4–6.

Robots Slither by Ryan Ann Hunter.

Hunter, Ryan Ann. *Robots Slither.* Illustrated by Julia Gorton. G. P. Putnam's Sons, 2004.
ISBN 0399237747. 40 p. Grades K–3.

Kent, Deborah. *Snake Pits, Talking Cures, and Magic Bullets: A History of Mental Illness.*
Twenty-First Century Books, 2003. ISBN 0761327045. 160 p. Grades 5–up.

Kerrod, Robin. *Universe* (Eyewitness Books). DK, 2003. ISBN 0789492385. 64 p. Grades 4–8.

Koss, Amy Goldman. *Where Fish Go in Winter: And Other Great Mysteries.* Illustrated by
Laura J. Bryant. Dial Books for Young Readers, 2002. ISBN 0803727046. 32 p.
Grades K–3.

***Planet Patrol* by Marybeth Lorbiecki.**

Lorbiecki, Marybeth. *Planet Patrol.* Illustrated by Nancy Meyers. Two-Can, 2005. ISBN 1587285142. 48 p. Grades 3–5.

Loy, Jessica. *Follow the Trail: A Young Person's Guide to the Great Outdoors.* Henry Holt, 2003. ISBN 0805061959. 48 p. Grades K–4.

MacDonald, Fiona. *Inside the Beagle with Charles Darwin.* Illustrated by Mark Bergin. Enchanted Lion, 2005. ISBN 1592700411. 48 p. Grades 4–6.

MacLeod, Elizabeth. *Albert Einstein: A Life of Genius.* Kids Can Press, 2003. ISBN 1553373960. 32 p. Grades 4–8.

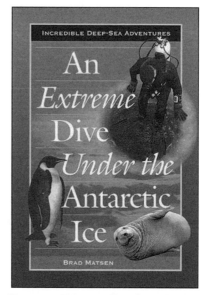

***An Extreme Dive under the Antarctic Ice*
by Brad Matsen.**

Matsen, Brad. *An Extreme Dive under the Antarctic Ice* (Incredible Deep-Sea Adventures). Enslow, 2003. ISBN 0766021904. 48 p. Grades 3–6.

Matsen, Brad. *The Incredible Record-Setting Deep-Sea Dive of the Bathysphere* (Incredible Deep-Sea Adventures). Enslow, 2003. ISBN 0766021882. 48 p. Grades 3–6.

Matsen, Brad. *The Incredible Submersible Alvin Discovers a Strange Deep-Sea World* (Incredible Deep-Sea Adventures). Enslow, 2003. ISBN 0766021890. 48 p. Grades 3–6.

Newquist, H. P. *The Great Brain Book: An Inside Look at the Inside of Your Head.* Illustrated by Keith Kasnot and Eric Brace. Scholastic Press, 2005. ISBN 0439458951, 160 p. Grades 4–8.

Nye, Bill. *Bill Nye the Science Guy's Great Big Book of Tiny Germs.* Illustrated by Bryn Barnard. Hyperion Books for Children, 2005. ISBN 0786805439. 48 p. Grades 4–6.

Oxlade, Chris. *Storm Warning: Tornadoes* (Turbulent Planet). Raintree, 2004. ISBN 1410910997. 48 p. Grades 4–6.

Oxlade, Chris. *Violent Skies: Hurricanes* (Turbulent Planet). Raintree, 2004. ISBN 1419011004. 48 p. Grades 4–6.

Reed, Jennifer. *Earthquakes: Disaster and Survival* (Deadly Disasters). Enslow, 2005. ISBN 0766023818. 48 p. Grades 4–6.

Rhatigan, Joe, and Veronika Alice Gunter. *Cool Chemistry Concoctions: 50 Formulas That Fizz, Foam, Splatter & Ooze.* Lark Books, 2005. ISBN 1597706206. 80 p. Grades 4–6.

***Zzz...: The Most Interesting Book You'll Ever Read about Sleep* by Trudee Romanek.**

Romanek, Trudee. *Zzz...: The Most Interesting Book You'll Ever Read about Sleep* (Mysterious You). Illustrated by Rose Cowles. Kids Can Press, 2002. ISBN 1550749447. 40 p. Grades 4–8.

Ross, Michael Elsohn. *Indoor Zoo* (You Are the Scientist). Carolrhoda Books, 2002. ISBN 0876146213. 48 p. Grades 1–5.

***Junk Lab* by Michael Elsohn Ross.**

Ross, Michael Elsohn. *Junk Lab* (You Are the Scientist). Carolrhoda Books, 2002. ISBN 0876146264. 48 p. Grades 1–5.

Ross, Michael Elsohn. *Kitchen Lab* (You Are the Scientist). Carolrhoda Books, 2002. ISBN 0876146256. 48 p. Grades 1–5.

Ross, Michael Elsohn. *Toy Lab* (You Are the Scientist). Carolrhoda Books, 2002. ISBN 0876144563. 48 p. Grades 1–5.

Royston, Angela. *Why Do Bones Break? And Other Questions about Movement* (Body Matters). Heinemann Library, 2002. ISBN 1403402019. 32 p. Grades 2–4.

Royston, Angela. *Why Do Bruises Change Color? And Other Questions about Blood* (Body Matters). Heinemann Library, 2002. ISBN 1403402027. 32 p. Grades 2–4.

Royston, Angela. *Why Do I Vomit? And Other Questions about Digestion* (Body Matters). Heinemann Library, 2002. ISBN 140340206x. 32 p. Grades 2–4.

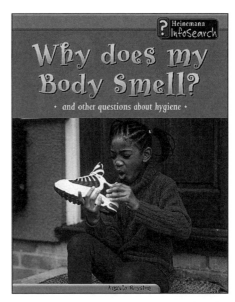

***Why Does My Body Smell? And Other Questions about Hygiene* by Angela Royston.**

Royston, Angela. *Why Does My Body Smell? And Other Questions about Hygiene* (Body Matters). Heinemann Library, 2002. ISBN 140340206x. 32 p. Grades 2–4.

Searle, Bobbi. *Electricity and Magnetism* (Fascinating Science Projects). Millbrook/Copper Beech, 2002. ISBN 0761327150. 48 p. Grades 3–5.

Simon, Seymour. *Destination: Space.* HarperCollins, 2002. ISBN 0688162894. 32 p. Grades 1–4.

Spilsbury, Louise, and Richard Spilsbury. *Blazing Bush and Forest Fires* (Awesome Forces of Nature). Heinemann Library, 2003. ISBN 140343722x. 32 p. Grades 4–7.

Spilsbury, Louise, and Richard Spilsbury. *Crushing Avalanches* (Awesome Forces of Nature). Heinemann Library, 2003. ISBN 1403437211. 32 p. Grades 4–7.

Spilsbury, Louise, and Richard Spilsbury. *Dreadful Droughts* (Awesome Forces of Nature). Heinemann Library, 2003. ISBN 1403437238. 32 p. Grades 4–7.

Spilsbury, Louise, and Richard Spilsbury. *Raging Floods* (Awesome Forces of Nature). Heinemann Library, 2003. ISBN 1403437246. 32 p. Grades 4–7.

Spilsbury, Louise, and Richard Spilsbury *Sweeping Tsunamis* (Awesome Forces of Nature). Heinemann Library, 2003. ISBN 1403437254. 32 p. Grades 4–7.

Thomas, Keltie. *Nature Shockers.* Illustrated by Greg Hall. Maple Tree Press, 2005. ISBN 1897066295. 64 p. Grades 4–6.

Torres, John. *Disaster in the Indian Ocean: Tsunami.* Mitchell Lane, 2005. ISBN 58415344x. 48 p. Grades 5–8.

***Microscopic Life* by Richard Walker.**

Walker, Richard. *Microscopic Life* (Kingfisher Knowledge). Kingfisher, 2004. ISBN 0753457784. 64 p. Grades 4–8.

Water Hole (24 Hours). DK, 2005. ISBN 0756611261. 48 p. Grades K–3.

Watts, Claire. *Heat Hazard: Droughts* (Turbulent Planet). Raintree, 2004. ISBN 1410910989. 48 p. Grades 4–6.

Watts, Claire. *White-Out: Blizzards* (Turbulent Planet). Raintree, 2004. ISBN 1410911012. 48 p. Grades 4–6.

***Avalanches* by Anne Ylvisaker.**

Ylvisaker, Anne. *Avalanches* (Natural Disasters). Capstone Press, 2003. ISBN 073681504x. 48 p. Grades 3–9.

Ylvisaker, Anne. *Droughts* (Natural Disasters). Capstone Press, 2003. ISBN 0736815058. 48 p. Grades 3–9.

Ylvisaker, Anne. *Ice Storms* (Natural Disasters). Capstone Press, 2003. ISBN 0736815066. 48 p. Grades 3–9.

Ylvisaker, Anne. *Landslides* (Natural Disasters). Capstone Press, 2003. ISBN 0736815074. 48 p. Grades 3–9.

Chapter  5

All Things Gross

There is no question that boys like books that are gross, and if you want to get them excited about reading, you have to give them what they want. Some books in this chapter are truly gross, like the ones about poop, germs, or body noises. Others are historical books (Pompeii, mummies, medieval dungeons, the history of medicine) with some gross aspects you can capitalize on to get kids interested. Either way, you can't go wrong with these gross books, guaranteed to entice boys of all ages.

NEW AND NOTABLE

Davies, Nicola. *Poop: A Natural History of the Unmentionable.* Illustrated by Neil Layton. Candlewick Press, 2004. ISBN 0763624373. 61 p. Grades 2–5.

"Grownups are shy about it … Horses ignore it … Dogs like to sniff it … And babies do it in their diapers … Poop, big jobs, number two" (page 7).

This book is filled with great information about poop, including:

- It is mostly made up of food that isn't used by the body when we eat. But it also includes germs, worn-out blood cells, and sometimes worms that try to live in our guts!

- Carnivores (meat eaters) don't poop as often as herbivores (plant eaters). Herbivores poop almost all of the time.

- Bat poop looks like runny jam.

- When whales eat lots of pink shrimp, their poop looks like giant blobs of strawberry ice cream.

- Rabbits poop underground and then eat their own poop. Then they poop above ground and don't eat that.

- Many animals have special areas in which they poop—just like we have bathrooms.

- Sloths each have their own bathroom area at the base of a tree. They poop every four days there.

- Hippos poop to be able to find their way back when they leave their homes—just like Hansel and Gretel left crumbs, they leave poop!

- A lot of animals love to eat other animals' poop. The most famous are dung beetles.

- More than twenty million bats live in Bracken Cave in Texas—and they poop fifty tons a day in that cave.

- Blue whales make the biggest poop in the world.

- Mayflies don't poop at all. They only live one day and they never eat—so they never poop.

Deem, James M. *Bodies from the Ash: Life and Death in Ancient Pompeii.* Houghton Mifflin, 2005. ISBN 0618473084. 50 p. Grades 3–up.

It was hot on August 24, A.D. 79, and the residents of Pompeii, a city of the Roman Empire, had recently experienced some small earthquakes. No one was too worried about it. No one realized that the earthquakes had been caused by the nearby Mount Vesuvius. Most people never knew that Mount Vesuvius was a volcano. It was a volcano about to blow.

Early that morning a small cloud of ash formed over Pompeii, and ash began to rain down. Some people near the volcano were concerned, but no one in Pompeii got worried until later, when the cloud began to release ash and stones. People went inside, but inside was not good enough. The fallout continued at a rate of five to six inches per hour, and, as it piled up all over the city, people began to try to escape.

But it did not take long for the situation to become a crisis. Bigger stones began to fall. By midnight, all the first-floor buildings and windows were blocked. You had to go out the second story to walk on the stones and ash in the street. Fires burned everywhere. Superhot, superfast gases and ash spread quickly down the mountain. They did not quite reach Pompeii itself, but by 7:30 in the morning, it was all over. Everyone alive in Pompeii was killed, buried in various kinds of material from the volcano.

It is amazing that almost two thousand years later, we have a timeline of what happened during the eruption.

The eruption covered Pompeii completely. People had forgotten it was ever there. A nearby city, Herculaneum, was discovered by people digging a canal, and in the 1700s, diggers started looking for Pompeii again. We no longer consider their methods to be remotely scientific, and they stole most of the good things they found, but among the objects they discovered were skeletons.

In time scientists discovered that they could fill the holes around the skeletons with plaster and have a perfect image of what the residents of Pompeii looked like as they were dying.

This is loaded with photographs and great information. The story of Pompeii and its destruction has fascinated people for centuries, and this is a great retelling.

Curse of the Pharaohs: My Adventures with the Mummies **by Zahi Hawass.**

Hawass, Zahi. *Curse of the Pharaohs: My Adventures with the Mummies*. National Geographic, 2004. ISBN 079226665x. 144 p. Grades 4–up.

Lots of people believe that the people who disturb mummies are cursed with terrible diseases or die soon after their discoveries. Is this true?

The man who wrote this book ought to know, because he has disturbed a *lot* of mummies. His name is Zahi Hawass, and he is a world-famous archaeologist and the head of Egypt's Supreme Council of Antiquities. A big part of his job is disturbing ancient mummies.

On the frontispiece of the book is a curse from the tomb of Petety. (Show the picture and read the curse.) Sometimes curses were put on tombs, most often because the people who were in charge of the government and the building were afraid that tomb robbers would come and steal everything. They were right. Tomb robbers usually came very quickly. In fact, Hawass believes that many of the tomb robbers were also the tomb builders. They seemed to know exactly where to find the tombs, even the ones that were well hidden. There was a great deal to steal, for the ancient rulers and wealthy people were buried with many valuable objects all around them.

Belief that there was a mummy's curse began in 1922, when Howard Carter opened the tomb of King Tutankhamun. This tomb had not been damaged by robbers in a major way and was an incredible discovery that made news all over the word. Show the students the picture on page 27 of a rope knot that held together the doors to one of the shrines in the tomb. This knot was tied by priests more than three thousand years before Carter arrived! Rumors began to start that the people who were in on the tomb discovery were dying horrible deaths, and a lot of people still believe that happened.

Hawass has had several strange experiences, one involving nightmares about two mummies who were children, a boy and a girl. He had moved the mummies into a museum, and he started thinking about why he was having nightmares. He had found another mummy near them, and he was quite certain that mummy was their father. Once he moved that mummy to the museum next to the children, his nightmares stopped. He does not understand why this happened.

This book has spectacular photographs. Show a few to your audience. The one of Ramses II on pages 104 and 105 is suitably gruesome and has a good story to go with it.

Tutankahmun: The Mystery of the Boy King
by Zahi Hawass.

Hawass, Zahi. *Tutankahmun: The Mystery of the Boy King.* National Geographic, 2005. ISBN 0792283546. 64 p. Grades 4–up.

Can you name one ancient Egyptian pharaoh? Just one? Who is it?

Most people would probably say Tutankhamun.

He wasn't an important king, and he didn't reign for very long. The pharaoh who came after him tried to erase his name from all of the important records.

But Tutankhamun had one thing going for him that no one else had. His tomb was never successfully robbed. His mummy remained in the same condition as when it was put in the tomb about three thousand years ago. And when that mummy was finally rediscovered in 1922, the world went "King Tut" crazy.

But who was he, really? What do we know about him? What did he look like? Was he married? Did he have children?

Zahi Hawass, who wrote this book, tells us the answers. Hawass is an important Egyptian archaeologist who directs excavations at the Giza Pyramids and the Valley of the Golden Mummies. When he was young, he even met a man who was present on the day the tomb was discovered.

You will be amazed at what we know now about Tutankhamun, although there are still many mysteries.

The pictures in this book are wonderful. Show the one on page 10 of the pharaoh as sculptors reconstructed his face based on images from a CT scanner or the one on page 51 showing a slice of King Tut's skull with embalming material stuck on the inside.

Lindsay, Judy. *The Story of Medicine from Acupuncture to X Rays.* Oxford University Press, in association with the British Museum Press, 2003, 2004. ISBN 0195219848. 40 p. Grades 4–8.

Medical treatment wasn't the greatest for most of human history. Part of the problem was simple: as far as we know, no one had dissected a human body before the 1300s. The first public dissection of a human body took place in 1315. So people did not really know what was *inside* a body and therefore could not really understand how it worked. Ancient Greeks and Romans dissected animal bodies, but that was often not particularly helpful. Animal anatomy tends to be very different from human anatomy.

Once people started dissecting bodies, though, they could not get enough bodies. The first ones publicly dissected were those of criminals. Later, criminals found the bodies for the doctors and students to dissect. They were called "Resurrection Men," and they dug up graveyards at night. The most famous were in Edinburgh, Scotland. Their last names were Burke and Hare. They couldn't keep up with the demand for bodies by digging them up at night, so they started murdering people!

Over the centuries, people figured out ways to help cure diseases. Many civilizations had doctors, including the ancient cultures of Egypt and Greece. People we call folk healers today found natural remedies, such as herbs. A famous Chinese emperor, Shen Nung, wrote an herbal manual recommending the use of herbs in treating diseases. Some of his treatments are still used today.

But the world has suffered greatly from not knowing what caused disease and how to treat it. People did not know about bacteria, and the importance of cleanliness, and the importance of keeping water for drinking separate from waste water.

The sections on surgery and on deadly diseases are particularly gruesome.

Kathy's Favorite Gross Books to Booktalk

◆ Lauber, Patricia. *What You Never Knew about Tubs, Toilets, and Showers* (Around the House History).

◆ Goodman, Susan E. *The Truth about Poop.*

◆ Davies, Nicola. *Poop: A Natural History of the Unmentionable.*

◆ MacDonald, Fiona. *A Medieval Castle.*

◆ Snedden, Robert. *Yuck! A Big Book of Little Horrors.*

◆ Ichord, Loretta Frances. *Toothworms and Spider Juice: An Illustrated History of Dentistry.*

◆ Fleischman, John. *Phineas Gage: A Gruesome but True Story about Brain Science.*

◆ McLafferty, Carla Killough. *The Head Bone's Connected to the Neck Bone: The Weird, Wacky and Wonderful X-Ray.*

◆ Senior, Kathryn. *You Wouldn't Want to Be Sick in the 16th Century: Diseases You'd Rather Not Catch.*

◆ Solway, Andrew. *What's Living in Your Bedroom?*

From *Gotcha for Guys! Nonfiction Books to Get Boys Excited About Reading* by Kathleen A. Baxter and Marcia Agness Kochel. Westport, CT: Libraries Unlimited. Copyright © 2007.

MacDonald, Fiona. *You Wouldn't Want to Be in a Medieval Dungeon! Prisoners You'd Rather Not Meet.* Illustrated by David Antram. Franklin Watts, 2003. ISBN 053112312x. 32 p. Grades 4–8.

What would it be like to be in a medieval jail? Imagine you are a soldier coming back from the war looking for a job. Would being a jailer work for you? What would conditions in a dungeon be like?

Well, right off the bat, it would be better to be a jailer than a prisoner any time.

There are all sorts of prisons, and you wouldn't want to be in any of them. Among the most unpleasant were the oubliette, which was long and narrow. They put prisoners down there on a rope and then forgot about them. Dying of thirst and hunger while hanging in the air is not fun. The "Little Ease" was a tiny chamber in a castle wall where prisoners could barely move. Some people were kept in cages hanging outside castle walls, and some were high up in towers.

Wherever prisoners were kept, you can be sure of one thing. Prisons were absolutely filthy. There were no beds and no bathrooms. Prisoners went to the bathroom *and* sleep on the floor. There were rats and lice. In most prisons, the prisoners were not fed unless someone (say, a family member) paid for their food. There was no heat. The water was completely unsanitary. Prisoners might get tortured, which was a horrible experience. Popular torturing instruments included the red-hot iron; the rack, which stretched prisoners out; the boot, which squeezed legs; and the thumbscrew, which squeezed fingers until the fingernails fell off.

You definitely would probably rather find another job unless you liked being cruel, for being a jailer in a medieval dungeon was indeed a cruel job. And being a prisoner was much, much worse.

Take a look at all of the illustrations in this interesting book.

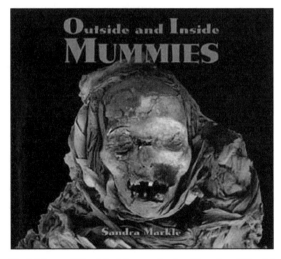

Outside and Inside Mummies **by Sandra Markle.**

Markle, Sandra. *Outside and Inside Mummies.* Walker, 2005. ISBN 0802789665. 40 p. Grades 4–7.

Most people have at least seen a photograph of a mummy, even if they have never seen a real one. But how could you see what is *inside* of a mummy?

For a long time, the only way to see inside any mummy was to cut it up and destroy it. But today, technology has enabled scientists to see what is actually inside the dead body of a mummy and learn all sorts of things from it, without hurting it at all.

On page 11, look at the spiral CT scanner photograph that even includes a piece of a pharaoh's lung!

This book is filled with great information. Did you know that the people who created the mummies removed the soft brain tissue from the head? They stuck a needle up the dead person's nose and pulled it out bit by bit. They did not think the brain was important—they believed that all it did was produce the snot that drips out of noses.

Scientists have learned what kind of injuries mummified people suffered as well as the kinds of diseases they had, and sometimes even what they ate.

At the end is a section that would make a great science fair project: make your own mummy. See it on pages 36 and 37.

You'll have a grand time reading this book with its amazing photographs.

Prelutsky, Jack. *What a Day It Was at School!* Pictures by Doug Cushman. Greenwillow Books, an imprint of HarperCollins, 2006. ISBN 0060823356. 40 p. Grades 2–5.

These funny poems about school add a lot of zest to a booktalk. "I Made a Noise This Morning" on page 18 fits in well with gross stuff (and will have every listener and the booktalker squirming in sympathy), "In the Cafeteria" on page 22 is as amusing as you would expect, and we can probably all relate to "My Backpack Weighs a Thousand Pounds" on page 7.

All of Prelutsky's poems can be sung—and singing is a great way to memorize them. Let the kids try out songs they know and see whether any of the poems and their tunes match.

*Achoo! The Most Interesting Book You'll
Ever Read about Germs* by Trudee Romanek.

Romanek, Trudee. *Achoo! The Most Interesting Book You'll Ever Read about Germs* (Mysterious You). Illustrated by Rose Cowles. Kids Can Press, 2003. ISBN 1553374509. 40 p. Grades 3–8.

In 1971, a boy was born with a condition called SCID, severe combined immune deficiency. His body was not able to fight off germs at all—and he lived his entire life inside a bubble.

Most people would not enjoy living in a bubble, and fortunately the human body fights germs in all sorts of ways. When people sneeze, for instance, they are fighting off germs. Long ago, people believed that the soul might escape when a person sneezed, and that is why they say "Bless you" or "Gesundheit" when you sneeze.

Germs had it pretty easy throughout most of our history, but in the 1880s, a chemist named Louis Pasteur did experiments and realized that bacteria made people sick. Beginning with his experiments, people began to realize that washing your hands and keeping clean was a good way to stay healthy.

This book is loaded with good information.

- Ear wax mixed with ink was used by medieval monks to make parchments.

- There is a recipe for fake snot on page 19.

- When you cough, air comes out of your body at about 760 miles per hour.

- Scientific studies prove that people with good attitudes about illness get well more often than people who believe that their illness will be terrible.

Singer, Marilyn. *What Stinks?* Darby Creek, 2006. ISBN 1581960358. 64 p. Grades 3–7.

A lot of things smell so bad that people say they stink. Women generally can smell things better than men, but kids smell things better than adults—so kids probably smell a lot of stinky things.

Not everyone around the world thinks exactly the same things smell bad. In the United States, for instance, we think that the natural odors of a body are not good—so we spend a lot of money on deodorants and perfume so people cannot smell our natural odors. In some other parts of the world, people like natural body odors.

You'll learn a lot of good information, such as:

- Komodo dragons sample other Komodo dragons' poop so they can see whether it is safe to stay around or whether they should get out. That poop can also tell if there are good things to eat in the area.

- All the rhinoceroses in the same neighborhood poop in the same place. After pooping, each rhino drags its feet through the poop. Other animals don't like that smell.

- Take a look at the photos of poop on page 8. Can you guess whose poop is whose?

- A lot of flowers that smell disgusting smell that way because they trap and kill insects inside them.

- Want a quick way to get bad breath? Put peeled cloves of garlic in your socks and walk around for at least seven hours. People won't want you to open your mouth!

- Bombardier beetles spray bad smelling stuff that is also boiling hot. Don't make one mad.

Kids will enjoy the fun facts and many colorful photographs.

What's Living in Your Bedroom?
by Andrew Solway.

Solway, Andrew. *What's Living in Your Bedroom?* (Hidden Life). Heinemann Library, 2004. ISBN 1403448450. 32 p. Grades 3–6.

You know one thing for sure. *You* live in your bedroom. But are you alone? Maybe you share a room with a pet or another human being or two, but is it possible there are other forms of life in the room with you? Think about it. What do you think might be in your bedroom?

This book gives us the answer, complete with photographs of some of the microscopic creatures that share living space with us.

Let's start with dust. Do you know what most of dust is made up of? "Household dust is a mixture of an amazing number of things. In addition to skin, there is hair, fibers from clothing, the droppings of insects and other tiny creatures, and living things such as pollen from plants, bacteria and other microbes. Dust is so complex a mixture that the dust from a particular place is different from the dust from anywhere else" (page 7). In fact, the number one ingredient in dust is skin—human skin. We are constantly getting rid of dead skin, and there it is—still in the same space with us. Show the picture on pages 6 and 7.

And then, of course, there are the dust mites. They are only about .008 inches long, and they have no eyes. They feel their way around. There could be as many as ten million mites living in your mattress. Take a look at the picture on page 8.

You'll also learn about bedbugs, fleas, carpet beetles, and clothes moths, among others. The photographs are great. Once you read this book, you'll never feel alone in your bedroom again. But is that a good thing?

Tanaka, Shelley. *Mummies: The Newest, Coolest & Creepiest from around the World.* Archaeological Consultation by Paul Bahn. A Madison Press Book/Harry N. Abrams, 2005. ISBN 0810957973. 48 p. Grades 4–7.

This book has some of the most gruesome photographs you will ever see.

Scientists are finding more and more mummies all of the time. As people build new homes, cities expand, and as glaciers melt, more and more of them simply turn up. Scientists are thrilled. They can study these ancient bodies and learn so much about how people lived in other times.

The world's oldest mummy makers were not in Egypt but in South America; we call them the Chinchorro. They prepared the body, cut the skull in half to remove the brain, and then put it back together, reinforcing it with other materials, such as paste, sticks, feathers, and clay. There is a great photograph of one of these mummies on page 7, along with one of the three Inca child mummies found in 1999. They were sacrificed to the gods about five hundred years ago, and it was considered a great honor. The mummies were frozen and were in such good condition that blood still filled their hearts and lungs. This enabled scientists to do DNA testing. Today a descendant of one of the girls lives in Washington, D.C.

Frozen mummies can carry disease, and researchers must be very careful. They could catch an ancient disease for which they have built up no immunity.

There are many mummies in Europe, too, including the peat bog mummies. One, the Grauballe Man, is about two thousand years old. He was found in Denmark in 1952. "His throat had been slit from ear to ear, and his right arm was twisted behind his back. His skin was so well preserved that researchers were able to take his fingerprints, yet the bog had dissolved all of his tooth enamel" (page 20). Show his picture on page 21.

This book is jam-packed with the latest, fascinating information about recent mummy discoveries.

NOT TO BE MISSED

Bagert, Brod. *Giant Children*. Pictures by Tedd Arnold. Dial Books for Young Readers, 2002. ISBN 0803725566. Unpaged. Grades 1–5. *Gotcha Covered.*

The class pet, a hamster, introduces these hysterically funny poems about the "giant" kids in the room (well, they do look like giants to a hamster!). Be sure to read "Booger Love."

Beattie, Owen. *Buried in Ice: Unlocking the Secrets of an Arctic Voyage* (Time Quest Book). A Scholastic/Madison Press Book, 1992. ISBN 0590438484. 64 p. Grades 4–8. *Gotcha.*

In 1845, the *Franklin* sailed through Arctic seas hoping to find a water passage across North America. The expedition never returned, and no one knew what exactly had happened to it until 1984, when researchers found not only the remains of the ship, but also several well-preserved frozen human bodies, which solved the mystery. Great stuff. Be sure to show the gruesome expressions on the faces of the frozen men on pages 56 and 57.

Berger, Melvin, and Gilda Berger. *Mummies of the Pharaohs: Exploring the Valley of the Kings*. National Geographic Society, 2001. ISBN 0792227734. 64 p. Grades 4–8. *Gotcha Again.*

Most of us probably believe that the pharaohs were buried in pyramids. Indeed, some of them were. But many were buried instead in the Valley of the Kings, where they believed their tombs would not be robbed. This is the story of that valley and especially of the most famous discovery there—that of the tomb of King Tutankhamen. Many fine color photographs add interest.

Branzei, Sylvia. *Grossology: The Science of Really Gross Things.* Illustrated by Jack Keely. Planet Dexter, 1995. ISBN 020140964X. 80 p. Grades 4–up.

Branzei, Sylvia. *Animal Grossology* (Grossology Series). Illustrated by Jack Keely. Price Stern Sloan, 2004. ISBN 0843110112. 80 p. Grades 4–up.

Branzei, Sylvia. *Grossology and You* (Grossology Series). Illustrated by Jack Keely. Price Stern Sloan, 2002. ISBN 0843177365. 80 p. Grades 4–up.

Branzei, Sylvia. *Hands-On Grossology* (Grossology Series). Illustrated by Jack Keely. Price Stern Sloan, 2003. ISBN 0843103051. 80 p. Grades 4–up.

   These books are, no doubt about it, really gross, and not for the weak of heart—or those fearful of censorship. They are not for every library (or librarian), but boys adore the cartoon illustrations and the wonderfully gross information contained inside. Did you know that we each eat about a quart of snot a day?

Buxbaum, Susan Kovacs, and Rita Golden Gelman. *Body Noises.* Illustrated by Angie Lloyd. Knopf, 1988. ISBN 0394857712. 56 p. Grades 4–6. *Gotcha.*

   This book is out of print, but if you still have a copy in your collection, stand it up or booktalk it and be astounded at how quickly it moves off the shelf. All kids are curious about why our bodies make such strange, often embarrassing noises.

Colman, Penny. *Corpses, Coffins, and Crypts: A History of Burial.* Henry Holt, 1997. ISBN 0689318944. 212 p. Grades 5–up. *Gotcha.*

   Funeral and burial customs differ all over the world and do change—but one, in America, has stayed the same for centuries. People bring food to the home of someone who is recently deceased. This somewhat scholarly book is loaded with interesting stories and information.

Colman, Penny. *Toilets, Bathtubs, Sinks and Sewers: A History of the Bathroom.* Atheneum, 1994. ISBN 0689318944. 70 p. Grades 4–8. *Gotcha.*

   After you read this book, you will be happy that you live in the age of running water, sinks, showers, and toilet paper. In the Middle Ages, Saint Francis of Assisi even said that one sign of a holy person was dirtiness. People were gross back in those days, and modern kids who read about them will be delighted.

Conrad, David. *Burps, Boogers, and Bad Breath* (Spyglass Books). Compass Point Books, 2002. ISBN 0756502284. 24 p. Grades 1–4.

   Simple information with fun photographs tells us exactly what causes some of the embarrassing things our bodies do.

Dahl, Roald. *Roald Dahl's Revolting Recipes.* Illustrated by Quentin Blake. Viking, 1994. ISBN 0670858366. 61 p. Grades 4–6. *Gotcha.*

   Each of the recipes in this titillating disgusting book is based on food described in Roald Dahl's children's books. Try making a mudburger today!

Day, Trevor. *Youch! It Bites: Real-Life Monsters Up Close.* Designed by Mike Jolley. Simon and Schuster Books for Young Readers, 2000. ISBN 0689834160. Unpaged. Grades 2–6. *Gotcha Again.*

Photos taken with a microscope show us wonderfully gross things. Did you know that a jellyfish is much more dangerous to people than a shark?

Deem, James. *Bodies from the Bog.* Houghton Mifflin, 1998. ISBN 0395857848. 42 p. Grades 4–8. *Gotcha.*

Bog bodies are inherently fascinating. Peat bogs preserve bodies, and when people dig up peat for fuel, they find them. Some are thousands of years old. When scientists study them, they learn all sorts of things about what they ate and what they wore—and sometimes why and how they died. Excellent photos will grab young readers.

Editors of Planet Dexter. *This Book Really Sucks! The Science behind Gravity, Flight, Leeches, Black Holes, Tornadoes, Our Friend the Vacuum Cleaner, and Most Everything Else.* Planet Dexter, 1999. ISBN 044844075X. 80 p. Grades 4–up.

This book's binding is an attention getter long before you even open it up. It looks like the bottom of a rubber bath mat—or suckers on an octopus arm. The title explains it all.

Filer, Joyce. *The Mystery of the Egyptian Mummy.* Oxford University Press in association with the British Museum, 2003. ISBN 0195219899. 48 p. Grades 4–8. *Gotcha Covered.*

This is the story of one particular mummy and the astounding amount of information that modern researchers have discovered about his life. It also includes a great deal of information about the reasons for and the process of mummification. Not an easy read, but mummy fans (and there are lots of them out there) will love it.

Fleischman, John. *Phineas Gage: A Gruesome but True Story about Brain Science.* Houghton Mifflin, 2002. ISBN 0618052526. 96 p. Grades 5–up. *Gotcha Covered.*

Phineas Gage, working with explosives on a railroad in 1848, had an accident that changed the knowledge of brain science in an extraordinary way. A huge stake went straight through his head—and he survived. But he wasn't exactly the same guy he had been before. What a story!

Getz, David. *Frozen Man* (A Redfeather Book). Illustrated by Peter McCarty. Henry Holt, 1994. ISBN 0805032614. 68 p. Grades 3–5. *Gotcha.*

The 5,300-year-old iceman found in the Italian Alps is the topic of yet another enticing book.

Goodman, Susan E. *The Truth about Poop.* Illustrated by Elwood H. Smith. Viking, 2004. ISBN 0670036749. 40 p. Grades 2–5. *Gotcha Covered.*

Although we would die if we didn't poop, we just plain don't like to talk about it much. But let's face it, poop is an inherently interesting topic to kids, and they may find out more than they wanted to know in this fun book, jam-packed with information.

Haduch, Bill. *Food Rules! The Stuff You Munch, Its Crunch, Its Punch, and Why You Sometimes Lose Your Lunch.* Illustrated by Rick Stromoski. Dutton, 2001. ISBN 052546419. 106 p. Grades 4–8. *Gotcha Again.*

    Did you know that 80 percent of the people in the world happily eat bugs? It certainly doesn't work for North Americans, but it's a fact. This is loaded with information kids will want to tell their friends. For example, are you aware that you spend about four full days a year just going to the bathroom?

Ichord, Loretta Frances. *Toothworms and Spider Juice: An Illustrated History of Dentistry.* Millbrook Press, 1999. ISBN 0761314652. 96 p. Grades 4–8. *Gotcha Again.*

    Information that sounds a little bit boring (a history of *dentistry?*) isn't in this delightfully gross history of dental practices for which we can only thank heaven we never had to endure. Did you know the belief that every tooth has a toothworm inside it is universal? *Every* culture around the world believed this. Scientists think it may be because when a tooth is pulled, the exposed pulp in it looks like it could be a worm.

Jackson, Donna M. *The Bone Detectives: How Forensic Anthropologists Solve Crimes and Uncover Mysteries of the Dead.* Little, Brown, 1996. ISBN 0316829358. 48 p. Grades 5–8. *Gotcha.*

    Forensic scientists helped detectives solve the mystery of a skull found in a campground in Saint Louis. This is a page-turner loaded with color photographs.

Janulewicz, Mike. *Yikes! Your Body, Up Close!* Designed by Mike Jolley. Edited by Dugald Steer. Simon & Schuster Books for Young Readers, 1997. ISBN 0689815204. 28 p. Grades 3–6. *Gotcha.*

    Each of these microscopic photos shows either a part of the human body or a parasite that lives on it. It's completely disgusting.

Kudalis, Eric. *Ice Mummies: Frozen in Time* (Mummies). Capstone Press, 2002. ISBN 0736813071. 32 p. Grades 3–9.

    Many frozen mummies have been found, and if we can keep them from melting, the fact that even their interior organs are preserved makes them enormously useful to scientists and historians. Numerous photos add to the "yuck" element.

Lauber, Patricia. *What You Never Knew about Tubs, Toilets, and Showers* (Around the House History). Illustrated by John Manders. Simon & Schuster Books for Young Readers, 2001. ISBN 0689824203. Unpaged. Grades 3–up. *Gotcha Again.*

    This is an all-time favorite nonfiction book to booktalk. It is filled with absolutely delicious gross information that will make young readers squeal with delight—and tell their friends. It looks like a book for younger children, but even young adults want to read it when they are told about the wonders it contains.

Lessem, Don. *The Iceman.* Crown, 1994. ISBN 051759596. 32 p. Grades 4–6. *Gotcha.*

    Gross pictures of the 5,300-year-old frozen man found in the Italian Alps in 1991 accompany a text filled with a lot of interesting information.

MacDonald, Fiona. *A Medieval Castle*. Illustrated by Mark Bergin. Peter Bedrick Books, 1990. ISBN 0-87226–340-1. 48 p. Grades 3–up. *Gotcha.*

You probably wouldn't expect to find this book in a chapter on gross stuff, but the double-page spread on pages 8 and 9 makes for an effective and gross booktalk. Point out the man on the right-hand side using the lavatory, and notice that the human waste is going straight into the moat. Imagine how it looked and smelled, both inside and outside the castle!

MacDonald, Fiona. *You Wouldn't Want to Be an Aztec Sacrifice! Gruesome Things You'd Rather Not Know*. Illustrated by David Antram. Created and designed by David Salariya. Franklin Watts, 2001. ISBN 0531162095. 32 p. Grades 4–8.

Aztec sacrifices were pretty gruesome—and their way of choosing victims to sacrifice was quite unusual. This explains exactly how it worked, and a subtitle like this makes *everyone* want to know.

Marrin, Albert. *Dr. Jenner and the Speckled Monster: The Search for the Smallpox Vaccine*. Dutton Children's Books, 2002. ISBN 0525469222. 120 p. Grades 4–8.

Twenty years ago, everyone believed that smallpox was a disease of the past. No one would ever get it again. Now they are not so sure. Is it still around? We sure hope not, because smallpox was one of the worst diseases anyone could get. It could scar you for life, leave you blind, or kill you. It killed thousands of people throughout history, including huge numbers of Native Americans. But there was a treatment that could help people become immune to it: vaccination. The first European who seriously researched how to do that was Edward Jenner. This is his amazing story.

Masoff, Joy. *Oh, Yuck! The Encyclopedia of Everything Nasty*. Illustrated by Terry Sirrell. Workman, 2000. ISBN 0761100711. 212 p. Grades 4–9. *Gotcha Covered.*

This giant paperback has an entry on almost every gross thing you can think of. It provides many happy hours of browsing to anyone who gets interested. And boys who see it will get interested. A surefire hit.

McLafferty, Carla Killough. *The Head Bone's Connected to the Neck Bone: The Weird, Wacky and Wonderful X-Ray*. Farrar, Straus & Giroux, 2001. ISBN 0374329087. 136 p. Grades 4–8.

A little over one hundred years ago, X-rays were an amazing new technology. In 1895, Dr. Wilhelm Conrad Roentgen was experimenting with Cathode rays when he noticed something unusual. He realized he could see inside his own hand! He could actually *see* his bones! When the news got out, everyone else got excited, too. In their excitement, they experimented with the strange new rays, never dreaming that what they were doing could be extremely dangerous. And then they found out how dangerous they were—and how beneficial as well. A good read.

Milton, Joyce. *Mummies*. Illustrated by Susan Swan. Grosset & Dunlap, 1996. ISBN 0448413264. 48 p. Grades 1–3. *Gotcha.*

An easy-to-read text and appealing illustrations provide a fine introduction to a topic that has fascinated people for centuries.

Monroe, Lucy. *Creepy Cuisine: Revolting Recipes That Look Disgusting but Taste Divine.*
Illustrations by Dianne O'Quinn Burke. Random House, 1992. ISBN 0679844023. 80
p. Grades 2–5. *Gotcha.*

If you have a copy of this paperback in your collection, dig it out now. The recipes
for such goodies as *Gory Gorilla Tonsils* and *Pus Pockets* crack kids up and make
them want to start cooking immediately.

Osborne, Mary Pope. *Pompeii: Lost and Found.* Frescoes by Bonnie Christensen. Knopf,
2006. ISBN 0375828893. Unpaged. Grades 1–5.

The pictures are the main attraction in this well-illustrated book about Pompeii.

Paulsen, Gary. *Guts: The True Stories behind* Hatchet *and the Brian Books.* Delacorte
Press, 2001. ISBN 0385326505. 148 p. Grades 5–8.

Paulsen's stories that inspired *Hatchet* and the other Brian books will amaze and
gross-out any audience. Be sure to mention the one food that made Paulsen himself
vomit: raw turtle eggs.

Prior, Natalie Jane. *The Encyclopedia of Preserved People: Pickled, Frozen and Mummified Corpses from around the World.* Crown, 2003. ISBN 0375922873. 64 p. Grades
4–8. *Gotcha Covered.*

This collection of information about how corpses from around the world have
been preserved, on purpose and by accident, is loaded with photographs and interesting information. It's a great book for browsing.

Putnam, James. *Mummy.* Photographed by Peter Hayman. Knopf, 1993. ISBN
0679838813. 64 p. Grades 4–up. *Gotcha.*

Eyewitness books aren't always favorites of adults, but kids love the brief tidbits
of information and the many color images. This one, with its grisly photographs of
mummies of all kinds, is a real winner.

Reinhard, Johan. *Discovering the Inca Ice Maiden: My Adventures on Ampato.* National
Geographic Society, 1998. ISBN 0792271424. 48 p. Grades 4–8.

This frozen mummy of a young girl has a tragic history. She was a human sacrifice about five hundred years ago, and this is the story of the discovery of her remains
and the research that scientists and historians did to find out more about her and the
time in which she lived.

Rollins, Barbara B., and Michael Dahl. *Blood Evidence* (Forensic Science). Edge
Books/Capstone Press, 2004. ISBN 0736824642. 32 p. Grades 3–9.

Did you know that it is practically impossible to get blood completely out of
clothing no matter how many times you wash it? Detectives and forensic scientists are
solving more mysteries all of the time using blood evidence.

Senior, Kathryn. *You Wouldn't Want to Be Sick in the 16th Century: Diseases You'd Rather Not Catch.* Illustrated by David Antram. Created and designed by David Salariya. Franklin Watts, 2002. ISBN 0531163660. 32 p. Grades 4–8. *Gotcha Covered.*

Kids don't realize how lucky we are today until they read how diseases were treated just a few hundred years ago. People did not know about germs, so things were not—to put it mildly—clean. This is the story of a boy who is apprenticed to learn medicine. Yuck!

Settel, Joanne, Ph.D. *Exploding Ants: Amazing Facts about How Animals Adapt.* Atheneum Books for Young Readers, 1999. ISBN 0689817395. 40 p. Grades 4–6. *Gotcha Again.*

This is a surefire winner. Show any kid the photos in the book, and you have hooked a reader. The photo of the toad eating the mouse and the accompanying information will knock them dead.

Showers, Paul. *What Happens to a Hamburger?* (Let's-Read-and-Find-Out Science Stage 2) (newly illustrated edition). Illustrated by Edward Miller. HarperCollins, 2001. ISBN 0060279486. 33 p. Grades 1–3.

The great Let's-Read-and-Find-Out Science books have wonderful new illustrations, and this depiction of what exactly happens to a hamburger after you eat it (it's not pretty) will delight young readers.

Simon, Seymour. *Out of Sight: Pictures of Hidden Worlds.* SeaStar Books, 2000. ISBN 1587170124. Unpaged. Grades 1–6. *Gotcha Again.*

Photographs of things taken through microscopes and telescopes are absolutely intriguing. Take a deep breath before you look at the tapeworm.

Singer, Marilyn. *Bottoms Up! A Book about Rear Ends.* Illustrated by Patrick O'Brien. Henry Holt, 1997. ISBN 0805042466. 32 p. Grades 3–5. *Gotcha Again.*

This is *not* a book about pooping, but rather some of the other interesting things that animals do with their behinds. (Think about a skunk.)

Sloan, Christopher. *Bury the Dead: Tombs, Corpses, Mummies, Skeletons and Rituals.* National Geographic, 2002. ISBN 0792271920. 64 p. Grades 3–6. *Gotcha Covered.*

Great photographs enliven this morbidly fascinating look at funeral rituals. Scientists find a great deal of information when they dig up graves. Studying graves can lead to important information about what people wore and about their health. One twelve-thousand-year-old grave found in Southeast Asia included a child buried with a puppy—our first real evidence that people kept pets that long ago. Some of the bones they have found have utensil marks on them, which probably means that the bodies were eaten.

Snedden, Robert. *Yuck! A Big Book of Little Horrors.* Simon & Schuster Books for Young Readers, 1996. ISBN 0689806760. 30 p. All ages. *Gotcha.*

Kids will never guess what these microscopic photos depict—but they are things we see and use almost every day. It truly is yucky, and impossible not to peruse.

Solheim, James. *It's Disgusting—and We Ate It! Food Facts around the World and throughout History.* Simon & Schuster Books for Young Readers, 1998. ISBN 0689806752. 44 p. Grades 4–8.

> All throughout history, in different times and places, people have eaten things we North Americans wouldn't go near today. Particularly interesting are the descriptions of what sailors used to eat while at sea. Rats were a delicacy because they were fresh meat!

Swanson, Diane. *Burp! The Most Interesting Book You'll Ever Read about Eating* (Mysterious You). Illustrated by Rose Cowles. Kids Can Press, 2001. ISBN 1550745999. 40 p. Grades 4–8. *Gotcha Again.*

> This is filled with intriguing facts about eating, including such goodies as this: we all normally carry around a cup of gas in our digestive system. We need to get rid of about ten cups a day! Or did you know that to get through the body, blood has to travel about sixty thousand miles of vessels—more than two times as long as a trip around Earth. The color illustrations are fun, too.

Tanaka, Shelley. *Discovering the Iceman: What It Was Like to Find 5,300 Year Old Mummy?* Illustrated by Laurie McGaw. A Hyperion/Madison Press Book, 1996. ISBN 0786802847. 48 p. Grades 4–6. *Gotcha.*

> In 1991, two men discovered a frozen body in the Alps. Frozen bodies are found there all the time, but this one was different. It turned out to be 5,300 years old. This is loaded with color photographs and intriguing illustrations.

Tanaka, Shelley. *Secrets of the Mummies: Uncovering the Bodies of Ancient Egyptians.* Illustrations by Greg Ruhl. A Hyperion/Madison Press Book, 1999. ISBN 0786804734. 48 p. Grades 4–6. *Gotcha Again.*

> Bad things happened to good mummies throughout the ages after they were buried. Not only did tomb robbers dig them up and destroy them, later visitors took them home and held mummy unwrapping parties. Some mummies were used to make medicine!
>
> Fortunately, today we preserve the mummies, and using modern techniques, we learn a lot about them without damaging them. This tells the story, with excellent photos and illustrations, of some of the mummies.

Trumble, Kelly. *Cat Mummies.* Illustrated by Laszlo Kubinyi. Clarion Books, 1996. ISBN 0395687071. 56 p. Grades 4–6. *Gotcha.*

> The ancient Egyptians not only mummified people, they mummified animals as well, especially cats. Cats were sacred to them, and that sometimes created problems. Thousands of cat mummies have been found, but they did not all come to a good end. This book has great information.

Bog Mummies: Preserved in Peat
by Charlotte Wilcox.

Wilcox, Charlotte. *Bog Mummies: Preserved in Peat* (Mummies). Capstone Press, 2002. ISBN 0736813063. 32p. Grades 3–9.

    Fine photographs of long-dead, beautifully preserved bodies highlight the interesting text.

Wilcox, Charlotte. *Mummies, Bones, and Body Parts*. Carolrhoda Books, 2000. ISBN 1575054280. 64 p. Grades 4–7. *Gotcha Again.*

    Scientists can learn a lot from human remains, and this book tells what they learn and how they do it. Excellent photos make this a standout.

WORTH READING

    Nonfiction books with "boy appeal" that have received positive reviews in *Booklist, Horn Book Guide,* and/or *School Library Journal.*

Davis, Kenneth. *Don't Know Much about Mummies* (Don't Know Much About). Illustrated by S. D. Schindler. HarperCollins, 2005. ISBN 0060287810. 48 p. Grades 4–6.

Helmer, Marilyn. *Yucky Riddles* (Kids Can Read). Illustrated by Eric Parker. Kids Can Press, 2003. ISBN 1553374487. 32 p. Grades K–3.

Kudalis, Eric. *The Royal Mummies: Remains from Ancient Egypt* (Mummies). Capstone Press, 2003. ISBN 073681308x. 32 p. Grades 3–9.

Morley, Jacqueline. *Inside the Tomb of Tutankhamun.* Illustrated by John James. Enchanted Lion, 2005. ISBN 159270042x. 48 p. Grades 4–6.

What's Living inside Your Body?
by Andrew Solway.

Solway, Andrew. *What's Living inside Your Body?* (Hidden Life). Heinemann Library, 2004. ISBN 1403448477. 32 p. Grades 4–8.

Solway, Andrew. *What's Living on Your Body?* (Hidden Life). Heinemann Library, 2004. ISBN 1403448485. 32 p. Grades 4–8.

Steinberg, David. *The Monster Mall: And Other Spooky Poems* (All Aboard Poetry Reader). Grosset & Dunlap, 2004. ISBN 0448435438. 48 p. Grades K–3.

Wilcox, Charlotte. *Animal Mummies: Preserved through the Ages* (Mummies). Capstone Press, 2003. ISBN 0736813055. 32 p. Grades 3–9.

Chapter  6

Animals

All kids love animals, whether pets, wild animals, or sea creatures. Boys especially seem to love animals that are scary—like bats, rats, piranhas, and sharks—or animals with strange and gross habits—like hyenas or naked mole rats. This chapter provides an array of animal books that will amaze and intrigue boys of all ages and reading abilities.

NEW AND NOTABLE

A Platypus, Probably by Sneed B. Collard III.

Collard, Sneed B., III. *A Platypus, Probably*. Illustrated by Andrew Plant. Charlesbridge, 2005. ISBN 1570915830. Unpaged. Grades 1–4.

What *is* a platypus, really? If you didn't know before, you will be amazed to learn about this extraordinary animal. Platypuses are half lizard, half beaver, and they live in rivers streams in Australia. They have been around since the time of the dinosaurs, and they are unlike any other mammal. Here are a few fun facts:

- They have a leather-soft, duck-like bill.

- They have webbed feet.

- They don't have teeth, so they crush their food on hard pads inside their bills.

- They rest in burrows along the water in which they live. One platypus can have many burrows.

- They lay eggs.

There are so many more wonderful things to learn about the platypus in this illustrated book. Show almost any picture—the book is crammed with colorful, interesting ones.

Conniff, Richard. *Rats! The Good, the Bad, and the Ugly.* Crown, 2002. ISBN 0375812075. 40 p. Grades 3–7.

Richard Conniff tells it like it is. Rats are among our closest companions in the animal world. They live where we do. They spread disease. They steal our food, invade our homes, and spread disease. "So they give most of use the willies" (page 8).

And there you have it, in a nutshell. The color photographs in this interesting book may even give you the willies. Rats are not animals that most of us feel comfortable even thinking about, but here are some facts:

- One rat in the United States can have as many as sixty or seventy babies in one year. The bandicoot rat in India can produce as many as fifteen thousand descendants in one year—children, grandchildren, and great- and great-great grandchildren.

- Rats can survive on their own at four weeks of age.

- Rats live all around the world. They hitchhike with human travelers.

- Rat teeth are powerful and have a bite with a force of twenty-four thousand pounds per square inch.

- Rats' eyes see well at night.

- A rat in a lab can swim for three days without drowning.

- Rats are very clean (really!) and clean themselves as soon as they wake up.

- Rats are very smart.

- Rat fleas spread disease.

- Rats eat a lot of food—twenty to thirty pounds per year.

- In spite of all this, some people keep them as pets.

Coren, Stanley. *Why Do Dogs Have Wet Noses?* Kids Can Press, 2006. ISBN 1553376579. 64 p. Grades 2–5.

Anybody who has a pet dog probably has a lot of questions about dogs. But so do a lot of other people. This has some great information about man's best friend.

- Dogs really did start out as wolves, and scientists can tell this because dogs can have babies with wolves—and jackals, coyotes, dingoes, and some kinds of foxes. This means they are a family.

- Greyhounds are amazingly fast. They can run at their top speed for as much as seven miles. Cheetahs can run faster, but only for a few seconds. Greyhounds can keep running at speeds of about thirty to thirty-five miles an hour.

- The most popular dog breed of all is the same in three countries: Britain, Canada, and the United States. Can you guess what it is? Find the answer on page 17. (It is the Labrador retriever.)

- Dogs have more than 220 million smell-detecting cells. Humans only have five million. No wonder dogs are sniffing all of the time!

- On page 39, you will learn how to get a dog to stop barking.

- Dogs can learn to understand about 120 to 150 words and hand signals.

- Male dogs raise their legs to pee on trees so they will give other animals the impression that they are actually bigger than they are. The higher up it goes, the bigger the dog must be.

Kids will love telling their friends about the facts in this book.

Kathy's Favorite Animal Books to Booktalk

- Cerullo, Mary M. *The Truth about Great White Sharks.*
- Halls, Kelly Milner. *Albino Animals.*
- Jackson, Donna M. *Hero Dogs: Courageous Canines in Action.*
- Jackson, Donna M. *The Bug Scientists.*
- Lauber, Patricia. *The True-or-False Book of Dogs.*
- McNulty, Faith. *How Whales Walked into the Sea.*
- Montgomery, Sy. *The Snake Scientist.*
- Montgomery, Sy. *The Tarantula Scientist.*
- Settel, Joanne, Ph.D. *Exploding Ants: Amazing Facts about How Animals Adapt.*
- Siy, Alexandra. *Mosquito Bite.*
- Turner, Pamela S. *Gorilla Doctors: Saving Endangered Great Apes.*
- Zeaman, John. *How the Wolf Became the Dog.*

From *Gotcha for Guys! Nonfiction Books to Get Boys Excited About Reading* by Kathleen A. Baxter and Marcia Agness Kochel. Westport, CT: Libraries Unlimited. Copyright © 2007.

Editors of Time for Kids with Adrienne Betz. *Sharks!* (Time for Kids Science Scoops Confident Reader 3). HarperCollins, 2005. ISBN 0060576332. 32 p. Grades 2–5.

This book is filled with great information and wonderful photos of sharks. Did you know that:

- Sharks have thousands of teeth.

- Sharks do not chew with their teeth—they grab things and bite them, but they do not chew.

- The ears of a shark are inside its head.

- More than five hundred kinds of sharks exist today.

- Baby sharks are called pups.

- You shouldn't wear bright orange and yellow around sharks because some of them really like those colors.

Kids will learn a lot from this interesting book. Show the double-page spread on pages 8 and 9.

Florian, Douglas. *Omnibeasts: Animal Poems and Paintings by Douglas Florian.* Harcourt, 2004. ISBN 0152050388. 96 p. Grades 2–5.

If you are doing booktalks about the animal kingdom, use this book for corresponding humorous poems. There may be a poem about the very animal you are discussing in this fun compilation of poems from Florian's earlier books. Some favorites are "The Anteater" on page 16, "The Army Ants" on page 15 (try this with *Army Ant Parade* by April Pulley Sayre), "The Praying Mantis" on page 40, "The Porcupine" on page 47, and "The Newt" on page 75.

Florian, Douglas. *Zoo's Who: Poems and Paintings by Douglas Florian.* Harcourt, 2005. ISBN 0152046399. 48 p. Grades K–5.

The funny, right-on poems and pictures will delight your audiences in this colorful anthology of animal poems. Try reading "The Manta Ray," "The Puffin," "The Ant," or "The Sloth."

Frattini, Stephanie. *Face-to-Face with the Cat.* Photos by Jean-Louis Klein and Marie-Luce Hubert, 2003. ISBN 1570914540. 26 p. Grades 2–4.

Young people who like cats and kittens will love looking at the pictures in this book—and learning about these animals that so many people love.
For instance:

- Cats can move so well because they have six hundred muscles that enable them to twist and turn.

- After cats mate, the female shoos the male away because he will not help her with her kittens.

- Kittens like to play with other animals—especially each other.

Show the picture on page 15.

Rickie and Henri: A True Story
by Jane Goodall.

Goodall, Jane. *Rickie and Henri: A True Story*. Pictures by Alan Marks. A Miniedition Book published by Putnam Young Readers Group, 2004. ISBN 069840002x. Unpaged. Grades K–3.

Rickie, a two-year-old baby chimpanzee, is torn from the mother who takes such loving care of her when her mother is killed by poachers in the Central African rainforest. The poachers put Rickie in a cage, and, starving and thirsty, she is put up for sale on a chain in a marketplace. There a good man rescues her and takes her home.

But when the man travels, his family does not want Rickie in the house and forces her to live outside. There, the only adult she can find is the family dog, Henri. Henri is bewildered at first, but soon he and the chimpanzee are the best of friends, and Rickie rides on him the way she rides on his mother.

Reading this book makes you realize how devastating it is for animals when human beings treat them savagely.

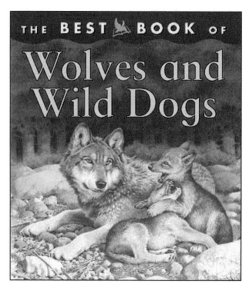

**The Best Book of Wolves and Wild Dogs
by Christiane Gunzi.**

Gunzi, Christiane. *The Best Book of Wolves and Wild Dogs.* Kingfisher, 2003. ISBN
0753455749. 32 p. Grades 3–5.

Gray wolves have been around for about one million years, and they are the largest members of the dog family. Although wolves once lived in many places around the
world, today they are found in only a few locations. But every single dog anywhere is
related to them.

This book is loaded with interesting illustrations and information about some of
the wild dogs around the world. Some of them are famous, such as the coyote, the
Golden jackal, and the Arctic fox, and some of them are rare and not as well known,
such as the Dhole from Asia, the Dingo from Australia, and the African hunting dog.

Fun facts include the following:

- The ancestor of all of the wolves is a mammal called the Eucyon, which lived
  around eight million years ago.

- Alpha male and female wolves are in charge of a wolf pack. They are the only
  pair that have young (show their picture on pages 10 and 11).

- Dingoes are the most feared predators in Australia. They cannot bark.

- African hunting dogs are unusual looking and can run up to thirty-four miles per
  hour.

Kids are guaranteed to learn something worth sharing when they read this book.

Hoose, Phillip. *The Race to Save the Lord God Bird.* Melanie Kroupa Books/Farrar, Straus
& Giroux, 2004. ISBN 0374361738. 196 pages. Grades 5–up.

Scientists believe that 99 percent of all species that ever lived on Earth are extinct.
The dodo bird, the passenger pigeon, and the dinosaurs have all died out. So what does
it matter if another animal or plant becomes extinct? Who really cares?

We all should. Most of the extinctions that have happened throughout history
were caused by natural disasters, some we do not yet understand. But the current wave
of extinctions is being caused by one of Earth's creatures: human beings. Humans are

changing the Earth in major ways for their own benefit, without thinking what those changes are doing to other creatures.

One of the animals that until recently was believed to be extinct is the ivory-billed woodpecker. It lived for thousands of years in the vast forests that once covered so much of what is now the United States. But by the time John James Audubon painted it almost two hundred years ago, it was beginning to be rare and hard to find.

A beautiful, huge, noisy bird, the ivory-billed woodpecker was difficult to see but always easy to hear. In 1809, bird artist Alexander Wilson shot ivory-billed woodpeckers so that he could get a good look at them and paint them more accurately. Once he wounded one slightly and made the bad mistake of taking it to his hotel room, where it practically trashed the place. These birds had not only powerful, dangerous bills but also needle-sharp barbs on their tongues. They were good at ripping bark off trees and finding the grubs they loved to eat.

One of its names given to these birds was the "Lord God Bird," so-called, it is believed, because people would see it and say "Lord God, what a bird!"

The story of this magnificent animal is also the story of the disappearance of our ancient forests. Scientists realized that the birds needed a lot of space, a lot of trees in which to live and thrive, and, as industrialists paid for those trees to be cut down, the birds began to starve to death.

This book is filled with amazing stories of bird-watching history. At the beginning, people killed bird after bird, supposedly just to get a good look at them. Then they went through great hardships to see and photograph them, being careful not to disturb them or their habitat. Even Nazi prisoners of war have a part in the story. It's a compelling read, made even more interesting by the incredible news that ivory-billed woodpeckers were sighted in Arkansas in 2005.

Jackson, Donna M. *ER Vets: Life in an Animal Emergency Room.* Houghton Mifflin, 2005. ISBN 0618436634. 66 p. Grades 4–7.

Life-threatening emergencies happen every day—to people and to animals. Emergency room vets haven't been around for a long time, but veterinary science has a long history. From the beginnings of time, people tried to take care of the wounds and illnesses of their domestic animals, and horse doctors became experts on those animals from the Middle Ages through the1800s.

But by the late 1700s, people started having more and more pets. They moved to the cities to live and no longer had to care for their farm animals. The first veterinarians cared only for horses, but after World Wars I and II more and more people had companion animals. Today more than 60 percent of American households have pets. They need doctors to take care of them.

Dr. Tim Hackett is an ER vet. He loves the excitement of his job and the knowledge that he can save an animal from dying. He always knew he wanted to be a vet, and today he is a good one. As a man, he is in the minority: 75 percent of the vets in the United States today are women.

All sorts of terrible things happen to animals. There are some great stories here. Look at the photo of the dog who got too close to a porcupine (ouch!) on page 14, the cat who got shot by an arrow on page 15, the dog who got bitten by a rattlesnake on page 24, and many other interesting photographs.

There is great information here, such as what you need in an animal first-aid kit, codes ER teams use to communicate (BDLD means a "big dog attacked a little dog," BDLC means a "big dog attacked a little cat") and what kinds of things mean an animal is in an emergency situation.

The photographs are great. Kids who like animals will devour this book.

Jenkins, Steve, and Robin Page. *I See a Kookaburra! Discovering Animal Habitats around the World*. Houghton Mifflin, 2005. ISBN 0618507647. Unpaged. Grades K–4.

Steve Jenkins loves animals and puzzles, and it shows in his interesting and beautiful books. In this one, he illustrates six animal habitats—a desert, a tide pool, a jungle, a savanna, a forest, and a pond. In each picture, you can find, if you search really hard, six different animals. You'll also always find an ant, because ants live in all of these environments. On the next pages, you can see whether you found all the animals and what they were. Finally, in the back of the book is information about every animal in the pictures. See how good you are at doing the puzzles—and see how many animals you can identify without looking at the second pages.

Kennedy, Senator Edward M. *My Senator and Me: A Dog's-Eye View of Washington, D.C.* Illustrated by David Small. Scholastic, 2006. ISBN 0439650771. Unpaged. Grades 1–4.

Do you know whether your U.S. senator has a dog?

Well, Senator Edward Kennedy has one, a Portuguese water dog named Splash, and this is the story of Splash's life as a senator's dog in Washington, D.C.

One reason Senator Kennedy chose Splash to be his dog is that Portuguese water dogs are good swimmers, and loyal, smart and loving. Splash goes to work with his senator, rides the senate tram with his senator (it's one of his favorite things to do—show the illustration), and even plays fetch with the senator, right on the Capitol lawn. He barks when he feels he needs to help out, and he knows to be quiet and still sometimes—so he won't get kicked out.

This is a fun book. Kids will enjoy reading about Splash and his life—and they'll learn a little bit about how the U.S. Senate works—and they will laugh at the wonderful illustrations by David Small.

Great White Sharks by Sandra Markle.

Markle, Sandra. *Great White Sharks* (Animal Predators). Carolrhoda Books, 2004. ISBN 157505731x. 40 p. Grades 3–7.

An exciting true story awaits readers of this book.

A female great white shark, swimming along about twenty to thirty feet below the surface of the ocean, looks for food. Her white belly blends in with the sky to animals beneath her, but her dark blue-gray back hides her from animals (and people) above her as they look into the ocean. This shark listens carefully to see whether any prey might be near, and then she smells. She has a keen sense of smell, and she smells seals—one of her favorite foods.

The amazing photographs in the book show her teeth and her chase after the seals. She always hopes to find one alone. Seals staying close together are more difficult to catch. She can dazzle us with her ability to leap out of the water, even though she weighs almost as much as a large car. She goes after a seal separated a bit from the group and she bites, fast and hard.

- How often does she have to eat?

- This shark is pregnant. She will have babies, and how do they develop in the womb and what happens to them after they are born?

- Does she eat already-dead animals?

All of these questions and a lot more are answered in this beautiful book. Show the picture on page 15.

Hyenas **by Sandra Markle.**

Markle, Sandra. *Hyenas* (Animal Scavengers). Lerner, 2005. ISBN 0822531941. 40 p. Grades 2–5.

Spotted hyenas kill and eat other animals. But brown hyenas are different. They usually eat animals that are already dead—and they can eat any part of that animal. They wait for other animals to finish eating, and then they go for it.

This is the story of a female hyena, an adult about the size of a German shepherd. She lives in the Kalahari Desert in southern Africa. She has teeth and jaws so powerful that they can easily crush bones. She lives with a clan, usually mostly females and cubs, and they take care of each other. When she has a baby cub, she takes care of it until it is about three months old. Then she hauls it to the communal den, where the cub can live and play with other cubs and be nursed by any of the adult females. This last fact is extremely important, for if something happens to a cub's mother, that cub can still survive.

There are some wonderful photos of these unusual animals in this book.

Montgomery, Sy. *Search for the Golden Moon Bear: Science and Adventure in the Asian Tropics*. Houghton Mifflin, 2004. ISBN 0618356509. 80 p. Grades 5–8.

Sy Montgomery is a writer who loves to travel and go to exciting places. She also loves to write about animals and the people who do research on those animals. And she likes to take photographs. Put all of these things together, and you have some very interesting and unusual books.

Sometimes we think that just about everything that can be discovered about planet Earth has already been discovered, but this is just plain wrong. People are discovering new animals all of the time, and some of those animals are pretty big. Sy got interested in a story Dr. Gary Galbreath, a biologist, told her about a strange bear, small and gold in color, that he had seen on a trip to China in 1988. Ever since he saw that bear, he had wanted to go back to see if he could find more—and if he could learn something about them. Sy couldn't wait to help out. She volunteered to pull hairs out of the bears they saw so scientists could do DNA testing on them.

Their trip started out in Cambodia. Sy figured not all of the bears would want to have someone pulling out their hairs, so she took along ammunition to help them get through the experience. The ammunition? Marshmallows and sweetened condensed milk. Bears love sweet food! They worked, too.

Scientists have found many new animals in Cambodia, so it was a promising place to start. Our searchers ate unusual (to us!) foods, such as fried bug snacks. Show the picture of them on page 28. They found several of the golden bears, some in very sad situations, and they found other animals they'd never heard about either. Then they took the hairs they'd taken to a forensic scientist in the United States and let her go to work on them, analyzing the animals they had found and discovering which other animals they were related to.

It's an amazing story, loaded with fascinating photographs.

Schaefer, Lola M. *What's Up? What's Down?* Pictures by Barbara Bash. Greenwillow Books, an imprint of HarperCollins, 2003. ISBN 0060297581. Unpaged. Grades K–3.

If you were a mole living in a hole in the ground, what would be above you? What would be above that? And that? And then that?

Think about all of this. Then look at the pictures in this book and see what is above (and underneath) different things and beings on our planet Earth.

This is great fun to look through.

Show the first and the second two-page spreads. The format alone is unusual and very appealing.

Simon, Seymour. *Horses.* HarperCollins, 2006. ISBN 0060289457. Unpaged. Grades K–3.

Horses and human beings have lived and worked together for thousands and thousands of years. The first horses, or the ancestors of the first horses, lived about fifty-five million years ago. They were about the size of medium dogs. By about ten million years ago, horses were as big as ponies are today, and about two million years ago, horses we would recognize today appeared.

This book has some excellent photographs and great information about horses, such as the following:

- Horses can see in almost a complete circle because their eyes are on each side of their heads.

- There are three types of horse breeds, hotbloods, such as Arabian horses; coldbloods, known for their ability to work, such as Clydesdales; and warmbloods, which are most of the horses kept today.

- There were no horses in North or South America before the Spaniards invaded in the 1500s bringing horses with them.

And lots more! This is a fun read.

***Killer Fish* by Andrew Solway.**

Solway, Andrew. *Killer Fish* (Wild Predators). Heinemann Library, 2004. ISBN 1403457689. 48 p. Grades 4–8.

    Because water covers almost three-quarters of Earth, there are a lot of animals living in it. As on land, there is a food chain. At the top of the food chain are the most powerful beings. On land and in the water, there is no being more powerful than a human being, and we humans kill many fish and predatory animals. We are a great danger to even the most dangerous fish.

    This book, with many photographs, tells us the story of some of the most fearsome fish. Piranhas live in rivers, and they are famous mostly for their razor-sharp teeth. They do not grow to be very big; the biggest are only about two feet long. They have a great sense of smell and can smell one drop of blood in fifty-three gallons of water. They hunt in groups, called schools, and spread out to catch their prey. Some humans who must take special care not to be eaten by piranhas are the surfers who ride the Pororoca up the Amazon River. The Pororoca is a tidal bore, creating a wall of water up to sixteen feet high. Surfers love to ride these waves, but they need to be very careful if they fall.

    Barracudas are known for their teeth too. They usually live in warm waters around coral reefs, and can go from zero to thirty-five miles per hour in just a few seconds. They rush up to their prey and eat it. Sometimes they chop the prey in half with their teeth.

    Cookie-cutter sharks like to feed on creatures bigger than they are. They just take a bite out of the dolphins and tunas they find.

    The northern pike sometimes eats fish that are longer that it is. It swims around with the tail of that fish hanging out of its mouth until the head is digested!

    Other fish discussed in the book include sharks, the red lionfish, the European catfish, the marlin, the bluefin tuna, and many others.

    Kids will learn many facts about killer fish.

Thomson, Sarah L. *Amazing Whales!* (An I Can Read Book). Photographs provided by the Wildlife Conservation Society. HarperCollins, 2005. ISBN 00605446x. 32 p. Grades K–3.

"A blue whale is as long as a basketball court. Its eyes are as big as softballs. Its tongue weighs as much as an elephant. It is the biggest animal that has ever lived on Earth—bigger than any dinosaur" (pages 2–3).

There are also many other kinds and sizes of whales, and this book is a fine introduction to them, with lots of color pictures. Kids will have a great time telling their friends what you have learned.

Turner, Pamela S. *Gorilla Doctors: Saving Endangered Great Apes.* Houghton Mifflin, 2005. ISBN 0618445552. 64 p. Grades 3–6.

There are only about seven hundred mountain gorillas left in the world. They all live in a small region in Africa, the only place where gorillas ever lived naturally. They have people who help them and care passionately about them, but they are an endangered group. The tourists who come to see them spend a great deal of money, which helps the poor people who live near them.

This book introduces readers to some of the people who take care of the gorillas. Some of them are gorilla doctors, who are concerned that the gorillas are getting diseases from human beings.

It is the story of several gorillas in the Rwandan Parc National des Volcans. Bad things of all sorts have happened to them. People set snares to catch small antelopes, but gorillas get caught in them—and if the snares are too tight, they can be seriously injured.

Gorillas have been killed because baby gorillas are valuable. Some poachers, who steal and kill the gorillas illegally, have killed many adults just to get one baby. The book also tells us about an orphaned gorilla baby, stolen by poachers, and how the humans are able to help her.

The pictures are just great. You'll enjoy learning about these extraordinary animals.

Wheeler, Lisa. *Mammoths on the Move.* Illustrated By Kurt Cyrus. Harcourt, 2006. ISBN 015204700x. Unpaged. Grades K–3.

Fourteen thousand years ago

The North was mostly ice and snow.

But woolly mammoths didn't care—

These beasts had comfy coats of hair.

Mammoths lived in the north during the times when they could eat the grass and arctic moss, but when it became too cold, mammoths, like birds today, migrated south for the winter. This is the true story of what could have happened to a mammoth herd as it made its way south, a route full of all sorts of dangers.

There are beautiful pictures—show the one of the wild cat about to attack a mammoth.

NOT TO BE MISSED

Ackerman, Diane. *Bats: Shadows in the Night.* Photographs by Merlin Tuttle. Crown, 1997. ISBN 0517709198. 30 p. Grades 4–7.

Bracken Cave, near San Antonio, Texas, is the home of more than twenty million bats. Every single one of them comes out of the cave at dusk to feed. This is loaded with color photographs of that event and lots of other great information about these helpful—and a little scary—creatures.

Arnold, Caroline. *African Animals.* Morrow Junior Books, 1997. ISBN 0688141153. 48 p. Grades 1–3.

What land animal can weigh as much as a truck—up to fourteen thousand pounds? If you guessed an elephant, you are right, and facts like that intrigue and delight readers. Fine photos illustrate the text.

Arnold, Caroline. *Hawk Highway in the Sky: Watching Raptor Migration.* Photographs by Robert Kruidnier. A Gulliver Green Book/Harcourt Brace, 1997. ISBN 0152008683. 48 p. Grades 4–6.

Thirty-one species of hawks, eagles, and falcons live in North America. We still have much to learn about them, but one of the greatest mysteries we have concerns their migration. How on earth do birds find their way on long journeys? Illustrated with color photographs, this will intrigue any browser.

Arnosky, Jim. *A Manatee Morning.* Simon & Schuster, 2000. ISBN 0689816049. 32 p. Grades K–3.

This is a fine read-aloud as well as an attractive introduction to manatees.

Arnosky, Jim. *Watching Water Birds.* National Geographic Society, 1997. ISBN 0792270738. 32 p. Grades 2–5.

Arnosky's love of water birds is contagious. The colorful illustrations show them in all of their glory, and the book includes a delightful array of fascinating facts. Did you know that loons can swim faster than trout? Great stuff.

Bare, Colleen. *Sammy: Dog Detective.* Cobblehill/Dutton, 1998. ISBN 0525652531. 32 p. Grades 1–3. *Gotcha.*

Sammy is not only a family pet, but also a partner in a K-9 unit. His partner is a police officer *and* the father of the family to which Sammy belongs. This book describes his life and his training and is illustrated with photographs.

Barrett, Jalma. *Lynx* (Wildcats of North America). Photographs by Larry Allan. Blackbirch Press, 1999. ISBN 1567112595. 24 p. Grades 3–5. *Gotcha Again.*

Is there a wild cat kids don't love reading about? Lynx live mostly in Canada, but a few live in forests in parts of the United States. They are solitary creatures, and we do not know as much about them as we do about many other animals. Great photos highlight the text.

Batten, Mary. *The Winking, Blinking Sea: All about Bioluminescence*. Millbrook Press, 2000. ISBN 0761315500. Unpaged. Grades 3–5. *Gotcha Again.*

 Astonishing photos show us ocean animals that make their own light from chemicals inside their bodies.

Bishop, Nic. *The Secrets of Animal Flight*. Illustrated by Amy Bartlett Wright. Houghton Mifflin, 1997. ISBN 0395778484. 32 p. Grades 3–6. *Gotcha.*

 Some of the secrets of animal flight are just that—mysteries still unsolved by scientists. This is loaded with interesting information: bats are the only mammals that fly, some birds can travel up to two thousand miles without stopping, bees probably visit about one hundred flowers each every time they leave the nest. Fun.

Brandenburg, Jim. *Scruffy: A Wolf Finds Its Place in the Pack*. Edited by JoAnn Bren Guernsey. Walker, 1996. ISBN 0802784453. 32 p. Grades K–3. *Gotcha.*

 Jim Brandenburg learned a lot about wolves when he was sent to the Arctic Circle by *National Geographic*. He took many photos and observed one wolf pack in particular. He named one wolf Scruffy because that is how it looked. After long observation, he realized that Scruffy's job was to be the pack babysitter—and that he was a good one.

Cerullo, Mary M. *Coral Reef: A City That Never Sleeps*. Photographs by Jeffrey L. Rotman. Cobblehill Books/Dutton, 1996. ISBN 0525651934. 58 p. Grades 4–8. *Gotcha Again.*

 Unusually shaped plants and shrubs in coral reefs are really the skeletons of millions of sea animals. Bright and colorful, with photographs to prove it, coral reefs are among the most stunning sights on our planet. What goes on in these exotic places is like life in a great big city.

Cerullo, Mary. *The Octopus: Phantom of the Sea*. Photographs by Jeffrey L. Rotman. Cobblehill Books/Dutton, 1997. ISBN 0525651993. 58 p. Grades 4–6. *Gotcha.*

 This book concentrates on the biggest octopus of them all, the giant Pacific octopus, which can reach a length of twenty feet. Octopuses are surprisingly intelligent (and sometimes very creative!) and are real loners—they do not like to be with other octopuses except during the mating season. They have eight arms, and if one is amputated or otherwise lost, it will grow back. Includes great information and color photographs.

Cerullo, Mary M. *The Truth about Great White Sharks*. Photographs by Jeffrey L. Rottman. Illustrations by Michael Wertz. Chronicle Books, 2000. ISBN 0811824675. 48 p. Grades 4–8. *Gotcha Again.*

 White sharks are so dangerous that most of the human beings who study live ones stay in cages—so the sharks can't get in! A shark bite is a terrible thing, and we do not know as much about these animals as we might if they didn't scare us so much. Contains wonderful photos.

Collard, Sneed B. III *Beaks*! Illustrated by Robin Brickman. Charlesbridge, 2002. ISBN 1570913870. Unpaged. Grades K–3. *Gotcha Covered.*

 If you have never really thought about how different various birds' beaks are from each other, this book will surprise you. Beaks can do all sorts of things and help birds get their food in many ways. Colorful pictures show the differences.

Curtis, Patricia. *Animals You Never Even Heard Of.* Sierra Club Books, 1997. ISBN 0871565943. 32 p. Grades K–3. *Gotcha.*

When you read the names of these animals, you'll realize how little you know. Fine color photographs accompany the text, which describes animals such as the caracal, the babirusa, the jabiru, the okapi, the pudu, and the pygmy loris, among others.

Darling, Kathy. *Arctic Babies.* Photographs by Tara Darling. Walker, 1996. ISBN 0802784135. 32 p. Grades K–3. *Gotcha.*

This entire series about animal babies is hugely appealing. Everyone in your audience will want to know more about these adorable animals.

Darling, Kathy. *Lemurs: On Location.* Photographs by Tara Darling. Lothrop, Lee & Shepard/Morrow, 1998. ISBN 0688125395. 40 p. Grades 4–6. *Gotcha.*

Lemurs are found only on the island of Madagascar, an island that was once a part of the African continent. Lemurs' leaping ability is unbelievable. They can leap higher than their length. The pictures will make you want to go out and see a lemur in person.

Davies, Nicola. *Bat Loves the Night.* Illustrated by Sarah Fox-Davies. Candlewick Press, 2001. ISBN 0763612022. 32 p. Grades K–3.

A pipistrelle bat is realistically portrayed in this beautifully designed book that is loaded with facts. This makes a fine read-aloud.

Davies, Nicola. *Surprising Sharks.* Illustrated by James Croft. Candlewick Press, 2003. ISBN 0763621854. 29 p. Grades K–3. *Gotcha Covered.*

Simple, brightly colored illustrations will attract kids to this excellent introduction to sharks. Several sharks are pictured in the text and many others are shown on the endpapers—all labeled. Two full-page spreads show the anatomy of the shark, and the author points out that sharks do kill people, about six every year—but that every year people kill one hundred million sharks. Sharks' worst enemy by far is human beings. Kids will love this.

Davis, Gibbs. *Wackiest White House Pets.* Illustrated by David A. Johnson. Scholastic Press, 2004. ISBN 0439443733. Unpaged. Grades 3–5. *Gotcha Covered.*

The presidents of the United States and their families must like pets. They've had more than four hundred of them in the more than two hundred years they've lived in the White House. Granted, a lot of the pets were cats and dogs, but there were more unusual animals, such as an alligator and two grizzly bears. This has a lot of good stories and fun illustrations.

DuQuette, Keith. *They Call Me Woolly: What Animal Names Can Tell Us.* G. P. Putnam's Sons, 2002. ISBN 0399234454. 32 p. Grades K–3. *Gotcha Covered.*

How do animals get their names? Why do we call a certain snake a "rattlesnake"? How about the Tasmanian devil? This provides fun, thought-provoking information for younger children.

Earle, Sylvia A. *Hello, Fish! Visiting the Coral Reef.* With photographs by Wolcott Henry. National Geographic, 1999. ISBN 0792271033. Unpaged. *Gotcha Again.*

Oceanographer Sylvia Earle tells us that 97 percent of Earth's water is in oceans. Extraordinary photos show some of the life that lives in the coral reefs.

Earle, Sylvia A. *Sea Critters*. With photographs by Wolcott Henry. National Geographic, 2000. ISBN 0792271815. 32 p. Grades 1–4. *Gotcha Again.*

   Easy to read and fun to browse, this title includes beautiful photographs of many of the animals that live in the ocean.

Florian, Douglas. *bow wow meow meow: it's rhyming cats and dogs.* Harcourt, 2003. ISBN 0152163956. 48 p. Grades K–4.

Florian, Douglas. *Mammalabilia.* Poems and paintings by Douglas Florian. Voyager Books/Harcourt 2003. ISBN 0152050248. 48 p. Grades 2–5.

Fredericks, Anthony D. *Cannibal Animals: Animals That Eat Their Own Kind.* Franklin Watts, 1999. ISBN 0531164209. 64 p. Grades 3–5. *Gotcha Again.*

   Animals do eat each other, and the ways in which they do it are utterly surprising. We know about the black widow spiders and praying mantises, but sand tiger sharks eat their siblings inside their mother's womb! You can hardly put this one down.

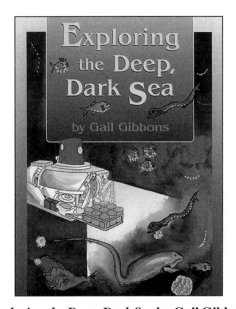

***Exploring the Deep, Dark Sea* by Gail Gibbons.**

Gibbons, Gail. *Exploring the Deep, Dark Sea*. Little, Brown, 1999. ISBN 0516309451. Unpaged. Grades 1–4. *Gotcha Again.*

   Although very little of the ocean floor has been explored so far, scientists are amazed at what they have found there. Some areas are six miles deep, and they are so dark that submersible vehicles have to turn on their lights at about 1,500 feet. Many of the sea creatures here are bioluminescent—that is, they create their own light. Great stuff.

Gibbons, Gail. *Rabbits, Rabbits and More Rabbits!* Holiday House, 2000. ISBN 0823414868. Unpaged. Grades 1–3. *Gotcha Again.*

   Rabbits live on every continent except Antarctica, and they have looked pretty much the same for almost sixty-five million years. The largest ones can weigh as much as twenty-four pounds. They're interesting and kids love them. (Gail Gibbons, whose simple, colorful books are extraordinarily popular, has dozens of books about animals. Titles especially interesting to boys are listed later in this chapter.)

Goldin, Augusta. *Ducks Don't Get Wet* (Let's Read and Find Out Science Book). Illustrated by Helen K. Davie. HarperCollins, 1999. ISBN 006027882X. 32 p. Grades K–3. *Gotcha Again.*

Ducks really do not get wet, and this newly and beautifully illustrated edition of an old classic explains exactly why.

Goodall, Jane. *The Chimpanzees I Love: Saving Our World and Theirs.* A Byron Preiss Book/Scholastic Press, 2001. ISBN 043921310x. 80 p. Grades 4–8. *Gotcha Covered.*

Jane Goodall fell in love with chimpanzees when she was a small child. She had a stuffed chimpanzee she called Jubilee back then, and she loves chimpanzees just as much today. She has devoted her life to them, to researching how they live and how they behave, and she has discovered all sorts of wonderful things about them. There are some fine photographs and a riveting story here.

Graham-Barber, Lynda. *Spy Hops and Belly Flops: Curious Behavior of Woodland Animals.* Illustrated by Brian Lies. Houghton Mifflin, 2004. ISBN 061822291x. Unpaged. Grades K–2. *Gotcha Covered.*

This colorful and unusual look at the behavior of woodland animals is sure to delight younger children—and serve as a fun read-aloud for older boys to read to younger ones.

Halls, Kelly Milner. *Albino Animals.* Darby Creek Publishing, 2004. ISBN 1581960123. 72 p. Grades 4–8. *Gotcha Covered.*

Albino animals are found throughout nature, including among human beings. Beings with albinism have no pigment, so they appear white. What we can see is their blood, which makes some parts of their bodies look pinkish. This book is jam-packed with great photographs of albino animals and information about the problems they face. To name just a couple, they sunburn very easily, and they have no protective coloring (or camouflage) and so are frequently killed by predators when they are very young. This is a great browsing book that pulls you right into the text.

Hickman, Pamela. *Animals Eating: How Animals Chomp, Chew, Slurp and Swallow.* Illustrated by Pat Stephens. Kids Can Press, 2001. ISBN 1550745778. 40 p. Grades 2–4. *Gotcha Again.*

How on earth can snakes eat things bigger than they are? Did you know that crocodiles carry stones in their stomachs to help them grind food and keep them down low in the water? You'll find great stuff in this book.

Holub, Joan. *Why Do Cats Meow?* Illustrations by Anna DiVito. Dial Books for Young Readers, 2001. ISBN 0803725035. 48 p. Grades 1–3. *Gotcha Again.*

Easy-to-read, with lots of color photos, this book about cat behavior is a great choice for cat lovers.

Holub, Joan. *Why Do Dogs Bark?* Illustrations by Anna DiVito. Dial Books for Young Readers, 2001. ISBN 0803725043. 48 p. Grades 2–3. *Gotcha Again.*

Holub, Joan. *Why Do Rabbits Hop? And Other Questions about Rabbits, Guinea Pigs, Hamsters, and Gerbils.* Illustrations by Anna DiVito. Dial Books for Young Readers, 2003. ISBN 0803727712. 48 p. Grades 1–3. *Gotcha Covered.*

The whys and wherefores of animal behavior are always intriguing. Did you know that the biggest rabbit, the Flemish giant, can weigh as much as twenty-two pounds?

Hopkins, Lee Bennett (selected by). *A Pet for Me: Poems* (An I Can Read Book). Pictures by Jane Manning. HarperCollins, 2003. ISBN 0060291117. Unpaged. Grades K–3.

This easy-to-read poetry book includes a nice selection of poems about pets. Try "I Would Like to Have a Pet" by Karla Kuskin, "Old Slow Friend" by Alice Schertle, "Tarantula" by Fran Haraway, or "Ant Farm" by Madeline Comora. It's a great book to use with any story about pets.

Jackson, Donna M. *Hero Dogs: Courageous Canines in Action.* Megan Tingley Books/Little, Brown, 2003. ISBN 0316826812. 48 p. Grades 3–6. *Gotcha Covered.*

When the World Trade Center towers were attacked on September 11, 2001, people were buried in the rubble of the buildings. Some were dead, and some were alive. Almost all of them were hard to find. Searchers could not do it alone. They needed help. And the best help they could find came from dogs. Lots of photographs of various types of hero dogs help us to realize what a great contribution these animals make.

Jarrow, Gail, and Paul Sherman. *Naked Mole Rats.* Carolrhoda Books, 1996. ISBN 0876149956. 48 p. Grades 3–6. *Gotcha.*

Naked mole rats may win the contest for the ugliest mammal. Living in eastern Africa, they inhabit complex tunnel systems, underground. Like bees, the naked mole rats have queens—and their queens can have as many as nine hundred babies. The pictures are fun to show to an audience.

Jenkins, Priscilla Belz. *A Safe Home for the Manatees.* Illustrated by Martin Classen. HarperCollins, 1997. ISBN 0060271493. 32 p. Grades 1–3. *Gotcha.*

Manatees look a little like hippopotamuses, and they are distant relatives of elephants. These gentle, endangered animals each eat up to one hundred pounds of plants a day, and their environment is changing rapidly—so many humans and boats are coming into the area off the coast of Florida where they live that they are dying off. Fascinating information about a sad topic.

Jenkins, Steve. *Actual Size.* Houghton Mifflin, 2004. ISBN 0618375945. Unpaged. Grades K–3. *Gotcha Covered.*

These pictures show several animals and animal body parts at actual size—and the actual sizes of many of these things will surprise you. Put your hand up against the pictures in the book and see how big or small animals can be.

Jenkins, Steve, and Robin Page. *What Do You Do with a Tail Like This?* Houghton Mifflin, 2003. ISBN 0618256288. Unpaged. Grades K–3. *Gotcha Covered.*

Each spread show five animal parts—noses, eyes, tails, feet, and mouths. And it asks us to guess which animals the body parts belong to and what they do with them. The stunning illustrations were awarded a 2004 Caldecott Honor.

Kirk, Daniel. *Dogs Rule!* Hyperion Books for Children, 2003. ISBN 0786819499. 48 p. Grades 1–4. *Gotcha Covered.*

These funny poems, illustrated by colorful, dead-on illustrations, can also be sung. A CD is included.

Landstrom, Lee Ann. *Nature's Yucky! Gross Stuff that Helps Nature Work.* Illustrated by Constance R. Bergum. Mountain Press Publishing, 2003. ISBN 0878424741. Unpaged. Grades K–4. *Gotcha Covered.*

Many things that people consider to be gross and disgusting are normal, natural, and wonderful when they happen in nature. Animals whose behavior includes pooping on their legs are among the "yucky" subjects covered in this colorful book.

Lauber, Patricia. *The True-or-False Book of Dogs.* Illustrated by Rosalyn Schanzer. HarperCollins, 2003. ISBN 0060297670. 32 p. Grades 1–4. *Gotcha Covered.*

Every single dog is originally descended from a wolf. It's hard to believe, especially since they all look so different. Here we learn how they changed over the years and why they are so diverse—and why they make good pets and behave the way they do. It even has a chart of how dogs' bodies reveal their feelings. Fun illustrations light up an equally delightful text.

Lewin, Ted. *Tooth and Claw: Animal Adventures in the Wild.* HarperCollins, 2003. ISBN 0688141056. 98 p. Grades 4–up.

Ted Lewin has an interesting life. He likes to have adventures, to take photographs of them and draw them, and then he likes to write books about them. Ted has seen a Bengal tiger lunge at him while he was riding an elephant, surprised a rattlesnake, and run into a huge bull shark when he was swimming, among other things. How would *you* handle some of these situations?

Markle, Sandra. *Growing Up Wild: Penguins.* Atheneum Books for Young Readers, 2002. ISBN 0689818874. 32 p. Grades 2–4. *Gotcha Covered.*

Penguins are more popular than ever with kids, and this colorful book is full of them. Learn how the penguins build nests, how the parents take turns warming and guarding it, how the chicks grow up, and the dangers they face.

Markle, Sandra. *Outside and Inside Bats.* Atheneum Books for Young Readers, 1997. ISBN 0689811659. 40 p. Grades 1–5. *Gotcha.*

Bats are appealingly creepy creatures, and the information given here only makes them more fascinating. Lots of good photos enhance the text.

Markle, Sandra. *Wolves: Growing Up Wild.* Atheneum Books for Young Readers, 2001. ISBN 0689818866. 32 p. Grades 2–4. *Gotcha Again.*

Baby wolves have babysitters—not just their moms, but real babysitters from their wolf packs. This book has good photos and great information to go along with them.

Matthews, Dawn. *Harp Seal Pups.* Photographs by Dan Guravich. Simon & Schuster Books for Young Readers, 1997. ISBN 0689800142. 34 p. Grades 2–5. *Gotcha.*

Harp seal pups are born in only four places—safe places where their enemies the polar bears cannot find them. Babies weigh about fifteen pounds each when they are born but about eighty pounds when they are only twelve days old. The color photographs are irresistible.

McMillan, Bruce. *Nights of the Pufflings.* Photo-illustrated by Bruce McMillan. Houghton Mifflin, 1995. ISBN 0395708109. 32 p. Grades 1–3. *Gotcha.*

Pufflings are the babies of puffins, birds that return every year to the same island off the coast of Iceland to lay their eggs and raise their chicks. Captivating photographs show the first flights of these young birds, who are not very good flyers and who are helped by the village children when they accidentally crash.

McMillan, Bruce. *Wild Flamingos.* Photo-illustrated by Bruce McMillan. Houghton Mifflin, 1997. ISBN 0395845459. 32 p. Grades 2–4. *Gotcha.*

Flamingos are colorful and beautiful—and they get their color from the foods they eat. The pink color comes mainly from eating shrimp! If they stop eating it, they are not pink anymore. Great photographs highlight the interesting text.

McNulty, Faith. *How Whales Walked into the Sea.* Illustrated by Ted Rand. Scholastic Press, 1999. ISBN 0590898302. Unpaged. Grades 2–5. *Gotcha Again.*

Unless you already know a lot about them, most of the information in this wonderful book on whales will probably be new to you. Do you know that whales were once land animals with legs and fur?

Montgomery, Sy. *Encantado: Pink Dolphin of the Amazon.* With photographs by Dianne Taylor-Snow. Houghton Mifflin, 2002. ISBN 0618131035. 73 p. Grades 4–8. *Gotcha Covered.*

Two places in the whole world have pink dolphins, and both of them are in South America. We don't have many photographs, especially because there is only one in captivity, at the Pittsburg Zoo. But this book has a lot of those photographs and good information about how these dolphins are both alike and different from their brothers and sisters who live in the oceans. Fascinating.

Page, Debra. *Orcas around Me: My Alaskan Summer.* Illustrated by Leslie W. Bowman. Albert Whitman, 1997. ISBN 0807561371. 40 p. Grades 2–4. *Gotcha.*

Taiga lives in Alaska, and his family makes money in the summer by fishing for salmon. He gets to see a lot of different animals in the water, and this is the story of a day in which the family's small boat was surrounded by killer whales. It's an exciting story.

Perry, Phyllis J. *Freshwater Giants, Hippopotamus, River Dolphins, and Manatees.* Franklin Watts, 1999. ISBN 0531116816. 64 p. Grades 3–5. *Gotcha Again.*

Most animals that live in rivers are small, but not these. These breathtaking giants will catch anyone's interest. Manatees are the only ones who live in the wild in North America, but all of these animals will intrigue young readers.

Pfeffer, Wendy. *Dolphin Talk: Whistles, Clicks, and Clapping Jaws* (Let's-Read-and-Find-Out Science, Level 2). Illustrated by Helen K. Davie. HarperCollins, 2003. ISBN 0064452107. 33 p. Grades 1–3. *Gotcha Covered.*

Dolphins *are* very intelligent, and they *do* communicate with each other, but not in the exact same ways that human beings do. This provides great information for early readers.

Pringle, Laurence. *Bats! Strange and Wonderful.* Illustrated by Meryl Henderson. Boyds Mills Press, 2000. ISBN 15639733278. 32 p. Grades K–3. *Gotcha Again.*

Bats are one of the most helpful animals to human beings—and yet they creep most of us out. Pringle leaps to the defense of these unusual animals.

Robbins, Ken. *Thunder on the Plains: The Story of the American Buffalo.* Atheneum Books for Young Readers, 2001. ISBN 0689830254. Unpaged. Grades 2–4. *Gotcha Again.*

Historians believe that in 1875 there were fifty million buffalo in the United States. By 1900, there were almost none. What happened? The unfortunate answer is that Americans killed them. They were in the way of the railroads and the farmers, and so they killed as many as they could. This is a horrifying story, with good photos and a somewhat happy ending.

Ryder, Joanne. *Little Panda: The World Welcomes Hua Mei at the San Diego Zoo.* Simon & Schuster, 2001. ISBN 0689843100. 32 p. Grades K–3.

Hua Mei, the first giant panda to be born and survive in captivity in the Western Hemisphere, is the subject of this fine read-aloud. Many color photos and good scientific information are included.

Stefoff, Rebecca. *Penguin* (Living Things). Benchmark Books, 1998. ISBN 0761404465. 32 p. Grades 1–3. *Gotcha Again.*

Everyone likes to look at penguins, perhaps the most unusual looking of all the birds. They may all look the same to us, but each penguin is different. Do you know that penguins mate for life? That there are penguin "babysitters"? This has excellent photos and good information.

Swanson, Diane. *Animals Eat the Weirdest Things.* Illustrated by Terry Smith. Henry Holt, 1998. ISBN 080505846X. 64 p. Grades 4–6. *Gotcha Again.*

We all know that beavers eat wood, but here you will learn about animals that eat all sorts of interesting things—including blood, dung, vomit, and rotting flesh.

Swinburne, Stephen R. *Coyote: North America's Dog*. Boyds Mills Press, 1999. ISBN 1563977656. 32 p. Grades 4–6. *Gotcha Again.*

> Coyotes are dogs that are native to North America. They have always lived here, and there are a lot of them still around. They eat just about everything and adapt easily to different environments. Swinburne's many photographs are excellent.

Swinburne, Stephen R. *Unbeatable Beaks*. Illustrated by Joan Paley. Henry Holt, 1999. ISBN 0805048022. Unpaged. Grades 1–3. *Gotcha Again.*

> You have probably never thought much about beaks, so this book will get you thinking. Beaks are shaped differently according to the job they have to do, and this is wonderful information.

Tildes, Phyllis Limbacher. *Calico's Cousins: Cats from around the World*. Charlesbridge, 1999. ISBN 0881066846. Unpaged. Grades 1–3. *Gotcha Again.*

> Huge, delightful pictures show us some of the many unusual—and usual—breeds of cats around the world. Cat lovers will find this irresistible.

Wallace, Karen. *Gentle Giant Octopus*. Illustrated by Mike Bostock. Candlewick Press, 1998. 076360318X. 30 p. Grades 1–3. *Gotcha Again.*

> Tantalizing pictures show us this extraordinary animal, which is very intelligent and can do all sorts of things human beings cannot.

Weaver, Robyn. *Meerkats* (Bridgestone Animals). Bridgestone Books, 1999. ISBN 0736800662. 24 p. Grades 2–4. *Gotcha Again.*

> Anybody who ever saw the movie *The Lion King* became at least a little interested in meerkats. Belonging to the mongoose family, they are unusual and intriguing animals. Good photos demonstrate their behavior. More books in this series are listed in the "Worth Reading" books later in this chapter.

Wilcox, Charlotte. *The Chihuahua* (Learning about Dogs). Capstone Press, 1999. ISBN 0736801588. 48 p. Grades 4–up. *Gotcha Again.*

Wilcox, Charlotte. *The Weimeraner* (Learning about Dogs). Capstone Press, 1999. ISBN 0736801634. 48 p. Grades 4–up. *Gotcha Again.*

> Kids who are deciding which kind of a dog they want for a pet, as well as kids who love to read about animals, will enjoy the information and the excellent photographs in these two books, which are filled with good stories about how the breeds came into existence, as well as advice on taking care of these dogs.
>
> Others in the series are listed in the "Worth Reading" books later in this chapter.

Zeaman, John. *How the Wolf Became the Dog* (Before They Were Pets). Franklin Watts, 1998. ISBN 0531114597. 64 p. Grades 4–6. *Gotcha Again.*

> When students hear about this book, they want to have it read it aloud on the spot. It contains great information about the evolution of the wolf into the beloved family pet.

Zeaman, John. *Why the Cat Chose Us* (Before They Were Pets). Franklin Watts, 1998. ISBN 0531114589. 64 p. Grades 4–6. *Gotcha Again.*

How did cats, the most independent of animals, ever become household pets? What made people want to own a cat? Good color photos accompany the fun information.

WORTH READING

Nonfiction books with "boy appeal" that have received positive reviews in *Booklist, Horn Book Guide*, and/or *School Library Journal.*

Arnold, Katya. *Elephants Can Paint Too!* Simon & Schuster Books for Young Readers, 2005. ISBN 0689865851. 40 p. Grades 1–3.

Arnosky, Jim. *All about Sharks*. Scholastic, 2003. ISBN 0590481665. 32 p. Grades K–3.

Arnosky, Jim. *Hook, Line & Sinker: A Beginner's Guide to Fishing, Boating, and Watching Water Wildlife*. Scholastic, 2005. ISBN 0439455847. 192 p. Grades 4–6.

***Grey Wolf* by Jill Bailey.**

Bailey, Jill. *Grey Wolf* (Animals under Threat). Heinemann Library, 2005. ISBN 140345583x. 48 p. Grades 4–6.

Benchley, Peter. *Shark Life: True Stories about Sharks & the Sea*. Adapted by Karen Wojtyla. Delacorte, 2005. ISBN 0385731094. 196 p. Grades 4–8.

Berger, Melvin. *Penguins Swim but Don't Get Wet and Other Amazing Facts about Polar Animals* (Speedy Facts). Scholastic, 2004. ISBN 0439625351. 48 p. Grades 3–8.

Big Cats (Eye Wonder). DK, 2002. ISBN 0789485486. 48 p. Grades K–3.

***Hermit Crabs* by Tristan Boyer Binns.**

Binns, Tristan Boyer. *Hermit Crabs* (Keeping Unusual Pets). Heinemann Library, 2004.
ISBN 1403408254. 48 p. Grades 4–8.

Binns, Tristan Boyer. *Potbellied Pigs* (Keeping Unusual Pets). Heinemann Library, 2004.
ISBN 1403408289. 48 p. Grades 4–8.

***Untamed: Animals around the World*
by Steve Bloom.**

Bloom, Steve. *Untamed: Animals around the World.* Illustrated by Emmanuelle Zicot.
Harry N. Abrams, 2005. ISBN 0810959569. 75 p. Grades 4–7.

Brend, Stephen. *Gorilla* (Natural World). Raintree, 2002. ISBN 0739852280. 48 p. Grades
2–5.

Butler, John. *Whose Nose and Toes?* Viking Children's Books, 2004. ISBN 0670059048. 24 p. Grades K–2.

Chottin, Ariane. *Little Foxes* (Born to Be Wild). Gareth Stevens, 2005. ISBN 0836844351. 24 p. Grades 3–5.

Chottin, Ariane. *Little Leopards* (Born to Be Wild). Gareth Stevens, 2005. ISBN 0836844386. 24 p. Grades 3–5.

Claybourne, Anna. *Cheetah* (Natural World). Raintree, 2003. ISBN 0739860569. 48 p. Grades 3–6.

Claybourne, Anna. *Giant Panda* (Animals under Threat). Heinemann Library, 2005. ISBN 1403455821. 48 p. Grades 4–6.

Coile, D. Caroline. *How Smart Is Your Dog? 30 Fun Science Activities with Your Pet.* Sterling, 2003. ISBN 0806976772. 96 p. Grades K–3.

Little Gorillas by Bernadette Costa-Prades.

Costa-Prades, Bernadette. *Little Gorillas*. Gareth Stevens, 2005. ISBN 0836844378. 23 p. Grades 3–5.

Cotton, Jacqueline S. *Polar Bears* (Pull Ahead Books). Lerner, 2004. ISBN 0822537761. 32 p. Grades K–3.

Dalgliesh, Sharon. *Working Dogs* (Farm Animals). Chelsea House, 2005. ISBN 079108275x. 32 p. Grades K–3.

Deady, Kathleen W. *Great White Sharks* (Predators in the Wild). Capstone High-Interest Books, 2001. ISBN 0736807861. 48 p. Grades 3–9.

Deady, Kathleen W. *Grizzly Bears* (Predators in the Wild). Capstone High-Interest Books, 2002. ISBN 0736810633. 48 p. Grades 3–9.

Dornfield, Margaret. *Bats* (Animals Animals). Benchmark Books, 2004. ISBN 0761417540. 46 p. Grades 2–5.

Editors of Time for Kids. *Bats!* (Time for Kids Science Scoops). HarperCollins, 2005. ISBN 0060576391. 32 p. Grades 1–3.

Estigarribia, Diana. *Cheetahs* (Animals Animals). Benchmark Books, 2004. ISBN 0761417494. 46 p. Grades 2–5.

Faiella, Graham. *Whales* (All Aboard Reading). Grosset & Dunlap, 2002. ISBN 0448428377. 48 p. Grades K–3.

Fraser, Mary Ann. *Where Are the Night Animals?* (Let's-Read-and-Find-Out Science, Stage 1). HarperCollins, 1999. ISBN 0064451763. 32 p. Grades K–3.

Gibbons, Gail. *Bats.* Holiday House, 1999. ISBN 0823414574. Unpaged. Grades 1–3.

Gibbons, Gail. *Penguins!* Holiday House, 1998. ISBN 0823413888. Unpaged. Grades 1–3.

Gibbons, Gail. *Pigs.* Holiday House, 1999. ISBN 0823414418. Unpaged. Grades 1–3.

Gordon, Sharon. *Guess Who Bites* (Bookworms: Guess Who). Benchmark Books, 2004. ISBN 0761417664. 32 p. Grades K–3.

Gordon, Sharon. *Guess Who Dives* (Bookworms: Guess Who). Benchmark Books, 2003. ISBN 0761415548. 32 p. Grades K–3.

Gordon, Sharon. *Guess Who Hides* (Bookworms: Guess Who). Benchmark Books, 2003. ISBN 0761415556. 32 p. Grades K–3.

Gordon, Sharon. *Guess Who Hisses* (Bookworms: Guess Who) Benchmark Books, 2004. ISBN 0761417672. 32 p. Grades K–3.

Gordon, Sharon. *Guess Who Hops* (Bookworms: Guess Who). Benchmark Books, 2004. ISBN 0761417648. 32 p. Grades K–3.

Gordon, Sharon. *Guess Who Roars* (Bookworms: Guess Who). Benchmark Books, 2003. ISBN 0761415564. 32 p. Grades K–3.

Gordon, Sharon. *Guess Who Runs* (Bookworms: Guess Who). Benchmark Books, 2004. ISBN 076141763X. 32 p. Grades K–3.

Gordon, Sharon. *Guess Who Swoops* (Bookworms: Guess Who). Benchmark Books, 2003. ISBN 076141553x. 32 p. Grades K–3.

Greenberg, Dan. *Leopards* (Animals Animals). Benchmark Books, 2002. ISBN 0761414487. 48 p. Grades 2–5.

Greenberg, Dan. *Whales* (AnimalWays). Benchmark, 2002. ISBN 0761413898. 104 p. Grades 4–8.

Greenberg, Dan. *Wolves* (Animals Animals). Benchmark, 2002. ISBN 0761414479. 48 p. Grades 2–5.

Gunzi, Christine. *The Best Book of Endangered and Extinct Animals* (Best Book of). Kingfisher, 2004. ISBN 0753457571. 32 p. Grades 3–6.

Hall, Katy, and Lisa Eisenberg. *Turkey Riddles* (Dial Easy-to-Read). Dial Books for Young Readers, 2002. ISBN 0803725302. 40 p. Grades K–3.

Handford, Tom. *Chinchillas* (Keeping Unusual Pets). Heinemann Library, 2003. ISBN 1403402809. 48 p. Grades 4–8.

Critter Riddles **by Marilyn Helmer.**

Helmer, Marilyn. *Critter Riddles* (Kids Can Read). Illustrated by Eric Parker. Kids Can Press, 2003. ISBN 1553374452. 32 p. Grades K–3.

Hirschi, Ron. *Dolphins* (Animals Animals). Benchmark, 2002. ISBN 0761414436. 48 p. Grades 2–5.

Hirschi, Ron. *Searching for Grizzlies*. Boyds Mills Press, 2005. ISBN 1590780140. 32 p. Grades 3–5.

Hiscock, Bill. *The Big Caribou Herd: Life in the Arctic National Wildlife Refuge.* Boyds Mills Press, 2003. ISBN 1590780108. 32 p. Grades 1–4.

Hoena, Blake. *Dogs ABC: An Alphabet Book* (A+ Alphabet Books). Capstone Press, 2004. ISBN 0736826068. 32 p. Grades K–3.

Holmes, Kevin. *Warthogs.* Bridgestone Books, an imprint of Capstone Press, 1999. ISBN 0736800670. 24 p. Grades 2–4.

Holub, Joan. *Why Do Horses Neigh?* (Dial Easy-to-Read). Dial Books for Young Readers, 2004. ISBN 0803727704. 48 p. Grades K–3.

Inskipp, Carol. *Killer Whale* (Animals under Threat). Heinemann Library, 2005. ISBN 1403455848. 48 p. Grades 4–6.

Inskipp, Carol. *Koala* (Animals under Threat). Heinemann Library, 2005. ISBN 1403455856. 48 p. Grades 4–6.

Jango-Cohen, Judith. *Armadillos* (Animals Animals) Benchmark Books, 2004. ISBN 076141617x. 46 p. Grades 2–5.

Jango-Cohen, Judith. *Crocodiles* (Animals Animals). Benchmark, 2002. ISBN 0761414460. 48 p. Grades 2–5.

Jango-Cohen, Judith. *Flying Squirrels* (Pull Ahead Books). Lerner, 2004. ISBN 0822537729. 32 p. Grades K–3.

Jango-Cohen, Judith. *Freshwater Fishes* (Perfect Pets). Benchmark, 2002. ISBN 0761413987. 32 p. Grades 2–5.

Jango-Cohen, Judith. *Gorillas* (Animals Animals). Benchmark, 2002. ISBN 0761414448. 48 p. Grades 2–5.

Jango-Cohen, Judith. *Octopuses* (Animals Animals). Benchmark Books, 2004. ISBN 0761416145. 46 p. Grades 2–5.

Jango-Cohen, Judith. *Rhinoceroses* (Animals Animals). Benchmark Books, 2004. ISBN 0761417532. 46 p. Grades 2–5.

Jeffrey, Laura S. *Birds: How to Choose and Care for a Bird* (American Humane Pet Care Library). Enslow, 2004. ISBN 0766025152. 48 p. Grades 3–6.

Jeffrey, Laura S. *Cats: How to Choose and Care for a Cat* (American Humane Pet Care Library). Enslow 2004. ISBN 0766025160. 48 p. Grades 3–6.

Jeffrey, Laura S. *Dogs: How to Choose and Care for a Dog* (American Humane Pet Care Library). Enslow 2004. ISBN 0766025209. 48 p. Grades 3–6.

Jeffrey, Laura S. *Fish: How to Choose and Care for a Fish* (American Humane Pet Care Library). Enslow 2004. ISBN 0766025179. 48 p. Grades 3–6.

Jeffrey, Laura S. *Hamsters, Gerbils, Guinea Pigs, Rabbits, Ferrets, Mice, and Rats: How to Choose and Care for a Small Mammal* (American Humane Pet Care Library). Enslow 2004. ISBN 0766025187. 48 p. Grades 3–6.

Jeffrey, Laura S. *Horses: How to Choose and Care for a Horse* (American Humane Pet Care Library). Enslow 2004. ISBN 0766025195. 48 p. Grades 3–6.

Jenkins, Steve. *What Do You Do When Something Wants to Eat You?* Houghton Mifflin, 1997. ISBN 0395825148. 32 p. Grades 1–3.

Jonas, Anne. *Little Elephants* (Born to Be Wild). Gareth Stevens, 2005. ISBN 0836844343. 24 p. Grades 3–5.

Kalz, Jill. *Cheetahs* (Let's Investigate). The Child's Word, 2003. ISBN 1583412328. 32 p. Grades 1–4.

Kane, Karen. *Chimpanzees* (Early Bird Nature Books). Lerner, 2004. ISBN 082252418x. 48 p. Grades 1–4.

Kane, Karen. *Mountain Gorillas.* Photographs by Gerry Ellis. Lerner, 2001. ISBN 0822530406. 48 p. Grades 2–4.

Kaner, Etta. *Animal Talk: How Animals Communicate through Sight, Sound and Smell.* Kids Can Press, 2002. ISBN 155074982x. 40 p. Grades 3–6.

Keller, Charles. *Animal Jokes* (Giggle Fit). Illustrated by Steve Harpster. Sterling, 2003. ISBN 1402704380. 48 p. Grades K–3.

Kelsey, Elin. *Strange New Species: Astonishing Discoveries of Life on Earth.* Maple Tree Press, 2005. ISBN 1897066317. 96 p. Grade 5–up.

Kendall, Patricia. *Dolphins* (In the Wild). Raintree, 2003. ISBN 0739849050. 32 p. Grades 1–3.

Kendall, Patricia. *Gorillas* (In the Wild). Raintree, 2003. ISBN 0739854976. 32 p. Grades 1–3.

Kendall, Patricia. *Grizzly Bears* (In the Wild). Raintree, 2003. ISBN 0739854992. 32 p. Grades 1–3.

Kendall, Patricia. *Leopards* (In the Wild). Raintree, 2003. ISBN 0739854968. 32 p. Grades 1–3.

Kendall, Patricia. *Lions* (In the Wild). Raintree, 2003. ISBN 0739849077. 32 p. Grades 1–3.

Kendall, Patricia. *Tigers* (In the Wild). Raintree, 2003. ISBN 0739849093. 32 p. Grades 1–3.

Kite, L. Patricia. *Leeches* (Early Bird Nature Books). Lerner, 2004. ISBN 0822530546. 48 p. Grades 1–4.

Knight, Tim. *Dramatic Displays* (Amazing Nature). Heinemann Library, 2003. ISBN 1403407215. 32 p. Grades 2–5.

Knight, Tim. *Ferocious Fighters* (Amazing Nature). Heinemann Library, 2003. ISBN 140341145X. 32 p. Grades 2–5.

Powerful Predators **by Tim Knight.**

Knight, Tim. *Powerful Predators* (Amazing Nature). Heinemann Library, 2003. ISBN 1403411476. 32 p. Grades 2–5.

Landau, Elaine. *Fierce Cats* (Fearsome, Scary, and Creepy Animals). Enslow, 2003. ISBN 0766020622. 48 p. Grades 3–5.

Landau, Elaine. *Killer Bees* (Fearsome, Scary, and Creepy Animals). Enslow, 2003. ISBN 0766020614. 48 p. Grades 3–5.

Landau, Elaine. *Scary Sharks* (Fearsome, Scary, and Creepy Animals). Enslow, 2003. ISBN 0766020584. 48 p. Grades 3–5.

Laskey, Elizabeth. *Giant and Teeny* (Wild Nature). Heinemann Library, 2004. ISBN 1403449570. 32 p. Grades 4–8.

***Gross and Gory* by Elizabeth Laskey.**

Laskey, Elizabeth. *Gross and Gory* (Wild Nature). Heinemann Library, 2004. ISBN 1403449597. 32 p. Grades 4–8.

Laskey, Elizabeth. *Speedy and Slow* (Wild Nature). Heinemann Library, 2004. ISBN 1403449589. 32 p. Grades 4–8.

Laskey, Elizabeth. *Weird and Wonderful* (Wild Nature). Heinemann Library, 2004. ISBN 1403449600. 32 p. Grades 4–8.

Laubach, Cynthia. *Raptor! A Kid's Guide to Birds of Prey.* Storey, 2002. ISBN 1580174752. 118 p. Grades 4–8.

Leach, Michael. *Moose* (Natural World). Raintree, 2003. ISBN 0739860569. 48 p. Grades 3–6.

Leach, Michael. *Wolf* (Natural World). Raintree, 2002. ISBN 0739852310. 48 p. Grades 3–6.

Levine, Michelle. *Foxes* (Pull Ahead Books). Lerner, 2004. ISBN 0822537745. 32 p. Grades K–3.

Levine, Michelle. *Jumping Kangaroos* (Pull Ahead Books). Lerner, 2005. ISBN 082252421x. 32 p. Grades K–3.

Lockwood, Sophie. *Polar Bears* (World of Mammals). The Child's World, 2005. ISBN 1592965016. 40 p. Grades 5–8.

Lockwood, Sophie. *Sea Otters* (World of Mammals). The Child's World, 2005. ISBN 1592965008. 40 p. Grades 5–8.

Lynch, Wayne. *Falcons.* Illustrated by Sherry Neidigh. Photographs by Wayne Lynch. NorthWord Books for Young Readers, 2005. ISBN 1559719125. 48 p. Grades K–3.

Lynch, Wayne. *Hawks* (Our Wild World). NorthWord Books for Young Readers, 2004. ISBN 1559718854 47 p. Grades 4–8.

Lynch, Wayne. *Owl.* Illustrated by Sherry Neidigh. Photographs by Wayne Lynch. NorthWord Books for Young Readers, 2005. ISBN 1559719141. 48 p. Grades K–3.

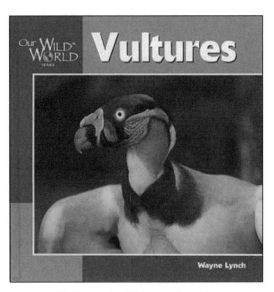

Vultures **by Wayne Lynch.**

Lynch, Wayne. *Vultures.* Illustrated by Sherry Neidigh. Photographs by Wayne Lynch. NorthWord Books for Young Readers, 2005. ISBN 1559719176. 48 p. Grades K–3.

MacQuitty, Miranda. *Sharks and Other Scary Sea Creatures* (DK Secret Worlds). DK, 2002. ISBN 0789485346. 96 p. Grades 3–7.

Marie, Christiane. *Little Giraffes* (Born to Be Wild). Gareth Stevens, 2005. ISBN 083684436x. 24 p. Grades 3–5.

Markle, Sandra. *Killer Whales* (Animal Predators). Lerner, 2004. ISBN 157505728X. 40 p. Grades 2–5.

Markle, Sandra. *Lions* (Animal Predators). Lerner, 2004. ISBN 1575057271. 40 p. Grades 2–5.

Markle, Sandra. *Outside and Inside Big Cats.* Atheneum Books for Young Readers, 2003. ISBN 0689822995. 40 p. Grades 3–8.

Markle, Sandra. *Outside and Inside Giant Squid.* Walker, 2003. ISBN 0802788726. 40 p. Grades 3–8.

Markle, Sandra. *Owls* (Animal Predators). Lerner, 2004. ISBN 1575057298. 40 p. Grades 2–5.

Markle, Sandra. *Polar Bears* (Animal Predators). Lerner, 2004. ISBN 1575057301. 40 p. Grades 2–5.

Markle, Sandra. *Vultures* (Animal Scavengers). Lerner, 2005. ISBN 082253195z. 40 p. Grades 3–5.

Markle, Sandra. *Wolves* (Animal Predators). Lerner, 2004. ISBN 1575057328. 40 p. Grades 2–5.

Martin-James, Kathleen. *Building Beavers* (Pull-Ahead Books). Lerner, 2000. ISBN 0822536285. 32 p. Grades K–3.

Mason, Adrienne. *Owls* (Kids Can Press Wildlife Series). Kids Can Press, 2004. ISBN 1553376234. 32 p. Grades 4–8.

McDaniel, Melissa. *Monkeys* (Animals Animals). Benchmark Books, 2004. ISBN 0761416151. 46 p. Grades 2–5.

McKerley, Jennifer. *Man o'War: Best Racehorse Ever.* Illustrated by Terry Widener. Random House Children's Books, 2005. ISBN 0375931643. 48 p. Grade 1–3.

McNicholas, June. *Ferrets* (Keeping Unusual Pets). Heinemann Library, 2003. ISBN 1403402817. 48 p. Grades 4–8.

McNicholas, June. *Rats* (Keeping Unusual Pets). Heinemann Library, 2003. ISBN 1403402833. 48 p. Grades 4–8.

Montarde, Helen. *Little Wolves* (Born to Be Wild). Gareth Stevens, 2005. ISBN 0836844408. 24 p. Grades 3–5.

Murray, Julie. *American Curl Cats* (Buddy Books: Animal Kingdom). ABDO , 2005. ISBN 1591973015. 24 p. Grades K–3.

Murray, Julie. *Blue Whales* (Buddy Books: Animal Kingdom). ABDO , 2005. ISBN 1591973031. 24 p. Grades K–3.

Murray, Julie. *Bottle-Nosed Dolphins* (Buddy Books: Animal Kingdom). ABDO , 2005. ISBN 159197304x. 24 p. Grades K–3.

Murray, Julie. *Clydesdale Horses* (Buddy Books: Animal Kingdom). ABDO , 2005. ISBN 1591973066. 24 p. Grades K–3.

Murray, Julie. *Cows* (Buddy Books: Animal Kingdom). ABDO, 2005. ISBN 1591973104. 24 p. Grades K–3.

Murray, Julie. *Elephants* (Buddy Books: Animal Kingdom). ABDO, 2005. ISBN 1591973147. 24 p. Grades K–3.

Murray, Julie. *Hammerhead Sharks* (Buddy Books: Animal Kingdom). ABDO, 2005. ISBN 1591973198. 24 p. Grades K–3.

Murray, Julie. *Jack Russell Terriers* (Buddy Books: Animal Kingdom). ABDO, 2005. ISBN 159197321x. 24 p. Grades K–3.

Murray, Julie. *Pandas* (Buddy Books: Animal Kingdom). ABDO, 2005. ISBN 1591973295. 24 p. Grades K–3.

Murray, Julie. *Sheep* (Buddy Books: Animal Kingdom). ABDO, 2005. ISBN 159197335x. 24 p. Grades K–3.

Murray, Julie. *Tiger Sharks* (Buddy Books: Animal Kingdom). ABDO, 2005. ISBN 1591973368. 24 p. Grades K–3.

Murray, Julie. *Vampire Bats* (Buddy Books: Animal Kingdom). ABDO, 2005. ISBN 1591973139. 24 p. Grades K–3.

Murray, Peter. *Tigers* (World of Mammals). The Child's World, 2005. ISBN 1592964982. 40 p. Grades 5–8.

Nelson, Kristin L. *Spraying Skunks* (Pull Ahead Books). Lerner, 2003. ISBN 0822546701. 32 p. Grades K–3.

Nelson, Robin. *Pet Fish* (First Step Nonfiction: Classroom Pets). Lerner, 2002. 082251267x. 24 p. Grades K–2.

Nelson, Robin. *Pet Guinea Pig* (First Step Nonfiction: Classroom Pets). Lerner, 2002. ISBN 0822512688. 24 p. Grades K–2.

Nelson, Robin. *Pet Hamster* (First Step Nonfiction: Classroom Pets). Lerner, 2002. ISBN 0822512696. 24 p. Grades K–2.

Nelson, Robin. *Pet Hermit Crab* (First Step Nonfiction: Classroom Pets). Lerner, 2002. ISBN 082251270x. 24 p. Grades K–2.

Nye, Bill. *Bill Nye the Science Guy's Big Blue Ocean*. Illustrated by John Dykes. Hyperion Books for Children, 1999. ISBN 0786842210. 48 p. Grades 3–5.

Ogle, Belinda. *Cockatiels* (Keeping Unusual Pets). Heinemann Library, 2004. ISBN 1403408246. 48 p. Grades 4–8.

Orme, David. *Orangutan* (Animals Under Threat). Heinemann Library, 2005. ISBN 1403455864. 48 p. Grades 4–6.

Parker Barbara. *Cheetahs* (Early Bird Nature Books). Lerner, 2004. ISBN 0822530538. 48 p. Grades 1–4.

Parker, Barbara Keevil. *Giraffes* (Early Bird Nature Books). Lerner, 2005. ISBN 0822524198. 48 p. Grades K–3.

Parker, Steve. *Seal* (Natural World). Raintree, 2003. ISBN 0739860569. 48 p. Grades 3–6.

Patent, Dorothy Hinshaw. *White-Tailed Deer* (Early Bird Nature Books). Lerner, 2004. ISBN 082253052x. 48 p. Grades 1–4.

Penny, Malcolm. *Hidden Hibernators* (Amazing Nature). Heinemann Library, 2004. ISBN 1403447047. 32 p. Grades 2–5.

Penny, Malcolm. *Kangaroo* (Natural World). Raintree, 2003. ISBN 0739860569. 48 p. Grades 3–6.

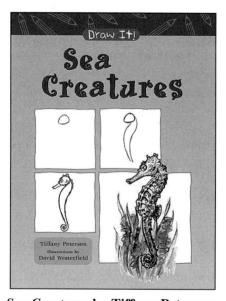

***Sea Creatures* by Tiffany Peterson.**

Peterson, Tiffany. *Sea Creatures* (Draw It!). Illustrated by David Westerfield. Heinemann Library, 2003. ISBN 1403402124. 32 p. Grades 3–6.

Piehl, Janet. *Chattering Chipmunks* (Pull Ahead Books). Lerner, 2005. ISBN 0822524201. 32 p. Grades K–3.

Pringle, Laurence. *Whales! Strange and Wonderful.* Illustrated by Meryl Henderson. Boyds Mills Press, 2003. ISBN 1563974398. 32 p. Grades K–3.

Pyers, Greg. *Snails Up Close* (Minibeasts Up Close). Raintree, 2005. ISBN 1410915328. 32 p. Grades K–3.

Caribou **by Susan E. Quinlan.**

Quinlan, Susan E. *Caribou* (Carolrhoda Nature Watch). Carolrhoda Books, 2004. ISBN 1575055791. 48 p. Grades 4–6.

Quinlan, Susan. *The Case of the Monkeys That Fell from the Trees and Other Mysteries in Tropical Nature.* Boyds Mills Press, 2003. ISBN 1563979020. 171 p. Grades 4–8.

Redmond, Shirley Ray. *Tentacles! Tales of the Giant Squid* (Step into Reading). Random House Children's Books, 2003. ISBN 0375913076. 48 p. Grades K–3.

Richardson, Adele. *Manatees: Peaceful Plant-Eaters* (The Wild World of Animals). Bridgestone Books, 2002. ISBN 0736813950. 24 p. Grades 1–4.

Richardson, Adele. *Owls: Flat-Faced Flyers* (The Wild World of Animals). Bridgestone Books, 2002. ISBN 0736813969. 24 p. Grades 1–4.

Riley, Joelle. *Pouncing Bobcats* (Pull Ahead Books). Lerner, 2002. ISBN 0822506866. 32 p. Grades K–3.

Rockwell, Anne. *My Pet Hamster* (Let's-Read-and-Find-Out Science). Illustrated by Bernice Lum. HarperCollins, 2002. ISBN 0060285648. 40 p. Grades K–2.

Rounds, Glen. *Beaver.* Holiday House, 1999. ISBN 082341440X. Unpaged. Grades 1–3.

Ruth, Maria Mudd. *Hawks and Falcons* (Animals Animals). Benchmark Books, 2004. ISBN 0761416161. 48 p. Grades 2–5.

Ruth, Maria Mudd. *Owls* (Animals Animals). Benchmark Books, 2004. ISBN 0761417524. 46 p. Grades 2–5.

Schaefer, Lola. *Armadillos* (My Big Backyard). Heinemann Library, 2004. ISBN 1403450447. 24 p. Grades K–3.

Schaefer, Lola. *Deer* (My Big Backyard). Heinemann Library, 2004. ISBN 1403450455. 24 p. Grades K–3.

Schaefer, Lola. *Javelinas* (My Big Backyard). Heinemann Library, 2004. ISBN 1403450463. 24 p. Grades K–3.

Schaefer, Lola. *Squirrels* (My Big Backyard). Heinemann Library, 2004. ISBN 1403450498. 24 p. Grades K–3.

Schafer, Susan. *Horses* (Perfect Pets). Benchmark, 2002. ISBN 0761413952. 32 p. Grades 2–5.

Schlaepfer, Gloria G. *Elephants* (AnimalWays). Benchmark, 2002. ISBN 0761413901 104 p. Grades 4–8.

Setford, Steve. *Predator: Animals with the Skill to Kill* (DK Secret Worlds). DK, 2003. ISBN 0789497050. 96 p. Grades 4–8.

Simon, Seymour. *Gorillas*. HarperCollins, 1999. ISBN 0060274735. Unpaged. Grades 3–5.

Simon, Seymour. *Killer Whales* (See More Reader). North-South/Sea Star, 2002. ISBN 1587171414. 32 p. Grades K–3.

Simon, Seymour. *Wild Bears* (See More Reader). North-South/Sea Star, 2002. ISBN 1587171449. 32 p. Grades K–3.

Sims, Neil. *Penguins* (Science Links). Chelsea House, 2003. ISBN 0791074285. 32 p. Grades 3–6.

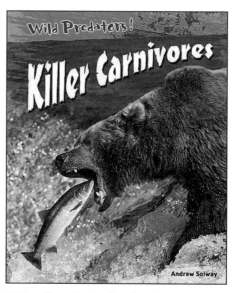

Killer Carnivores **by Andrew Solway.**

Solway, Andrew. *Killer Carnivores* (Wild Predators!). Heinemann Library, 2005. ISBN 1403465673. 48 p. Grades 4–6.

Solway, Andrew. *Killer Cats* (Wild Predators!). Heinemann Library, 2005. ISBN 1403465657. 48 p. Grades 4–6.

Solway, Andrew. *Sea Hunters: Dolphins, Whales, and Seals* (Wild Predators!). Heinemann Library, 2005. ISBN 140346569x. 48 p. Grades 4–6.

Solway, Andrew. *What's Living in Your Backyard?* (Hidden Life). Heinemann Library, 2004. ISBN 1403448434. 32 p. Grades 4–8.

Solway, Andrew. *What's Living in Your Classroom?* (Hidden Life). Heinemann Library, 2004. ISBN 1403448469. 32 p. Grades 4–8.

Solway, Andrew. *What's Living in Your Kitchen?* (Hidden Life). Heinemann Library, 2004. ISBN 1403448442. 32 p. Grades 4–8.

Souza, D. M. *Skunks Do More than Stink!* Millbrook Press, 2002. ISBN 0761325034. 32 p. Grades K–3.

Spilsbury, Richard. *Bengal Tiger* (Animals under Threat). Heinemann Library, 2004. ISBN 1403448582. 48 p. Grades 4–8.

Spilsbury, Richard. *Great White Shark* (Animals under Threat). Heinemann Library, 2004. ISBN 1403448604. 48 p. Grades 4–8.

Stefoff, Rebecca. *Dogs* (AnimalWays). Benchmark, 2002. ISBN 0761413936. 112 p. Grades 4–8.

Stefoff, Rebecca. *Tigers* (AnimalWays). Benchmark, 2002. ISBN 076141391x. 104 p. Grades 4–8.

Stein, Sara. *Great Pets! An Extraordinary Guide to More than 60 Usual and Unusual Family Pets.* Photographs by Edward Justice. Storey Kids, 2003. ISBN 158017504x. 358 p. Grades 4–6.

Stewart, Melissa. *Small Birds* (Perfect Pets). Benchmark, 2002. ISBN 0761413979. 32 p. Grades 2–5.

Stewart, Melissa. *Sloths* (Carolrhoda Nature Watch). Carolrhoda Books, 2004. ISBN 1575055775. 48 p. Grades 4–6.

Stone, Lynn M. *Bald Eagles* (Early Bird Nature Books). Lerner, 2003. ISBN 0822530341. 48 p. Grades 1–4.

***Gray Wolves* by Lynn M. Stone.**

Stone, Lynn M. *Gray Wolves* (Early Bird Nature Books). Lerner, 2003. ISBN 08225303503. 48 p. Grades 1–4.

Stone, Lynn M. *Tigers* (Carolrhoda Nature Watch). Carolrhoda Books, 2004. ISBN 1575055783. 48 p. Grades 4–6.

Strong, Mike. *Shark! The Truth Behind the Terror* (High Five Reading). Capstone Press, 2003. ISBN 0736895477. 48 p. Grades 3–9.

Sullivan, Jody. *Beavers: Big-Toothed Builders* (The Wild World of Animals). Bridgestone Books, 2002. ISBN 0736813926. 24 p. Grades 1–4.

Swanson, Diane. *Coyotes* (Welcome to the World of Animals). Gareth Stevens, 2002. ISBN 0836833139. 32 p. Grades 1–5.

Swanson, Diane. *Octopuses* (Welcome to the World of Animals). Gareth Stevens, 2002. ISBN 0836833147. 32 p. Grades 1–5.

Swanson, Diane. *Porcupines* (Welcome to the World of Animals). Gareth Stevens, 2002. ISBN 0836833155. 32 p. Grades 1–5.

Swanson, Diane. *Skunks* (Welcome to the World of Animals). Gareth Stevens, 2002. ISBN 0836833171. 32 p. Grades 1–5.

Swinburne, Stephen R. *Black Bear: North America's Bear.* Boyds Mills Press, 2003. ISBN 159078023x. 32 p. Grades K–3.

Taylor, Leighton. *Octopuses* (Early Bird Nature Books). Photographs by Norbert Wu. Lerner, 2002. ISBN 082250068X. 48 p. Grades K–3.

Thomson, Sarah. *Amazing Gorillas!* (I Can Read Book). HarperCollins, 2005. ISBN 0060544597. 32 p. Grades K–3.

Thomson, Sarah L. *Tigers* (I Can Read). HarperCollins, 2004. ISBN 0060544503. 32 p. Grades K–3.

Townsend, John. *Incredible Birds* (Incredible Creatures). Raintree, 2004. ISBN 1410905276. 56 p. Grades 4–8.

Townsend, John. *Incredible Fish* (Incredible Creatures). Raintree, 2004. ISBN 1410905292. 56 p. Grades 4–8.

Townsend, John. *Incredible Mammals* (Incredible Creatures). Raintree, 2004. ISBN 1410905314. 56 p. Grades 4–8.

Townsend, John. *Incredible Mollusks* (Incredible Creatures). Raintree, 2004. ISBN 1410905284. 56 p. Grades 4–8.

Townsend, John. *Incredible Reptiles* (Incredible Creatures). Raintree, 2004. ISBN 1410905322. 56 p, Grades 4–8.

Asian Elephant **by Matt Turner.**

Turner, Matt. *Asian Elephant* (Animals under Threat). Heinemann Library, 2005. ISBN 1403455813. 48 p. Grades 4–6.

***Wild Horses* by Julia Vogel.**

Vogel, Julia. *Wild Horses* (Our Wild World). NorthWord Books for Young Readers, 2004. ISBN 1559718811. 47 p. Grades 4–8.

***Seahorses* by Sally M. Walker.**

Walker, Sally M. *Seahorses* (Early Bird Nature Books). Lerner, 2003. ISBN 0822530511. 48 p. Grades 1–4.

Warhol, Tom, and Chris Reiter. *Eagles* (AnimalWays). Benchmark Books, 2003. ISBN 0761415785. 112 p. Grades 4–8.

Waters, Jo. *The Wild Side of Pet Birds* (Wild Side of Pets). Raintree, 2005. ISBN 1410914054. 32 p. Grades K–3.

Waters, Jo. *The Wild Side of Pet Hamsters* (Wild Side of Pets). Raintree, 2005. ISBN 1410914089. 32 p. Grades K–3.

Waters, Jo. *The Wild Side of Pet Mice and Rats* (Wild Side of Pets). Raintree, 2005. ISBN 1410914062. 32 p. Grades K–3.

Waters, Jo. *The Wild Side of Pet Rabbits* (Wild Side of Pets). Raintree, 2005. ISBN 1410914097. 32 p. Grades K–3.

Waxman, Laura Hamilton. *Diving Dolphins* (Pull Ahead Books). Lerner, 2002. ISBN 082250684x. 32 p. Grades K–3.

Webb, Sophie. *My Season with Penguins: An Antarctic Journal.* Houghton Mifflin, 2000. ISBN 0395922917. 48 p. Grades 4–up

Vampire Bats **by Anne Welsbacher.**

Welsbacher, Anne. *Vampire Bats* (Predators in the Wild). Capstone High-Interest Books, 2001. ISBN 073680787X. 48 p. Grades 3–9.

Welsbacher, Anne. *Wolves* (Predators in the Wild). Capstone High-Interest Books, 2001. ISBN 0736807888. 48 p. Grades 3–9.

Winner, Cherie. *Everything Dolphin: What Kids Really Want to Know about Dolphins* (Kids' FAQ). NorthWord Books for Young Readers, 2004. ISBN 155971042X. 64 p. Grades 4–8.

Woodward, John. *Clever Camouflage* (Amazing Nature). Heinemann Library, 2004. ISBN 1403447039. 32 p. Grades 2–5.

Woodward, John. *Pesky Parasites* (Amazing Nature). Heinemann Library, 2004. ISBN 1403447071. 32 p. Grades 2–5.

Zemlicka, Shannon. *Prickly Porcupines* (Pull Ahead Books). Lerner, 2002. ISBN 0822506858. 32 p. Grades K–3.

Chapter 7

Creepy-Crawly Creatures: Bugs, Reptiles, and Amphibians

To some they are scary, but to others they are the most fascinating things on Earth. Cockroaches, killer bees, worms, snakes, komodo dragons, alligators, spiders, and other unpopular creatures tend to appeal to young male readers, who pore over detailed photos and memorize facts about them. For boys who like creepy-crawly creatures, these books are guaranteed to satisfy.

NEW AND NOTABLE

Cowley, Joy. *Chameleon, Chameleon*. Illustrated with photographs by Nic Bishop. Scholastic, 2005. ISBN 0439666538. Unpaged. Grades K–3.
    This spectacular companion to *The Red-Eyed Tree Frog* by the same duo follows a few hours in the life of a panther chameleon from the island of Madagascar. As it awakes, hungry, it searches for food and encounters danger before the happy ending. The photographs are stunning. Show the one of the chameleon with its tongue fully extended.

Outside and Inside Killer Bees
by Sandra Markle.

Markle, Sandra. *Outside and Inside Killer Bees.* Walker, 2004. ISBN 0802789064. 40 p. Grades 3–7.

It makes most people feel a little nervous when they just hear the words "killer bees." Every once in a while we hear that those bees may be heading north into the United States, but so far we have not seen many of them. Scientists believe it may be too cold for them. And that is a good thing for us.

Killer bees are hybrid bees. It's not easy to tell them apart from regular honeybees by looking at them, but their behavior is very different. Most bees that we call honeybees are actually European honeybees. They were brought into all parts of the world, including Brazil. There they did not produce as much honey as expected, and in 1956, beekeepers imported some African bees to see if production could be increased. It was a big mistake.

These new Africanized bees turned out to be almost super-bees. Africanized bees have stung and killed almost eight hundred people. They also kill a lot of animals. Even wild animals are afraid of them. Their sting is no more deadly than that of Europeanized bees, but they attack in large groups, and they attack in just three seconds.

This topic is both scary and interesting, and the pictures and information about the lives of these frightening bees is just great.

This book has incredible photographs of these bees. Take a look at the photo of a bee that has just stung someone on page 5. The bee is dying. Stinging kills these bees. Then take a look at the photograph of the stinger on page 12, and you will see the reason why that happens.

Pfeffer, Wendy. *Wiggling Worms at Work* (Let's-Read-and-Find-Out Science). Illustrated by Steve Jenkins. HarperCollins, 2004. ISBN 0060284498. 33 p. Grades K–3.

Some people think worms are gross and don't want to touch them. Other people think they are incredibly interesting. A lot of people look at them and see bait for catching fish. But worms are some of the most helpful creatures on Earth.

Worms eat almost anything, and they break up earth, making tunnels and turning hard earth into something crumbly. The earth and food they eat pass through their bodies, making something called worm castings, which make great fertilizer.

This book is loaded with great information about worms.

Did you know that:

- Worms have no backbones. They can even tie themselves up in knots.

- Worms breathe through their skins. If they get too hot in the sun, they dry up and may die.

And much, much more!

The Bumblebee Queen **by April Pulley Sayre.**

Sayre, April Pulley. *The Bumblebee Queen.* Illustrated by Patricia J. Wynne. Charlesbridge, 2005. ISBN 1570913625. Unpaged. Grades K–3.

The fact is that most people are not very happy to see a bumblebee. They're afraid they will get stung, and that hurts.

But bumblebees are interesting, especially the queens.

Bumblebee queens sleep underneath the ground, all alone, all winter long. All the other bees die above ground before winter comes. The queens sometimes go as long as six months without eating. When they dig out, they look for a good place to build a nest, and then they get ready to lay their eggs, which only take five days to hatch. The queen bee works like crazy, taking care of them. Within just a few weeks, she has helpers. The babies are born.

The life of a bumblebee queen is an extraordinary thing. Read it and find out what happens—and how long she lives.

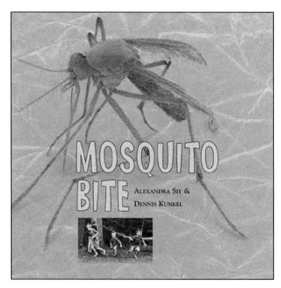

***Mosquito Bite* by Alexandra Siy.**

Siy, Alexandra. *Mosquito Bite.* Illustrated by Dennis Kunkel. Charlesbridge, 2005. ISBN 1570915911. 32 p. Grades 2–5.

A girl and a boy play hide-and-go-seek on a humid summer evening. The boy hides behind an old tractor tire that used to be a swing and is bitten by a mosquito. He doesn't even really notice it.

But the mosquito is fighting for her life and for the lives of her unborn children. And, thanks to microscopic photographs, we see exactly what she looks like and how she and her babies live and develop.

These photographs are color enhanced to make it easier to see the different parts of the insects' bodies, and they are amazing.

Nobody likes mosquitoes much. And no wonder! They have been around since the time of the dinosaurs, and not only do they bite, they also spread diseases because of those bites. The mosquito is the deadliest animal on Earth. One disease they spread, malaria, is responsible for killing about two million people every year.

Take a look at these great photographs and interesting information.

Any of the microscopic photographs, properly called photomicrographs, are great to show your audience.

Thomson, Sarah L. *Amazing Snakes!* (An I Can Read Book). Photographs provided by the Wildlife Conservation Society. HarperCollins, 2006. ISBN 00605446335. 32 p. Grades K–3.

A lot of people don't like snakes, but anyone who does not like them may feel differently after they read this book.

There are more than two thousand kinds of snakes on Earth. Some can climb trees. Some can swim in water. Some can dig underground, and some can even jump off branches. They are truly amazing creatures.

Snakes can swallow things that are bigger than their heads. If people's mouths and bodies were built like snakes, they could swallow a watermelon. Snakes hunt animals like rats, which are good animals to hunt (human beings don't much like rats, and they spread diseases). And other animals hunt them.

Young readers will enjoy the fine pictures and good information in this book. Show the picture of a snake eating some poor creature on pages 14–15.

NOT TO BE MISSED

Arnosky, Jim. *All about Rattlesnakes*. Scholastic, 1997. ISBN 0590467948. 28 p. Grades 1–3. *Gotcha.*
    Arnosky's simple, beautifully illustrated books give us just the facts, always told in an entertaining fashion. One fact about rattlesnakes: we are much more dangerous to them than they are to us.

Arnosky, Jim. *All about Turtles*. Written and illustrated by Jim Arnosky. Scholastic, 2000. ISBN 0590481495. Unpaged. Grades 1–3. *Gotcha Again.*
    Yet another winner for young children by the always interesting Arnosky. Look at the life-size illustration of a snapping turtle.

Berger, Melvin. *Spinning Spiders* (Let's Read and Find Out Science, Level 2). Illustrated by S. D. Schindler. HarperCollins, 2003. ISBN 0060286962. 33 p. Grades 1–3.
    Spiderwebs are all around us when we go outside, but how are they made? How do the spiders do it? In simple text and beautiful pictures, we learn how it happens. This is a lovely entry in one of the most popular nonfiction series of all time.

Cerullo, Mary M. *Sea Turtles: Ocean Nomads*. Photographs by Jeffrey L. Rotman. Dutton Children's Books, 2003. ISBN 0525466495. 40 p. Grades 3–6. *Gotcha Covered.*
    Imagine an animal that is beautiful and graceful in the water but clumsy and awkward on land. Imagine an animal that always returns to the beach where it was born to lay its own eggs. Imagine that many of those beaches are now being developed, with buildings erected on the original nest sites. Sea turtles are an endangered species. Scientists estimate that only one baby out of a thousand makes it to adulthood. Loaded with beautiful color photographs, this will intrigue animal lovers.

Cowley, Joy. *The Red-Eyed Tree Frog*. Illustrated with photographs by Nic Bishop. Scholastic, 1999. ISBN 0590871757. Unpaged. Grades K–2. *Gotcha Again.*
    Nonfiction for young children does not get any better than this story of a hungry red-eyed tree frog searching for his dinner. The spectacular photos by Nic Bishop are enthralling.

Darling, Kathy. *Chameleons: On Location*. Photographs by Tara Darling. Lothrop, Lee & Shepard, 1997. ISBN 0688125379. 40 p. Grades 4–6. *Gotcha.*
    There are 128 species of chameleons, and the information here is as compelling as the topic. Chameleons are not in charge of their color changes, which often give a lot of information about what is happening to the chameleon—is it scared, sleepy, sick, or angry?

Darling, Kathy. *Komodo Dragon: On Location.* Photographs by Tara Darling. Lothrop, Lee & Shepard, 1997. ISBN 0688137776. 40 p. Grades 4–6. *Gotcha.*

Komodo dragons live on the island for which they were named, in Indonesia. These carnivorous animals can reach almost eleven feet in length, and they are pretty scary. Baby dragons come out of their eggs measuring eighteen inches long. Excellent photos highlight the text.

George, Linda. *Vipers* (Snakes). Capstone High-Interest Books, 2002. ISBN 0736809104. 48 p. Grades 4–up. *Gotcha Covered.*

Vipers are those poisonous snakes with long, hollow fangs. Those fans are hinged; they lie flat against the roof of the snake's mouth and only swing forward, locking into place when the snake is ready to bite its victim. The color photos are compelling and include one of a viper biting a rodent.

Heiligman, Deborah. *Honeybees.* Illustrated by Carla Golembe. National Geographic Society, 2002. ISBN 0792266781. 32 pages. Grades K–3. *Gotcha Covered.*

Bright, colorful illustrations accompany a fine introduction to an animal that scares a lot of people and fascinates almost everyone.

Jackson, Donna M. *The Bug Scientists.* Houghton Mifflin, 2002. ISBN 0618108688. 48 p. Grades 3–6. *Gotcha Covered.*

There are a lot more insects than there are human beings on our planet, and this is the story of some of the scientists who study them—and of some of the astonishing things they have learned from their studies. There is even an interview with a man who directs insects in movies such as *Jurassic Park.* Lots of color photograph make this a fine browsing book, too.

Jenkins, Martin. *Chameleons Are Cool.* Illustrated by Sue Shields. Candlewick Press, 1997, 1998. ISBN 0763601446. 30 p. Grades 1–3. *Gotcha Again.*

Although they are very cool, by any standards, chameleons don't make very good pets. One unusual feature they possess is that each of their eyes can look in a different direction.

Kite, L. Patricia. *Blood-Feeding Bugs and Beasts.* Millbrook Press, 1996. ISBN 1562945998. 48 p. Grades 4–6. *Gotcha.*

One picture is worth a thousand words, and these will entice even the most reluctant readers into wanting to find out more. A more satisfying set of "creepy" creatures never existed.

Kite, L. Patricia. *Cockroaches.* Lerner, 2001. ISBN 0822530465. 48 p. Grades 3–5. *Gotcha Again.*

Most people hate them, but cockroaches definitely have staying power. They've been on Earth since before the dinosaurs, and they eat just about everything. They are ugly but interesting, and they have quite a history.

Landau, Elaine. *Your Pet Iguana.* Children's Press, 1997. ISBN 0516203878. 47 p. Grades 1–3. *Gotcha.*

Iguanas are really cool pets, at least to everyone who wants one. But they are not the easiest pets to own. Colorful pictures and good information pair to make an appealing book.

Lasky, Kathryn. *Interrupted Journey: Saving Endangered Sea Turtles.* Photographs by Christopher G. Knight. Candlewick Press, 2001. ISBN 0763606359. Unpaged. Grades 2–5. *Gotcha Again.*

One of the most solitary animals in the world is the sea turtle, and it is also one of the most endangered. It comes back to the beach where it was born to lay its eggs, and, because those beaches are getting more and more built up by human developers, the sea turtle has no place to go and so it dies. This is the story of those turtles and how human beings are trying to fix the problem.

Martin, Patricia A. Fink. *Animals That Walk on Water.* Franklin Watts, 1997. ISBN 0531202976. 64 p. Grades 3–5. *Gotcha.*

Have you ever heard of a "Jesus Christ" lizard? Its real name is the basilisk lizard, but Mexicans gave it the other name because it really can walk on water! Water has a skin on it that enables some creatures to walk on it, and others merely look like they are walking on water. Whether they are or not, it's interesting information for kids.

Montgomery, Sy. *The Snake Scientist.* Photographs by Nic Bishop. Houghton Mifflin, 1999. ISBN 0395871697. 48 p. Grades 4–6. *Gotcha Covered.*

Bob Mason is the snake scientist, and, boy, does he have an interesting job. About fifty miles north of Winnipeg, Canada, he works in the Narcisse Wildlife Management Area. There, thousands of garter snakes live, and they bruminate (which is similar to "hibernate") all winter long. When they wake up in the spring, piles of snakes, more than you could find anywhere else in the world, are ready for action. They are looking for mates—and the way they go about finding a mate is truly astonishing. Wonderful color photographs show us exactly what happens.

Montgomery, Sy. *The Tarantula Scientist.* Photographs by Nic Bishop. Houghton Mifflin, 2004. ISBN 0618147993. 80 p. Grades 4-9. *Gotcha Covered.*

Sam Marshall, who lives in Ohio, is the Tarantula Scientist. He has a lot to learn, because we do not know much about tarantulas—and a lot of the things we think we know are wrong. This is a book loaded with color photographs, particularly about the goliath bird-eater tarantula, which can have a leg spread of almost twelve inches. Sam goes to South America to study them, and captures them to study further in his laboratory in Ohio.

Murawski, Darlyne A. *Bug Faces.* National Geographic, 2000. ISBN 0792275578. Unpaged. Grades 1–4. *Gotcha Again.*

National Geographic, renowned for its beautiful photographs, does not fail us in this book of surprising close-up photos of bugs. The information is equally pleasing.

Patent, Dorothy Hinshaw. *Flashy Fantastic Rainforest Frogs.* Illustrations by Kendahl Jan Jubb. Walker, 1997. ISBN 0802786154. 32 p. Grades 2–4. *Gotcha Again.*

Fans of frogs will be happy campers when you show them this book, generously illustrated with pictures of many kinds of rainforest frogs, including the Poison Dart Frog, which has enough poison in its skin to kill more than one hundred people.

Patent, Dorothy Hinshaw. *Slinky Scaly Slithery Snakes.* Illustrations by Kendahl Jan Jubb. Walker, 2000. ISBN 0802787436. 32 p. Grades 2–4. *Gotcha Again.*

Filled with colorful illustrations, this book gives us a lot of basic information about snakes, including some very gross stuff.

Sayre, April Pulley. *Army Ant Parade.* Illustrated by Rick Chrustowski. Henry Holt, 2002. ISBN 0805063536. Unpaged. Grades K–3.

When these ants go marching, it is best for anyone in their path to get out of the way. They eat just about anything they run into, including small birds, reptiles, amphibians, and mice. This is a simple look at a very interesting subject.

Simon, Seymour. *Crocodiles and Alligators.* HarperCollins, 1999. ISBN 0060274735. Unpaged. Grades 3–6. *Gotcha Again.*

Crocodiles were around at the same time as the dinosaurs were, and we still don't know why they didn't become extinct, too. Excellent photographs show some of the different kinds, including the gharial and the caiman.

Wechsler, Doug. *Bizarre Bugs.* Photographs by Doug Wechsler. Cobblehill Books/Dutton, 1995. ISBN 0525651810. 35 p. Grades 4–6. *Gotcha.*

A lot of people call all insects bugs, but this is not accurate. There may be as many as thirty million species of insects. The great color photographs show many fascinating behaviors insects exhibit—and many unusual insects.

WORTH READING

Nonfiction books with "boy appeal" that have received positive reviews in *Booklist, Horn Book Guide,* and/or *School Library Journal.*

Arnosky, Jim. *All about Frogs.* Scholastic, 2002. ISBN 0590481649. 32 p. Grades K–3.

Barraclough, Sue. *Ants* (Creepy Creatures). Raintree, 2005. ISBN 1410915050. 24 p. Grades K–2.

Barraclough, Sue. *Bees* (Creepy Creatures). Raintree, 2005. ISBN 1410915042. 24 p. Grades K–2.

Barraclough, Sue. *Earthworms* (Creepy Creatures). Raintree, 2005. ISBN 1410915069. 24 p. Grades K–2.

Barraclough, Sue. *Mosquitoes* (Creepy Creatures). Raintree, 2005. ISBN 1410915077. 24 p. Grades K–2.

Behler, Deborah, and John Behler. *Snakes* (AnimalWays). Benchmark, 2002. ISBN 0761412654. 112 p. Grades 4-8.

Birch, Robin. *Ants Up Close* (Minibeasts Up Close). Raintree, 2004. ISBN 1410911373. 32 p. Grades 1–4.

Birch, Robin. *Bees Up Close* (Minibeasts Up Close). Raintree, 2004. ISBN 1410911381. 32 p. Grades 1–4.

Birch, Robin. *Cockroaches Up Close* (Minibeasts Up Close). Raintree, 2004. ISBN 141091139x. 32 p. Grades 1–4.

Birch, Robin. *Head Lice Up Close* (Minibeasts Up Close). Raintree, 2004. ISBN 1410911403. 32 p. Grades 1–4.

Birch, Robin. *Mosquitoes Up Close* (Minibeasts Up Close). Raintree, 2004. ISBN 1410911411. 32 p. Grades 1–4.

Birch, Robin. *Spiders Up Close* (Minibeasts Up Close). Raintree, 2004. ISBN 1410911497. 32 p. Grades 1–4.

Creepy Crawlies **by Jim Bruce.**

Bruce, Jim. *Creepy Crawlies* (Question Time). Kingfisher, 2002. ISBN 0753453428. 32 p. Grades K–3.

Bugs (Eye Wonder). DK, 2002. ISBN 0789485524. 48 p. Grades K–3.

Burnie, David. *Bug Hunter.* DK/Smithsonian, 2005. ISBN 0756610303. 72 p. Grades 4–6.

Dixon, Norman. *Lowdown on Earthworms.* Fitzhenry & Whiteside, 2005. ISBN 1550411148. 32 p. Grades 2–4.

Editors of Time for Kids. *Ants!* (Time for Kids Science Scoops). HarperCollins, 2005. ISBN 0060576413. 32 p. Grades 1–3.

Editors of Time for Kids. *Bees!* (Time for Kids—Science Scoops). HarperCollins, 2005. ISBN 0060576431. 32 p. Grades 1–3.

Editors of Time for Kids. *Snakes!* (Time for Kids—Science Scoops). HarperCollins, 2005. ISBN 0060576375. 32 p. Grades 1–3.

Editors of Time for Kids. *Spiders!* (Time for Kids—Science Scoops). HarperCollins, 2005. ISBN 0060576359. 32 p. Grades 1–3.

Ethan, Eric. *Black Widow Spiders* (Dangerous Spiders). Gareth Stevens, 2004. ISBN 0836837657. 24 p. Grades K–3.

Ethan, Eric. *Brown Recluse Spiders* (Dangerous Spiders). Gareth Stevens, 2004. ISBN 0836837665. 24 p. Grades K–3.

Ethan, Eric. *Funnel-Web Spiders* (Dangerous Spiders). Gareth Stevens, 2004. ISBN 0836837673. 24 p. Grades K–3.

Ethan, Eric. *Hobo Spiders* (Dangerous Spiders). Gareth Stevens, 2004. ISBN 0836837681. 24 p. Grades K–3.

Ethan, Eric. *Tarantulas* (Dangerous Spiders). Gareth Stevens, 2004. ISBN 083683769X. 24 p. Grades K–3.

***Yellow Sac Spiders* by Eric Ethan.**

Ethan, Eric. *Yellow Sac Spiders* (Dangerous Spiders). Gareth Stevens, 2004. ISBN 0836837703. 24 p. Grades K–3.

Lizards: Weird and Wonderful
by Margery Facklam.

Facklam, Margery. *Lizards: Weird and Wonderful.* Illustrated by Alan Male. Little, Brown, 2003. ISBN 0316173460. 32 p. Grades 2–4.

Florian, Douglas. *Lizards, Frogs, and Polliwogs.* Harcourt, 2001. ISBN 015202591x. 48 p. Grades 2–5.

Gilpin, Daniel. *Centipedes, Millipedes, Scorpions & Spiders* (Animal Kingdom Classification). Compass Point Books, 2005. ISBN 0756512549. 48 p. Grades 4–6.

Greenberg, Dan. *Lizards* (AnimalWays). Benchmark, 2003. ISBN 0761415807. 112 p. Grades 4-8.

Greenberg, Dan. *Spiders* (Animals Animals). Benchmark, 2002. ISBN 0761412638. 48 p. Grades 2–5.

Gunzi, Christiane. *The Best Book of Snakes* (Best Book of). Kingfisher, 2003. ISBN 0753455781. 32 p. Grades 3–6.

Gutman, Bill. *Becoming Best Friends with Your Iguana, Snake, or Turtle* (Pet Friends). Millbrook Press, 2001. ISBN 0761318623. 64 p. Grades 3–6.

Heathcote, Peter. *Lizards* (Keeping Unusual Pets). Heinemann Library, 2004. ISBN 1403408270. 48 p. Grades 4–8.

Heathcote, Peter. *Salamanders* (Keeping Unusual Pets). Heinemann Library, 2004. ISBN 1403408262. 48 p. Grades 4–8.

Hernandez-Divers, Sonia. *Geckos* (Keeping Unusual Pets). Heinemann Library, 2003. ISBN 1403402825. 48 p. Grades 4–8.

Hernandez-Divers, Sonia. *Snakes* (Keeping Unusual Pets). Heinemann Library, 2003. ISBN 1403402841. 48 p. Grades 4–8.

Holub, Joan. *Why Do Snakes Hiss? And Other Questions about Snakes, Lizards, and Turtles* (Dial Easy-to-Read). Dial Books for Young Readers, 2004. ISBN 0803730004. 48 p. Grades K–3.

Iorio, Nicole. *Spiders!* (Time for Kids Science Scoops). HarperCollins, 2005. ISBN 0060576359. 48 p. Grades K–3.

Landau, Elaine. *Creepy Spiders* (Fearsome, Scary, and Creepy Animals). Enslow, 2003. ISBN 0766020592. 48 p. Grades 3–5.

Landau, Elaine. *Fearsome Alligators* (Fearsome, Scary, and Creepy Animals). Enslow, 2003. ISBN 0766020606. 48 p. Grades 3–5.

Landau, Elaine. *Sinister Snakes* (Fearsome, Scary, and Creepy Animals). Enslow, 2003. ISBN 0766020576. 48 p. Grades 3–5.

Llewellyn, Claire. *Crocodile* (Starting Life). NorthWord Books for Young Readers, 2004. ISBN 1559719001. 24 p. Grades 1–3.

Markle, Sandra. *Crocodiles* (Animal Predators). Lerner, 2004. ISBN 1575057263. 40 p. Grades 2–5.

Markle, Sandra. *Snakes: Biggest! Littlest!* Boyds Mills Press, 2005. ISBN 1590781899. 32 p. Grades K–3.

Snakes **by Adrienne Mason.**

Mason, Adrienne. *Snakes* (Kids Can Press Wildlife Series). Illustrated by Nancy Gray Ogle. Kids Can Press, 2005. ISBN 1553376277. 32 p. Grades K–3.

McAuliffe, Emily. *Tarantulas* (Dangerous Animals). Capstone High-Interest Books, 1998. ISBN 1560656212. 48 p. Grades 3–9.

Murray, Julie. *Copperheads* (Buddy Books: Animal Kingdom). ABDO, 2005. ISBN 1591973090. 32 p. Grades K–3.

Murray, Julie. *Crocodiles* (Buddy Books: Animal Kingdom). ABDO, 2005. ISBN 1591973112. 24 p. Grades K–3.

Murray, Julie. *Frogs* (Buddy Books: Animal Kingdom). ABDO, 2005. ISBN 1591973155. 24 p. Grades K–3.

Murray, Julie. *Grasshoppers* (Buddy Books: Animal Kingdom). ABDO, 2005. ISBN 1591973171. 24 p. Grades K–3.

Murray, Julie. *Jumping Spiders* (Buddy Books: Animal Kingdom). ABDO, 2005. ISBN 1591973236. 24 p. Grades K–3.

Murray, Julie. *Lizards* (Buddy Books: Animal Kingdom). ABDO, 2005. ISBN 1591973252. 24 p. Grades K–3.

Murray, Julie. *Rattlesnakes* (Buddy Books: Animal Kingdom). ABDO, 2005. ISBN 1591973333. 24 p. Grades K–3.

Murray, Julie. *Salamanders* (Buddy Books: Animal Kingdom). ABDO, 2005. ISBN 1591973341. 24 p. Grades K–3.

Murray, Julie. *Wolf Spiders* (Buddy Books: Animal Kingdom). ABDO, 2005. ISBN 1591973392. 24 p. Grades K–3.

Myers, Jack. *On the Trail of the Komodo Dragon and Other Explorations of Science in Action.* Illustrated by John Rice. Boyds Mills Press, 1999. ISBN 1563977613. 63 p. Grades 4–6.

Nelson, Robin. *Pet Frog* (First Step Nonfiction: Classroom Pets). Lerner, 2002. ISBN 0822512718. 24 p. Grades K–2.

Platt, Richard. *Spiders' Secrets* (DK Readers). DK, 2002. ISBN 0789483726. 49 p. Grades K–3.

Pringle, Laurence. *Snakes! Strange and Wonderful.* Boyds Mills Press, 2004. ISBN 1590780035. 32 p. Grades K–3.

Pyers, Greg. *Butterflies Up Close* (Minibeasts Up Close). Raintree, 2005. ISBN 141091528x. 32 p. Grades K–3.

Pyers, Greg. *Grasshoppers Up Close* (Minibeasts Up Close). Raintree, 2005. ISBN 1410915298. 32 p. Grades K–3.

Pyers, Greg. *Ladybugs Up Close* (Minibeasts Up Close). Raintree, 2005. ISBN 410915301. 32 p. Grades K–3.

Pyers, Greg. *Pill Bugs Up Close* (Minibeasts Up Close). Raintree, 2005. ISBN 141091531x. 32 p. Grades K–3.

Pyers, Greg. *Wasps Up Close* (Minibeasts Up Close). Raintree, 2005. ISBN 1410915336. 32 p. Grades K–3.

Reinhart, Matthew. *Insect-lo-Pedia: Young Naturalist's Handbook.* Hyperion Books for Children, 2003. ISBN 0786805595. 48 p. Grades K–3.

Rockwell, Anne. *Little Shark.* Illustrated by Megan Halsey. Walker Books for Young Readers, 2005. ISBN 0802789552. 32 p. Grades K–3.

Schaefer, Lola. *Lizards* (My Big Backyard). Heinemann Library, 2004. ISBN 1403450471. 24 p. Grades K–3.

Schafer, Susan. *Snakes* (Perfect Pets). Benchmark, 2002. ISBN 0761413960. 32 p. Grades 2–5.

Silverstein, Alvin, Virginia Silverstein, and Laura Silverstein. *Creepy Crawlies* (What a Pet!). Twenty-First Century, 2003. ISBN 0761325115. 48 p. Grades 4–8.

Simon, Seymour. *Big Bugs.* Chronicle/Sea Star, 2005. ISBN 1587172534. 32 p. Grades K–3.

Simon, Seymour. *Spiders.* HarperCollins, 2003. ISBN 0060283912. 32 p. Grades K–3.

Solway, Andrew. *Deadly Reptiles* (Wild Predators!). Heinemann Library, 2005. ISBN 1403465681. 48 p. Grades 4–6.

Solway, Andrew. *Deadly Snakes* (Wild Predators). Heinemann Library, 2005. ISBN 1403457662. 48 p. Grades 4–8.

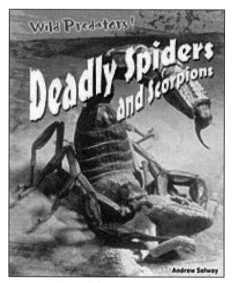

**Deadly Spiders and Scorpions
by Andrew Solway.**

Solway, Andrew. *Deadly Spiders and Scorpions* (Wild Predators). Heinemann Library, 2005. ISBN 1403457670. 48 p. Grades 4–8.

Spilsbury, Richard. *Alligator* (Animals Under Threat). Heinemann Library, 2004. ISBN 1403448574. 48 p. Grades 4–8.

Stewart, Melissa. *Maggots, Grubs, and More: The Secret Lives of Young Insects.* Millbrook Press, 2003. ISBN 0761326588. 64 p. Grades 4–6.

Swanson, Diane. *Snakes* (Welcome to the World of Animals). Gareth Stevens, 2002. ISBN 083683318x. 32 p. Grades 1–5.

Swinburne, Stephen R. *Turtle Tide: The Ways of Sea Turtles.* Illustrated by Bruce Hiscock. Boyds Mills Press, 2005. ISBN 1590780817. 32 p. Grades K–3.

Townsend, John. *Incredible Amphibians* (Incredible Creatures). Raintree, 2004. ISBN 141090525X. 56 p, Grades 4-8.

Townsend, John. *Incredible Arachnids* (Incredible Creatures). Raintree, 2004. ISBN 1410905268. 56 p, Grades 4–8.

Townsend, John. *Incredible Insects* (Incredible Creatures). Raintree, 2004. ISBN 1410905306. 56 p. Grades 4–8.

Walker, Sally M. *Crocodiles* (Carolrhoda Nature Watch). Carolrhoda Books, 2003. ISBN 1575053454. 48 p. Grades 4–6.

Waters, Jo. *The Wild Side of Pet Snakes* (Wild Side of Pets). Raintree, 2005. ISBN 1410914070. 32 p. Grades K–3.

Welsbacher, Anne. *Anacondas* (Predators in the Wild) Capstone High-Interest Books, 2001. ISBN 0736807853. 48 p. Grades 3–9.

Welsbacher, Anne. *Komodo Dragons* (Predators in the Wild). Capstone High-Interest Books, 2002. ISBN 0736810668. 48 p. Grades 3–9.

Everything Bug: What Kids Really Want to Know about Insects and Spiders by Cherie Winner.

Winner, Cherie. *Everything Bug: What Kids Really Want to Know about Insects and Spiders* (Kids' FAQ). NorthWord Books for Young Readers, 2004. ISBN 1559718909. 64 p. Grades 4–8.

Winner, Cherie. *Everything Reptile: What Kids Really Want to Know about Reptiles* (Kids' FAQ). NorthWord Books for Young Readers, 2004. ISBN 1559711469. 64 p. Grades 4–8.

Chapter _____ 8

Action and Innovation: Sports, the Military, Machines, Buildings, and Inventions

Boys want to read about the things they love, and for many boys that means topics such as motorcycles, skateboarding, sports, machines, inventions, and skyscrapers. They are interested in how things work and how they can do things themselves, and they like to read for information. These books cover a wide variety of topics of interest to a great many boys.

NEW AND NOTABLE

Adler, David A. *Joe Louis: America's Fighter.* Illustrated by Terry Widener. Gulliver Books/Harcourt, 2005. ISBN 0152164804. Unpaged. Grades 2–5.

Joseph Louis Barrow was the grandson of slaves, born in 1914, and the seventh of eight kids in a terribly poor family in Alabama. His father worked so hard and worried so much that when Joe was only two years old, his dad went into an insane asylum and never left.

Joe's mother remarried and moved to Detroit, and there Joe worked hard and found something he loved to do—box. He practiced and practiced, and when he signed up for his first fight, he wrote *Joe Louis* so big that there was no room for his last name—and thus he became Joe Louis the fighter.

And what a fighter he was! By the time he was twenty-one years old, he had his first professional fight. Four years later, he had a major fight, with a white man. And he won. Many white Americans hated Joe because he was African American.

By 1937, Joe was the heavyweight champion of the world, but it wasn't always easy.

This is his story and tells us how he got there and what happened along the way.

Barretta, Gene. *Now & Ben: The Modern Inventions of Ben Franklin.* Henry Holt, 2006. ISBN 0805079173. Unpaged. Grades K–3.

Almost everyone has heard of Benjamin Franklin. He was a very important man in American history for all sorts of reasons.

Some of those reasons were his inventions. Ben loved to invent things, and he liked inventions that helped people. Some of his inventions are still around today, sometimes changed a little, but the basic idea is still there.

Think of illustrations in newspapers. Ben was the first person to print a political cartoon in a newspaper in America.

He also invented bifocals. Ben got tired of switching two pairs of glasses back and forth, depending on whether he wanted to see something up close or something far away, so he invented a pair of glasses in which he could see both near and far.

The lightning rod was his idea, too. Ben wanted to keep lightning from striking and burning down buildings. He invented a metal rod that stood above the building—and that invention has not changed much over the years.

Ben even invented the second hand on a clock, and many more things, too.

Show your students any of the above two-page spreads. They are fun and the kids (and you) will learn a lot.

Burke, Jim. *Take Me Out to the Ball Game.* Lyrics by Jack Norworth. Introduction by Pete Hamill. Little, Brown, 2006. ISBN 0316758191. Unpaged. Grades 2–5.

In 1908, a songwriter named Jack Norworth was riding the elevated subway. He saw a poster that said "BASE BALL TODAY—POLO GROUNDS." All the New York Giants games were held at the Polo Grounds, and almost the whole city was baseball crazy. Store owners even closed down so they could go to the games. Jack wrote down some lyrics to a song about it, and then a composer named Harry Von Tilzer set them to music. And the song they came up with is one almost everyone can still sing today—*Take Me Out to the Ball Game.*

If you follow the song (and I bet you don't know the first verse), you will see the story of two young people going to the game—and in boxes of text in the book you will learn about the New York Giants, especially their pitcher, Christy Mathewson, whom many consider the greatest pitcher of all time. Read the facts and sing along with the story.

Demarest, Chris L. *Alpha Bravo Charlie: The Military Alphabet.* Margaret K. McElderry Books, 2005. ISBN 0689869282. Unpaged. Grades K–3.

This is just the ticket for young military buffs—a new kind of alphabet, one that tells and shows the military alphabet, including the signal flags that give each letter a color-coded shape. Big color illustrations show us examples of some military things the letters can stand for.

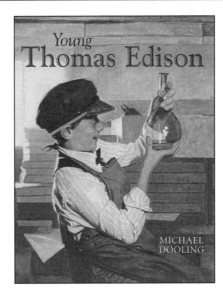

Young Thomas Edison **by Michael Dooling.**

Dooling, Michael. *Young Thomas Edison.* Holiday House, 2005. ISBN 0823418685. Unpaged. Grades K–3.

Before Thomas Alva Edison became the most famous inventor in American history, he was just a kid. His family called him Al.

But that kid just loved to experiment. By the time he was nine years old, in 1856, he had made his family's basement into a laboratory. He loved to mix up chemicals to see what would happen.

School was hard for Al. He'd had a disease called scarlet fever, and that made him hard of hearing. His teacher was not sympathetic to this, and his mother decided to homeschool Al. Fortunately, she was a good teacher.

When Al was twelve, he decided he needed a job to make more money for his experiments. He sold newspapers on the train from Port Huron, where he lived, to Detroit, and then he spent the day at the Detroit library, reading and learning even more. He took the train home again at night and sold more papers.

Somehow he made friends with the conductor, and pretty soon he set up a laboratory in the baggage car of the train. He had fun until the day some of his phosphorus caught on fire.

Al was quite a kid, with quite a dream—and he worked hard and learned a lot and made his dream come true.

Editors of YES Magazine. *Fantastic Feats and Failures.* Kids Can Press, 2004. ISBN 1553376331. 52 p. Grades 3–7.

Take a look at the picture on the title page. It is a feat that turned into a failure very quickly. The Tacoma Narrows Bridge opened on the fourth of July in 1940, and it immediately became apparent that there were problems with it. Major problems. "It swayed and rolled so much … that drivers would lose sight of cars ahead of them on the bridge. No wonder it was nicknamed Galloping Gertie" (page 26).

The engineer who designed the bridge had made a serious error in judgment. He did not allow wind flow, and the structure was open only four months before the bridge collapsed. At that time it was the third largest suspension bridge in the world.

Fortunately, no human beings died, but there is a fine picture of a man running as fast as he can on page 26.

This is a book about manmade structures, and about triumphs and mistakes. We learn what went wrong in these and more great engineering failures: the space shuttle *Challenger* disaster, the collapse of the walkways in the Hyatt Regency hotel in Kansas City, in which more than 200 people were injured and 114 died, the Leaning Tower of Pisa, and the World Trade Center buildings, which no one expected to collapse. Triumphs include the magnificent Brooklyn Bridge, the Eiffel Tower, and the Sydney Opera House—but the designers of these structures had to overcome many obstacles.

This is a fascinating read.

Fradin, Dennis Brindell. *With a Little Luck: Surprising Stories of Amazing Discoveries.* Dutton Children's Books, 2006. ISBN 0525471960. 183 p. Grades 4–up.

Lucky discoveries have changed the world, over and over again. In this book, the author tells us some incredible stories of real people who stumbled on or were searching for all sorts of wonderful things.

It starts with Isaac Newton, a boy born in England in 1642. Isaac did not do well in school. When he was twelve years old, he was at the bottom of his class of nearly one hundred kids. But Isaac was passionately interested in science, and his discoveries in later life changed science forever. He had wondered how the moon and the planets kept in orbit, and one day, he watched an apple fall, and it hit him. "The same force that pulled the apple to the ground also kept the planets in their orbits around the sun and the moon in orbit around the earth. Newton then figured out many details of how this force works" (p. 14). The force was, of course, gravity.

Mary Anning was a little girl in Lyme Regis, England, whose father collected and sold fossils that he found in the cliffs along the seashore in the early 1800s. When he died young, she started doing the work herself—and became the first person, at age thirteen, to discover the complete fossil of an *Ichthyosaurus*. The fossils she collected during her life are in museums all over the world.

Charles Goodyear was obsessed with rubber. It was a wonderful substance that repelled rain, and could be shaped and molded, but it cracked in cold weather and turned into sticky goo in warm weather. Most people had given up on it, but he was sure there had to be a way to make it useable. "Two giant obstacles stood in the way of his becoming an inventor: He had no scientific background and little talent for building things" (p. 37). He spent all of his money on the project, so much so that he went to prison for debt a few times. But one day an accidental discovery brought the answer: the rubber needed to be mixed with sulfur and heated, or *vulcanized*. The Goodyear Company was named after him. By the way, rubber got its English name because it was good at rubbing out pencil marks. Show the picture of Goodyear on page 42.

Read about the invention of anesthesia (how would you like to have surgery without it?), the discovery that fewer people died in hospitals if doctors washed their hands, the discovery of the (former) planet Pluto, and many more. This is a fun read.

Goodman, Susan E., and Michael J. Doolittle. *Skyscraper: From the Ground Up.* Knopf, 2004. ISBN 0375813098. Unpaged. Grades 3–5.

"Some artists paint and draw. Architects are artists who sculpt the city. … [they] can't make their projects look any way they want. They must design a building that is comfortable and safe. They must include ideas that owners have about their building. The city has its ideas too. City laws say that a building's shape must fit in with its neighbors and allow the sun to reach the streets below.

"The architect must juggle all these challenges. Plus one more. He wants the skyscraper to be beautiful."

Wow! That's quite a job.

This is the true story of a skyscraper designed by architect Gary Heaney and built in New York City, which has more skyscrapers more than 270 feet tall than any place in the world.

But skyscrapers, even though there are a lot of them, are not easy to build, and this colorful book, filled with fascinating photographs, will astound you. It's filled with fun facts, such as these:

- When workers need to use the world's biggest hammer to cut through bedrock, it makes so many vibrations that there are waves in toilet bowls a block away.

- When workers lay concrete, they get it all over their boots and pants. Sometimes they will carry around an extra ten pounds by the end of the day.

- Workers put up nets called "diapers" to keep bolts and concrete from falling on people walking near the construction site.

Award-Winning Nonfiction (That Boys Will Like!)

- Allen, Thomas B. *Remember Pearl Harbor: American and Japanese Survivors Tell Their Stories.* ALA Notable Children's Books

- Armstrong, Jennifer. *Shipwreck at the Bottom of the World: The Extraordinary True Story of Shackleton and the* Endurance. ALA Notable Children's Books

- Bartoletti, Susan Campbell. *Hitler Youth: Growing Up in Hitler's Shadow.* 2006 Sibert Honor Book, ALA Notable Children's Books

- Drez, Ronald. J. *Remember D-Day: The Plan, the Invasion, Survivor Stories.* ALA Notable Children's Books

- Giblin, James Cross. *The Life and Death of Adolf Hilter.* 2003 Sibert Medal Winner, ALA Notable Children's Books

- Jackson, Donna M. *The Bone Detectives: How Forensic Anthropologists Solve Crimes and Uncover Mysteries of the Dead.* ALA Notable Children's Books

- Jenkins, Steve. *The Top of the World: Climbing Mount Everest.* ALA Notable Children's Books

From *Gotcha for Guys! Nonfiction Books to Get Boys Excited About Reading* by Kathleen A. Baxter and Marcia Agness Kochel. Westport, CT: Libraries Unlimited. Copyright © 2007.

The building that is finished by the end of the book is the Random House building. Random House is a book publisher, and the building looks like three books between two bookends. It's beautiful!

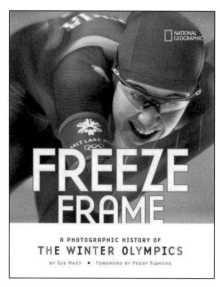

**Freeze Frame: A Photographic History of
the Winter Olympics by Sue Macy.**

Macy, Sue. *Freeze Frame: A Photographic History of the Winter Olympics*. Foreword by
  Peggy Fleming. National Geographic, 2006. ISBN 0792278879. 96 p. Grades 4–up.
  The modern Olympics started in 1896. But it included no cold weather sports.
Ice-skating was *supposed* to be part of the event, but there was no ice rink in Athens,
Greece, so it never made the program. By 1924, proponents of winter sports had organized the first winter Olympics, in Chamonix, France. There were lots of reasons not
to have an Olympics for winter sports. Very few countries had training facilities for
them, and the Scandinavian countries were the main ones that had Olympic-class athletes. Their athletes, in fact, were so good that they did not *want* a Winter Olympics.
They wanted something called the Nordic Games, an international sports competition
held every four years in Norway or Sweden. And they wanted to keep their
competition.
  But slowly, winter sports were making it into the Olympics—skating and ice
hockey were both in the 1920 games. And, after the 1924, it was official. Winter sports
would be equal to summer sports.
  Weather drives everyone crazy at the Winter Olympics. Either it snows too much,
or it doesn't snow at all; it may be too cold to hold an event or too warm. Sometimes it
might even rain. Almost every Winter Olympics has some kind of weather emergency.
  This is the story of those games, and of some of the most famous and successful
contestants. Sonja Henie of Norway, at age eleven, was the youngest contestant ever,
although she came in last that year, but she became the most successful figure of all
time—and later a great movie star in the United States. Eric Heiden of the United
States won five gold medals for speed skating in 1980, the most gold medals ever won
by a contestant at a single competition. Today he is a sports doctor and was the doctor
for the U.S. speed-skating team in 2002. He worries about some of the extreme sports,
such as snowboarding, that have been added to the Olympics recently. He is afraid
people could gravely injure themselves in these sports.

Terrible things have happened connected with the Winter Olympics. In 1961, an airplane carrying the entire U.S. figure skating team crashed in Belgium, killing everyone on board—all the skaters, their coaches, and family members. In 1994, U.S. figure skater Nancy Kerrigan was attacked and wounded by men associated with one of her competitors, Tanya Harding. They wanted Nancy to be too injured to compete, but their plan did not work. In other cases, judges have confessed to being bribed to make sure certain people won their competition.

This is a fascinating book, filled with great photographs. Young people will enjoy reading it.

Mann, Elizabeth. *Empire State Building* (A Wonder of the World Book). Mikaya Press, 2003. ISBN 1931414068. 48 p. Grades 3–5.

For a long time, the Empire State Building was the tallest building in the world. It is not anymore, but it is still one of the most famous. It has starred in a lot of movies. Maybe you saw it in *King Kong*, when the giant ape stood on top of it and fought off airplanes.

This is the story of how it came to be.

Award-Winning Nonfiction (That Boys Will Like!)

- Montgomery, Sy. *The Tarantula Scientist.* 2005 Sibert Honor Book, ALA Notable Children's Books

- Murphy, Jim. *Blizzard: The Storm That Changed America.* ALA Notable Children's Books, 2001 Sibert Honor Book

- Schyffert, Bea Uusma. *The Man Who Went to the Far Side of the Moon: The Story of* Apollo 11 *Astronaut Michael Collins.* 2004 Batchelor Honor Book, ALA Notable Children's Books

- Turner, Pamela S. *Gorilla Doctors: Saving Endangered Great Apes.* ALA Notable Children's Books

- Walker, Sally M. *Secrets of a Civil War Submarine: Solving the Mysteries of the* H.L. Hunley. 2006 Sibert Medal Winner, ALA Notable Children's Books

- Warren, Andrea. *Surviving Hitler: A Boy in the Nazi Death Camps.* 2002 Sibert Honor Book, ALA Notable Children's Books

From *Gotcha for Guys! Nonfiction Books to Get Boys Excited About Reading* by Kathleen A. Baxter and Marcia Agness Kochel. Westport, CT: Libraries Unlimited. Copyright © 2007.

First of all, it is a skyscraper, a type of building that hasn't been around for very long. To build skyscrapers, people had to have advanced technology, such as elevators and steel-framed buildings that were strong enough to bear the weight of all of the upper stories. That kind of technology hadn't been around very long when construction of the Empire State Building started in 1929. People began to build skyscrapers in the 1880s. If you have a small audience, show them the two photos on page 11. They show the same view of Manhattan in 1890 and then in 1921. You would hardly recognize it.

Demolition workers tore down the old Waldorf-Astoria hotel, and then the building of the Empire State Building started. Workers lined up to get the jobs, which paid well, although they involved working in very dangerous conditions (show the pictures on page 19). Workers would walk on beams high above the ground and climb cables in open air. Some of the best workers came from northern New York and from Canada.

They were Mohawks, and they seemed to be not afraid of heights at all. They were very skilled at working in high places. There were 3,500 workers on the site every day, and they did sixty different kinds of jobs.

This is an incredible story.

McDonough, Yona Zeldis. *Hammerin' Hank: The Life of Hank Greenberg.* Illustrations by Malcah Zeldis. Walker, 2006. ISBN 0802789978. Unpaged. Grades 1–4.

Hank loved baseball from the time he was a kid living in the Bronx. He went to the ballpark as often as he could and stayed all day. He was not a natural athlete: all of his life he had to work at his playing. But he worked hard, and he got very good at it.

He went to college for one semester, but he dropped out to play baseball. He could not get a job with a major league team, so he had to go to the minor leagues with the Detroit Tigers.

Finally, when he was twenty-two years old, in 1933, he moved up to the major league, playing for the Tigers. Although some baseball fans didn't like him and called him names because he was Jewish, he was a hero to many Jewish people around the United States—and to many baseball fans as well. He was good. In 1935, he was voted Most Valuable Player of both the National and American Leagues.

This is his story. When you read this colorful book, you will see why Hank Greenberg was a hero to so many people.

Stewart, Mark. *The New England Patriots* (Team Spirit). Norwood House Press, 2006. ISBN 1559530066. 48 p. Grades 2–5.

Meet the New England Patriots. They're an unusual football team, renowned for not relying on superstars to win. Instead, they play as a team—and they don't make a lot of mistakes. This is an exciting introduction to one of football's top winners.

Learn some great facts:

- In December 1982, the Patriots played the Miami Dolphins during a snowstorm. The snow was so bad that a snow plow had to keep plowing off the lines in the field. The Patriot's coach, Ron Meyer, had a great idea. He ordered the snowplow driver to clear off a spot so it would not be as slippery as the rest of the field. That way the kicker of an attempt at a field goal had a cleared-off spot in which to do his thing. The Patriots won and the Dolphins protested, but no one could find a rule against it.

- Steve Grogan played for the Patriots for fifteen years—but he had another job in the off-season. He was a dentist.

- "There is a lot more to a football uniform than what you see on the outside. Air can be pumped inside the helmet to give it a snug, padded fit. The jersey covers should pads, and sometimes a rib-protector called a 'flak jacket.' The pants include pads that protect the hips, thighs, tailbone, and knees" (page 15).

This book is just one in a brand new series about great teams. Check to see if the library has your favorite team. (See the "Worth Reading" section in this chapter for more titles.)

Sullivan, George. *Built to Last: Building America's Amazing Bridges, Dams, Tunnels, and Skyscrapers.* Scholastic Nonfiction, 2005. ISBN 0439517370. 128 p. Grades 4–up.

For more than two hundred years, Americans have celebrated their own ingenuity. George Sullivan's beautiful book, filled with photographs, tells us the story of seventeen engineering marvels.

One of the most original of them all is the Erie Canal, built between 1817 and 1825. It is still there, although now it is used for recreation more than business. When the Erie Canal was conceived and built, it was truly a radical idea, and it made a huge difference in the lives of many early Americans. What it did was connect the Great Lakes with the Hudson River, enabling goods to travel easily and inexpensively in both directions. Farmers who had moved west to the frontier could easily sell the goods they raised. "Before construction of the Erie Canal, it cost between $90 and $125 to ship a ton of wagon between Buffalo and New York City; afterward, the cost dropped to $4 a ton. By 1830, the cost of transporting flour on the Erie Canal had fallen to a penny a ton" (page 11).

Other amazing designs include the Capitol of the United States (the best known of all American buildings), the Brooklyn Bridge, the Flatiron Building, the Transcontinental Railroad, the Hoover Dam, the Golden Gate Bridge (workers who fell off of it while it was being constructed landed in safety nets), the Chesapeake Bay Bridge and Tunnel, and Boston's famous "Big Dig." Kids (and adults) will learn a lot of fun information from this book.

Show your audience the tall spread of the Flatiron Building on pages 38 and 39.

Sweetman, Bill. *Stealth Bombers: The B-2 Spirits* (War Planes). Capstone Press, 2001. 0736807918. 32 p. Grades 4–up.

Stealth bombers are very strange looking planes. In fact, the author of this book says they are basically flying wings. Most of the parts we are used to seeing on airplanes simply do not exist on a B-2—and that is why they are so extraordinary.

All of them are based at Whiteman Air Force Base in Missouri. Each plane costs 1.3 *billion* dollars to build. The shape of the plane makes it very difficult for them to be found on radar, unless they are directly overhead certain radar stations—which means that their pilots must always avoid those stations. They look no bigger than a bird on most radar screens.

The first B-2 went into service in 1993, and there will be no more because they are so expensive. The U.S. Air Force expects to use the ones in existence until 2020.

Tomecek, Stephen M. *What a Great Idea: Inventions That Changed the World.* Illustrated by Dan Stuckenschneider. Scholastic, 2003. ISBN 0590681443. 112 p. Grades 4–up.

Throughout history, people have been inventing things. Many times the same thing was invented in different places at about the same time. This book takes two pages not only to describe each invention but also to tell us about some of the huge changes they made in the way people lived. It's truly staggering information.

The book starts with a simple, simple object: the hand axe. Before people invented this tool, which was a stone that had been sharpened using other stones, they could eat only plants. The only meat they could eat usually came from dead animals that other animal predators had left. But the axe changed everything. Pretty soon people were eating a lot of meat because they could finally cut it.

In the opening paragraph of the introduction to the book, the author writes, "If you stop and think about it, it seems pretty amazing that humans have come to dominate the world. Let's face it—stripped down to our birthday suits, we're not really much a threat to the rest of the animal kingdom. Deer are faster, oxen are stronger, and lions have sharper teeth. Humans do have one major advantage, however, and that's our superior brains. Using our intelligence and imagination, we can solve problems and invent devices that not only protect us, but make our lives easier" (page 7).

Think of some changes that came about because of inventions. Who invented clothing? For a long time, people didn't wear anything. How did clothing change their lives? How did the axle change people's lives? The author of this book thinks the axle was a much more important invention than the wheel. How about writing and mathematics? They may not be kids' favorite subjects, but where would the world be without them?

Start reading this one, and you won't be able to stop.

NOT TO BE MISSED

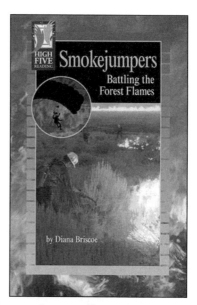

Smokejumpers: Battling the Forest Flames
by Diana Briscoe.

Briscoe, Diana. *Smokejumpers: Battling the Forest Flames* (High Five Reading). Capstone, 2003. ISBN 0736895485. 48 p. Grades 3–9.

Jumping into forests filled with raging fires may sound glamorous, but it is hard, dangerous work. Smokejumpers have to stay in great shape, working out sixty to ninety minutes a day. Good, basic information and easy to read.

Carrow, Robert. *Put a Fan in Your Hat! Inventions, Contraptions, and Gadgets Kids Can Build.* Illustrated by Rick Brown. McGraw-Hill, 1997. ISBN 0070116571. 139 p. Grades 4–6. *Gotcha.*

The title says it all. There are directions for making all sorts of inventions, contraptions, and gadgets in this interesting compendium.

Delano, Marfé Ferguson. *Inventing the Future: A Photobiography of Thomas Alva Edison.* National Geographic Society, 2002. ISBN 0792267214. 64 p. Grades 3–6. *Gotcha Covered.*

Thomas Edison wanted to invent things from the time he was a kid, and he got his first patent at age twenty-two. By the time he was twenty-three, he had hired fifty employees and opened his own manufacturing company and laboratory. Some of our greatest inventions came from his ideas and the work of his company. Excellent photographs and pictures give this book great appeal.

Glaser, Jason. *Bicycle Stunt Riding* (Extreme Sports). Capstone Books, an imprint of Capstone Press, 1999. ISBN 0736801677. 48 p. Grades 4–8.

BMX started in the 1970s, and stunt riding became inordinately popular in a short time period. Good photos add to the fun of this high interest book.

Haduch, Bill. *Go Fly a Bike! The Ultimate Book about Bicycle Fun, Freedom & Science.* Illustrated by Chris Murphy. Dutton Children's Books, 2004. ISBN 0525470247. 83 p. Grades 4–6.

Did you know that many of the same moves required to fly a plane are also required to ride a bicycle? No wonder the Wright brothers started working on their airplane in their bicycle shop. A fun book loaded with great information.

Harper, Cherise Mericle. *Imaginative Inventions: The Who, What, Where, When, and Why of Roller Skates, Potato Chips, Marbles, and Pie and More!* Megan Tingley Books/Little, Brown, 2001. ISBN 0316347256. 32 p. Grades 1–4. *Gotcha Covered.*

These poems about inventions are silly and fun, especially if you decide to sing them. They are a great introduction to a unit on inventions, or just to add some fun to your poetry time.

Hendrickson, Steve. *Enduro Racing* (Motorcycles). Capstone Books, an imprint of Capstone Press, 2000. ISBN 0736804773. 48 p. Grades 4–8.

The winners of Enduro races are not necessarily the fastest riders. Accuracy is far more important than speed in these races that take place on paths, not racecourses. You'll find out why it is a controversial sport in this interesting book.

Hendrickson, Steve. *Land Speed Racing* (Motorcycles). Capstone Books, an imprint of Capstone Press, 2000. ISBN 0736804765. 48 p. Grades 4–8.

There is really only one good reason why land speed racers compete: they want to know exactly how fast their vehicles can go. They do not speed on racecourses, but on large, flat areas, such as dry lake beds or the Bonneville Salt Flats. Amazing information!

Hendrickson, Steve. *Supercross Racing* (Motorcycles). Capstone Books, an imprint of Capstone Press, 2000. ISBN 073680479X 48 p. Grades 4–up.

Supercross racing makes use of many obstacles to make motorcycle racing more exciting. There are excellent color photos and good information on the skills stunts and the companies that sponsor supercross races.

Hunter, Ryan Ann. *Dig a Tunnel.* Illustrated by Edward Miller. Holiday House, 1999. ISBN 0823413918. Unpaged. Grades K–3. *Gotcha Again.*

Any book that combines digging and big machines cannot go wrong with young readers.

Jones, Charlotte Foltz. *Mistakes That Worked.* Illustrated by John O'Brien. A Doubleday Book for Young Readers, 1991. ISBN 0385320434. 82 p. Grades 4–6. *Gotcha Again.*

Many everyday items came about by mistake. Someone was trying to do something else, and got an unexpected result. Without mistakes, we would not have chocolate chip cookies, Post-It Notes, potato chips, popsicles, and many other things. Kids start by browsing but end up reading.

Macaulay, David. *Building Big.* Houghton Mifflin, 2000. ISBN 0395963311. 192 p. Grades 6–up. *Gotcha Again.*

Macaulay is renowned for his intricate, detailed art, which shows, with clear explanation, exactly how things were built. This is just the thing for budding engineers.

Matthews, Tom L. *Always Inventing: A Photobiography of Alexander Graham Bell.* National Geographic, 1999. ISBN 0792273915. 64 p. Grades 4–6. *Gotcha Again.*

Alexander Graham Bell didn't stop with the telephone. He kept inventing all of his interesting life. This is filled with photographs and compelling information about a curious and resourceful man.

Severance, John B. *Skyscrapers: How America Grew Up.* Holiday House, 2000. ISBN 0823414922. 112 p. Grades 4–8. *Gotcha Again.*

Before the late 1800s, there were tall buildings—the pyramids, the cathedrals, and some Hindu temples. But it took a lot of new inventions coming together to enable people to be able to start making the buildings we call skyscrapers. They needed elevators, steel structures, telephones, electric lighting, and modern plumbing (no one would want to go up and down twenty floors to go to the bathroom!). When all of these were available, the first skyscrapers were built—and they are still being built all over the world.

St. George, Judith. *So You Want to Be an Inventor?* Illustrated by David Small. Philomel Books, 2002. ISBN 0399235930. 50 p. Grades K–3.

It is not easy being an inventor, but it can be a wonderfully exciting and rewarding occupation. The Caldecott-Medal-winning duo of *So You Want to Be President* returns with another simple, humorous, and informative picture book.

Taylor, Barbara. *I Wonder Why Zippers Have Teeth and Other Questions about Inventions.* Kingfisher, 1995. ISBN 185697670X. 32 p. Grades 1–4. *Gotcha Again.*

These are excellent questions, with sometimes mind-boggling answers. Do you know that drinking straws (once made of paper) were invented to keep liquids cooler? Your glass or cup would not warm up when you held it in your hands if you were drinking from a straw. This is a fun one for browsing.

Wulffson, Don L. *The Kid Who Invented the Trampoline: More Surprising Stories about Inventions.* Dutton Children's Books, 2001. ISBN 0525466541. 128 p. Grades 4–8. *Gotcha Again.*

You would not expect to find it here, but this has some grand gross information. The stories of toilet paper, and the history of plumbing (or, better yet, the lack of plumbing, which is quite sickening to read about), toothbrushes and toothpaste, of which urine was an early and common ingredient, are facts kids will have to share with their friends. There are other, less gross inventions discussed as well, but all of them are so interesting that readers will have a hard time putting the book down.

Wulffson, Don. *Toys! Amazing Stories behind Some Great Inventions.* Illustrations by Laurie Keller. Henry Holt, 2000. ISBN 0805061967. 137 p. Grades 4–8. *Gotcha Again.*

Some toys and games have been around for a long time, such as backgammon, chess, checkers, playing cards, and the seesaw. But others are recent inventions. What do you think is the most popular board game in the United States?

Youngblood, Ed. *Dirt Track Racing* (Motorcycles). Capstone Books, an imprint of Capstone Press, 2000. ISBN 0736804749. 48 p. Grades 3–9.

Dirt track racing is one of the oldest types of motorcycle racing in North America. It began in the early 1900s, and developed over the years. Dirt track equipment is expensive and unusual—even the fuel costs four times as much as regular gasoline.

Youngblood, Ed. *Superbike Racing* (Motorcycles). Capstone Books, an imprint of Capstone Press, 2000. ISBN 0736804781. 48 p. Grades 3–9.

The American Motorcycle Association developed superbike racing in 1976. It's an unusual sport, in which some of the riders sort of resemble Darth Vader. Excellent photos highlight the informative text.

WORTH READING

Nonfiction books with "boy appeal" that have received positive reviews in *Booklist, Horn Book Guide,* and/or *School Library Journal.*

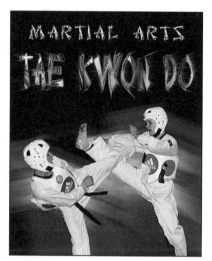

***Tae Kwon Do* by David Amerland.**

Amerland, David. *Tae Kwon Do* (Martial Arts). Gareth Stevens, 2004. ISBN 0836841956. 32 p. Grades 4–8.

Barr, Matt, and Chris Moran. *Snowboarding* (Extreme Sports). LernerSports, 2003. ISBN 0822512424. 32 p. Grades 4–8.

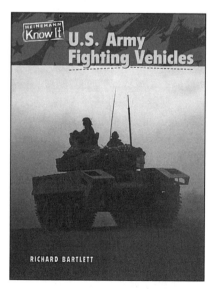

***U.S. Army Fighting Vehicles*
by Richard Bartlett.**

Bartlett, Richard. *U.S. Army Fighting Vehicles* (U.S. Armed Forces). Heinemann Library, 2003. ISBN 1403401896. 48 p. Grades 4–6.

Bell, Lonnie. *The Story of Coca-Cola* (Built for Success). Creative/Smart Apple 2003. ISBN 1583402926. 48 p. Grades 4–8.

Bledsoe, Glen, and Karen Bledsoe. *The World's Fastest Dragsters* (Built for Speed). Capstone Press, 2003. ISBN 0736815007. 48 p. Grades 3–9.

**The World's Fastest Indy Cars
by Glen Bledsoe and Karen Bledsoe.**

Bledsoe, Glen, and Karen Bledsoe. *The World's Fastest Indy Cars* (Built for Speed). Capstone Press, 2003. ISBN 0736815015. 48 p. Grades 3–9.

Buckley, James, Jr. *AFC North* (Inside the NFL). The Child's World, 2005. ISBN 1592965091. 48 p. Grades 4–6.

Buckley, James, Jr. *AFC South* (Inside the NFL). The Child's World, 2005. ISBN 1592965105. 48 p. Grades 4–6.

Buckley, James. *American League East* (Behind the Plate). The Child's World, 2005. ISBN 1592963595. 48 p. Grades 4–6.

Buckley, James. *A Batboy's Day*. DK, 2005. ISBN 0756612063. 32 p. Grades 1–3.

Buckley, James. *NASCAR*. DK, 2005. ISBN 0756611946. 72 p. Grades 5–up.

Buckley, James, Jr. *Super Bowl* (Eyewitness Books). DK, 2003. ISBN 0789488310. 64 p. Grades 4–6.

Campbell, Peter. *Old-Time Baseball: 1903 and the First Modern World Series.* Millbrook Press, 2002. ISBN 0761324666. 48 p. Grades 4–up.

Chesterman, Barnaby, and Bob Willingham. *Judo* (Martial Arts). Gareth Stevens, 2004. ISBN 0836841921. 32 p. Grades 4–8.

Clendening, John. *American League Central* (Behind the Plate). The Child's World, 2005. ISBN 1592963609. 48 p. Grades 4–6.

Collicutt, Paul. *This Car.* FSG, 2002. ISBN 0374399654. 32 p. Grades K–2.

Cook, Harry. *Karate* (Martial Arts). Gareth Stevens, 2004. ISBN 083684193x. 32 p. Grades 4–8.

Extreme Mountain Biking Moves
by Kathleen Deady.

Deady, Kathleen. *Extreme Mountain Biking Moves* (Behind the Moves). Capstone Press, 2003. ISBN 0736815139. 32 p. Grades 3–9.

Deady, Kathleen. *Extreme Rock Climbing Moves* (Behind the Moves). Capstone Press, 2003. ISBN 0736815147. 32 p. Grades 3–9.

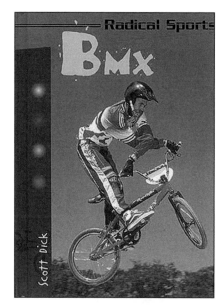

***BMX* by Scott Dick.**

Dick, Scott. *BMX* (Radical Sports). Heinemann Library, 2002. ISBN 1588106233. 32 p. Grades 4–up.

Fisher, David. *American League West* (Behind the Plate). The Child's World, 2005. ISBN 1592963587. 48 p. Grades 4–6.

Freeman, Gary. *Motocross* (Radical Sports). Heinemann Library, 2002. ISBN 1588106276. 32 p. Grades 4–up.

Frisch, Aaron. *Motocross* (World of Sport). Creative/Smart Apple, 2002. ISBN 158340161x. 32 p. Grades 4–9.

Gifford, Clive. *A World-Class Sprinter* (Making of a Champion). Heinemann Library, 2004. ISBN 1403446695. 48 p. Grades 4–8.

Gigliotti, Jim. *National League West* (Behind the Plate). The Child's World, 2005. ISBN 1592963633. 48 p. Grades 4–6.

Glidewell, Steve. *Inline Skating* (Extreme Sports). LernerSports, 2003. ISBN 0822512440. 32 p. Grades 4–8.

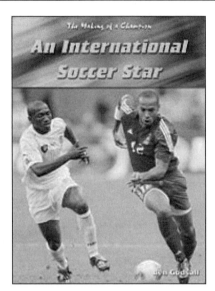

***An International Soccer Star* by Ben Godsal.**

Godsal, Ben. *An International Soccer Star* (Making of a Champion). Heinemann Library, 2005. ISBN 1403453659. 48 p. Grades 4–6.

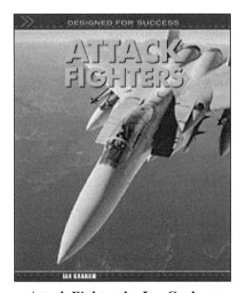

***Attack Fighters* by Ian Graham.**

Graham, Ian. *Attack Fighters* (Designed for Success). Heinemann Library, 2003. ISBN 140340769x. 32 p. Grades 4–8.

Graham, Ian. *Off-Road Vehicles* (Designed for Success). Heinemann Library, 2003. ISBN 1403407703. 32 p. Grades 4–8.

Graham, Ian. *Race Cars* (Designed for Success). Heinemann Library, 2003. ISBN 1403407711. 32 p. Grades 4–8.

Graham, Ian. *Sports Cars* (Designed for Success). Heinemann Library, 2003. ISBN 140340722x. 32 p. Grades 4–8.

Graham, Ian. *Superbikes* (Designed for Success). Heinemann Library, 2003. ISBN 1403407738. 32 p. Grades 4–8.

Graham, Ian. *Superboats* (Designed for Success). Heinemann Library, 2003. ISBN 1403407746. 32 p. Grades 4–8.

Haskins, Jim. *Champion: The Story of Muhammad Ali.* Illustrated by Eric Velasquez. Walker Books for Young Readers, 2002. ISBN 0802787843. 40 p. Grades 1–4.

Hedlund, Stephanie F. *Snowboarding* (Checkerboard: X-treme Sports Series). ABDO, 2003. ISBN 1577659295. 32 p. Grades 3–7.

Hedlund, Stephanie F. *Windsurfing* (Checkerboard: X-treme Sports Series). ABDO, 2003. ISBN 1577659317. 32 p. Grades 3–7.

Hill, Lee Sullivan. *Earthmovers* (Pull Ahead Books). Lerner, 2002. ISBN 0822506890. 32 p. Grades K–3.

Hill, Lee Sullivan. *Trains* (Pull Ahead Books). Lerner, 2002. ISBN 0822506920. 32 p. Grades K–3.

Hocking, Justin. *Awesome Obstacles: How to Build Your Own Skateboard Ramps and Ledges* (Skateboarder's Guide to Skate Parks, Half-Pipes, Bowls, and Obstacles). Rosen, 2005. ISBN 1404203370. 48 p. Grades 4–6.

Hocking, Justin. *Dream Builders: The World's Best Skate Park Creators* (Skateboarder's Guide to Skate Parks, Half-Pipes, Bowls, and Obstacles). Rosen, 2005. ISBN 1404203389. 48 p. Grades 4–6.

Hocking, Justin. *Off the Wall: A Skateboarder's Guide to Riding Bowls and Pools* (Skateboarder's Guide to Skate Parks, Half-Pipes, Bowls, and Obstacles). Rosen, 2005. ISBN 1404203397. 48 p. Grades 4–6.

Hocking, Justin. *Rippin' Ramps: A Skateboarder's Guide to Riding Half-Pipes* (Skateboarder's Guide to Skate Parks, Half-Pipes, Bowls, and Obstacles). Rosen, 2005. ISBN 1404203400. 48 p. Grades 4–6.

Hocking, Justin. *Taking Action: How to Get Your City to Build a Public Skate Park* (Skateboarder's Guide to Skate Parks, Half-Pipes, Bowls, and Obstacles). Rosen, 2005. ISBN 1404203419. 48 p. Grades 4–6.

Hocking, Justin. *Technical Terrain: A Skateboarder's Guide to Riding Skate Park Street Courses* (Skateboarder's Guide to Skate Parks, Half-Pipes, Bowls, and Obstacles). Rosen, 2005. ISBN 1404203427. 48 p. Grades 4–6.

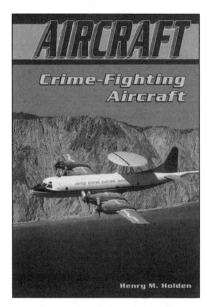

Crime-Fighting Aircraft
by Henry M. Holden.

Holden, Henry M. *Crime-Fighting Aircraft* (Aircraft). Enslow, 2002. ISBN 0766017184. 48 p. Grades 4–8.

Holden, Henry M. *Fire-Fighting Aircraft and Smoke Jumpers* (Aircraft). Enslow, 2002. ISBN 0766017206. 48 p. Grades 4–8.

Holden, Henry M. *Rescue Helicopters and Aircraft* (Aircraft). Enslow, 2002. ISBN 0766017192. 48 p. Grades 4–8.

Holden, Henry M. *The Supersonic X-15 and High-Tech NASA Aircraft* (Aircraft). Enslow, 2002. ISBN 0766017176. 48 p. Grades 4–8.

Horsley, Andy. *Skating* (Radical Sports). Heinemann Library, 2002. ISBN 158810625x. 32 p. Grades 4–up.

Howes, Chris. *Caving* (Radical Sports). Heinemann Library, 2002. ISBN 1588106268. 32 p. Grades 4–up.

Ingram, Scott. *A Basketball All-Star* (Making of a Champion). Heinemann Library, 2005. ISBN 1403453632. 48 p. Grades 4–6.

Ingram, Scott. *A Football Pro* (Making of a Champion). Heinemann Library, 2005. ISBN 1403453640. 48 p. Grades 4–6.

Jango-Cohen, Judith. *Dump Trucks* (Pull Ahead Books). Lerner, 2002. ISBN 0822506882. 32 p. Grades K–3.

Jango-Cohen, Judith. *Fire Trucks* (Pull Ahead Books). Lerner, 2002. 0822500779. 32 p. Grades K–3.

January, Brendan. *A Baseball All-Star* (Making of a Champion). Heinemann Library, 2005. ISBN 1403453624. 48 p. Grades 4–6.

Job, Chris. *BMX* (Extreme Sports). LernerSports, 2003. ISBN 0822512432. 32 p. Grades 4–8.

Jordan, Denise M. *Muhammad Ali: Meet the Champion* (Meeting Famous People). Enslow, 2003. ISBN 0766022722. 32 p. Grades 1–4.

Cars **by Nancy Smiler Levinson.**

Levinson, Nancy Smiler. *Cars* (Holiday House Readers). Holiday House, 2004. ISBN 0823416143. 32 p. Grades K–3.

Lichtenheld, Tom. *Everything I Know about Cars: A Collection of Made-Up Facts, Educated Guesses, and Silly Pictures about Cars, Trucks, and Other Zoomy Things.* Simon & Schuster Books for Young Readers, 2005. ISBN 0689843828. 40 p. Grades K–3.

Logan, Jim. *NFC South* (Inside the NFL). The Child's World, 2005. ISBN 1592965148. 48 p. Grades 4–6.

Marquez, Heron. *Roberto Clemente: Baseball's Humanitarian Hero* (Trailblazer Biography). Carolrhoda, 2005. ISBN 1575057670. 112 p. Grades 5–up.

Mason, Paul. *A World-Class Judo Champion* (Making of a Champion). Heinemann Library, 2004. ISBN 1403446733. 48 p. Grades 4–8.

Mason, Paul. *A World-Class Mountain Biker* (Making of a Champion). Heinemann Library, 2004. ISBN 1403446741. 48 p. Grades 4–8.

Mason, Paul. *A World-Class Swimmer* (Making of a Champion). Heinemann Library, 2004. ISBN 1403446717. 48 p. Grades 4–8.

Mason, Paul. *Skiing* (Radical Sports). Heinemann Library, 2002. ISBN 1588106284. 32 p. Grades 4–up.

McKendry, Joe. *Beneath the Streets of Boston: Building America's First Subway.* Godine, 2005. ISBN 1567922848. 48 p. Grades 4–6.

Middleton, Haydn. *A World-Class Marathon Runner* (Making of a Champion). Heinemann Library, 2004. ISBN 1403446709. 48 p. Grades 4–8.

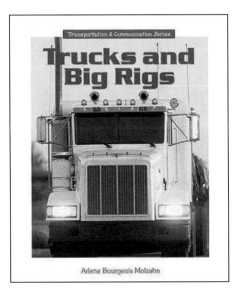

Trucks and Big Rigs
by Arlene Bourgeois Molzahn.

Molzahn, Arlene Bourgeois. *Trucks and Big Rigs* (Transportation and Communication). Enslow, 2003. ISBN 076602024x. 48 p. Grades 1–4.

Murphy, Frank. *Babe Ruth Saves Baseball!* Illustrated by Richard Walz. Random House Children's Books, 2005. ISBN 0375930485. 48 p. Grades K–3.

Nelson, Kristin L. *Farm Tractors* (Pull Ahead Books). Lerner, 2002. ISBN 0822506904. 32 p. Grades K–3.

Nelson, Kristin L. *Monster Trucks* (Pull Ahead Books). Lerner, 2002. ISBN 0822506912. 32 p. Grades K–3.

Nonnemacher, Klaus. *Kickboxing* (Martial Arts). Gareth Stevens, 2004. ISBN 0836841948. 32 p. Grades 4–8.

Osborne, Ian. *Mountain Biking* (Extreme Sports). LernerSports, 2003. ISBN 0822512459. 32 p. Grades 4–8.

Oxlade, Chris. *Car* (Take It Apart). Creative/Thameside, 2002. ISBN 1930643942. 32 p. Grades K–2.

Oxlade, Chris. *Plane* (Take It Apart). Creative/Thameside, 2002. ISBN 1930643950. 32 p. Grades K–2.

Oxlade, Chris. *Rock Climbing* (Extreme Sports). LernerSports, 2003. ISBN 0822512408. 32 p. Grades 4–8.

Peterson, Tiffany. *Watercraft* (Draw It!) Illustrated by David Westerfield. Heinemann Library, 2003. ISBN 1403402140. 32 p. Grades 3–6.

Pinchuck, Amy. *Make Amazing Toy and Game Gadgets* (Popular Mechanics for Kids). Illustrated by Teco Rodrigues. HarperCollins, 2002. ISBN 0688177263. 64 p. Grades 4–9.

Pinchuck, Amy. *Make Cool Gadgets for Your Room* (Popular Mechanics for Kids). Illustrated by Teco Rodrigues. HarperCollins, 2002. ISBN 0688177271. 64 p. Grades 4–9.

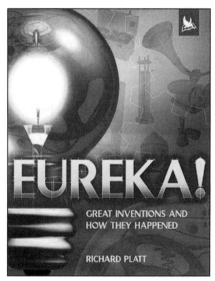

Eureka! Great Inventions and How They Happened **by Richard Platt.**

Platt, Richard. *Eureka! Great Inventions and How They Happened.* Kingfisher, 2003. ISBN 0753455803. 96 p. Grades 4–8.

Powell, Ben. *Skateboarding* (Extreme Sports). LernerSports, 2003. ISBN 0822512416. 32 p. Grades 4–8.

Readhead, Lloyd. *A World-Class Gymnast* (Hidden Life). Heinemann Library, 2004. ISBN 1403446725. 48 p. Grades 4–8.

Rielly, Robin. *Karate for Kids.* Tuttle, 2004. ISBN 0804835349. 48 p. Grades 4–8.

Ripley, Esther. *Solo Sailing* (DK Readers). DK, 2005. ISBN 0756609941. 48 p. Grades 4–6.

Rivera, Sheila. *Thunderbird* (Ultimate Cars). ABDO, 2004. ISBN 1591975832. 32 p. Grades 3–8.

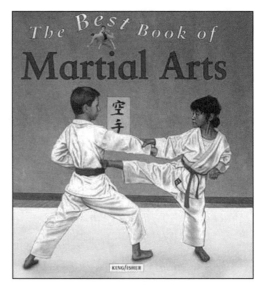

**The Best Book of Martial Arts
by Lauren Robertson.**

Robertson, Lauren. *The Best Book of Martial Arts* (Best Book of). Kingfisher, 2002. ISBN 0753454483. 32 p. Grades 3–6.

Romanek, Trudee. *Switched On, Flushed Down, Tossed Out: Investigating the Hidden Workings of Your Home.* Illustrated by Stephen MacEachern. Annick Press, 2005. ISBN 1550379038. 48 p. Grades 3–5.

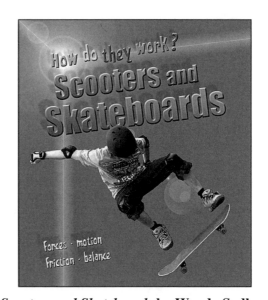

Scooters and Skateboards by Wendy Sadler.

Sadler, Wendy. *Scooters and Skateboards* (How Do They Work?). Heinemann Library, 2005. ISBN 1403468273. 32 p. Grades K–3.

Savage, Jeff. *Demolition Derby Cars* (Wild Rides!). Capstone Press, 2003. ISBN 0736815163. 32 p. Grades 3–9.

Savage, Jeff. *Go-Karts* (Wild Rides!). Capstone Press, 2003. ISBN 0736815171. 32 p. Grades 3–9.

Savage, Jeff. *Mountain Bikes* (Wild Rides!). Capstone Press, 2003. ISBN 073681519x. 32 p. Grades 3–9.

***Stunt Planes* by Jeff Savage.**

Savage, Jeff. *Stunt Planes* (Wild Rides!). Capstone Press, 2003. ISBN 0736815198. 32 p. Grades 3–9.

***The World's Fastest Pro Stock Trucks*
by Jeff Savage.**

Savage, Jeff. *The World's Fastest Pro Stock Trucks* (Built for Speed). Capstone Press, 2003. ISBN 0736815023. 48 p. Grades 3–9.

Savage, Jeff. *The World's Fastest Stock Cars* (Built for Speed). Capstone Press, 2003. ISBN 0736815031. 48 p. Grades 3–9.

Schaefer, A. R. *Extreme Freestyle Motocross Moves* (Behind the Moves). Capstone Press, 2003. ISBN 0736815120. 32 p. Grades 3–9.

Schaefer, A. R. *Extreme Wakeboarding Moves* (Behind the Moves). Capstone Press, 2003. ISBN 0736815155. 32 p. Grades 3–9.

Schwarz, Renee. *Birdhouses* (Kids Can Do It). Kids Can Press, 2004. ISBN 1553375491. 40 p. Grades 4–6.

Shange, Ntozake. *Float Like a Butterfly*. Illustrated by Edel Rodriguez. Hyperion/Jump at the Sun, 2002. ISBN 0786805544. 40 p. Grades K–3.

Sherman, Josepha. *The Story of Harley-Davidson* (Robbie Reader). Mitchell Lane, 2005. ISBN 158415358x. 32 p. Grades 2–5.

Silbaugh, John. *National League Central* (Behind the Plate). The Child's World, 2005. ISBN 1592963617. 48 p. Grades 4–6.

Simon, Seymour. *Amazing Aircraft* (See More Reader). North-South/Sea Star, 2002. ISBN 1587171791. 32 p. Grades K–3.

Simon, Seymour. *Giant Machines* (See More Reader). North-South/Sea Star, 2002. ISBN 1587171560. 32 p. Grades K–3.

Transformed: How Everyday Things Are Made **by Bill Slavin.**

Slavin, Bill. *Transformed: How Everyday Things Are Made*. Kids Can Press, 2005. ISBN 1553371798. 160 p. Grades 4–7.

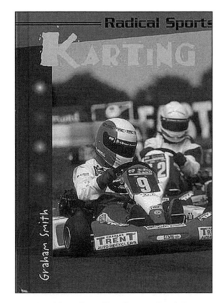

***Karting* by Graham Smith.**

Smith, Graham. *Karting* (Radical Sports). Heinemann Library, 2002. ISBN 1588106241. 32 p. Grades 4–up.

Smith, Ryan A. *Trading Cards: From Start to Finish.* Gale/Blackbirch, 2005. ISBN 1410303748. 48 p. Grades 3–5.

***How to Build Your Own Prize-Winning Robot* by Ed Sobey.**

Sobey, Ed. *How to Build Your Own Prize-Winning Robot* (Science Fair Success). Enslow, 2002. ISBN 0766016277. 128 p. Grades 5–up.

Stewart, Mark. *The Atlanta Braves* (Baseball). Norwood House, 2006. ISBN 1599530007. 48 p. Grades 3–6.

Stewart, Mark. *The Chicago Cubs* (Baseball). Norwood House, 2006. ISBN 1599530015. 48 p. Grades 3–6.

Stewart, Mark. *The Chicago White Sox* (Baseball). Norwood House, 2006. ISBN 1599530600. 48 p. Grades 3–6.

Stewart, Mark. *The Detroit Pistons* (Basketball). Norwood House, 2006. ISBN 1599530082. 48 p. Grades 3–6.

Stewart, Mark. *The Dallas Cowboys* (Football). Norwood House, 2006. ISBN 159953004x. 48 p. Grades 3–6.

Stewart, Mark. *The Indianapolis Colts* (Football). Norwood House, 2006. ISBN 1599530058. 48 p. Grades 3–6.

Stewart, Mark. *The Miami Heat* (Basketball). Norwood House, 2006. ISBN 1599530090. 48 p. Grades 3–6.

Stewart, Mark. *The New York Yankees* (Baseball). Norwood House, 2006. ISBN 1599530031. 48 p. Grades 3–6.

Stewart, Mark. *The Philadelphia Eagles* (Football). Norwood House, 2006. ISBN 1599530074. 48 p. Grades 3–6.

Stewart, Mark. *The Phoenix Spurs* (Basketball). Norwood House, 2006. ISBN 1599530104. 48 p. Grades 3–6.

Stewart, Mark. *The San Antonio Spurs* (Basketball). Norwood House, 2006. ISBN 1599530112. 48 p. Grades 3–6.

Teitelbaum, Michael. *National League East* (Behind the Plate). The Child's World, 2005. ISBN 1592963625. 48 p. Grades 4–6.

Van Cleaf, Kristin. *In-line Skating* (Checkerboard: X-treme Sports Series). ABDO, 2003. ISBN 1577659279. 32 p. Grades 3–7.

Van Cleaf, Kristin. *Rock Climbing* (Checkerboard: X-treme Sports Series). ABDO, 2003. ISBN 1577659309. 32 p. Grades 3–7.

Vieregger, K. E. *BMX Biking.* (Checkerboard: X-treme Sports Series). ABDO, 2003. ISBN 1577659260. 32 p. Grades 3–7.

Vieregger, K. E. *Skateboarding* (Checkerboard: X-treme Sports Series). ABDO, 2003. ISBN 1577659287. 32 p. Grades 3–7.

Walters, John. *AFC West* (Inside the NFL). The Child's World, 2005. ISBN 1592965113. 48 p. Grades 4–6.

Walters, John. *NFC West* (Inside the NFL). The Child's World, 2005. ISBN 1592965156. 48 p. Grades 4–6.

Welsh, Nick. *NFC East* (Inside the NFL). The Child's World, 2005. ISBN 1592965121. 48 p. Grades 4–6.

Wheeler, Jill C. *Beetle* (Ultimate Cars). ABDO, 2004. ISBN 1591975786. 32 p. Grades 3–8.

Wheeler, Jill C. *Camaro* (Ultimate Cars). ABDO, 2004. ISBN 1591975794. 32 p. Grades 3–8.

Wheeler, Jill C. *Maserati* (Ultimate Cars). ABDO, 2004. ISBN 1591975808. 32 p. Grades 3–8.

Wheeler, Jill C. *Mercedes-Benz* (Ultimate Cars). ABDO, 2004. ISBN 1591975816. 32 p. Grades 3–8.

Wheeler, Jill C. *Rolls-Royce* (Ultimate Cars). ABDO, 2004. ISBN 1591975821. 32 p. Grades 3–8.

Bulldozers **by Linda D. Williams.**

Williams, Linda D. *Bulldozers* (Pebble Plus: Mighty Machines). Capstone Press, 2004. ISBN 0736825932. 24 p. Grades K–3.

Winter, Jonah. *Roberto Clemente: Pride of the Pittsburgh Pirates.* Illustrated by Raul Colon. Atheneum Books for Young Readers, 2005. ISBN 0689856431. 40 p. Grades K–3.

Wood, Don. *A World-Class Boxer* (Making of a Champion). Heinemann Library, 2005. ISBN 1403453667. 48 p. Grades 4–6.

Woods, Bob. *AFC East* (Inside the NFL). The Child's World, 2005. ISBN 1592965083. 48 p. Grades 4–6.

Yoo, Paula. *Sixteen Years in Sixteen Seconds: The Sammy Lee Story.* Illustrated by Dom Lee. Lee and Low, 2005. ISBN 158430247x. 32 p. Grades K–3.

Zuehlke, Jeffrey. *Michael Phelps* (Amazing Athletes). Lerner, 2005 ISBN 0822524317. 32 p. Grades 2–4.

Chapter 9

Disasters and Unsolved Mysteries

Did UFOs land in Roswell? Why did the Hindenburg explode? Does the lost city of Atlantis exist? How did D. B. Cooper vanish into the wilderness? Mysteries and disasters are a surefire winner in a booktalk program. Boys and girls both will be clamoring to read about these fascinating, troubling, and mysterious events in history.

NEW AND NOTABLE

Fleischman, Sid. *Escape! The Story of the Great Houdini.* Greenwillow Books, 2006. ISBN 0060850944. 224 p. Grades 5–up.

The name Houdini is synonymous with magic, and even today it is a mystery how he performed some of his amazing feats. Harry Houdini's real name was not Houdini. It was Erich Weiss, and he was born in Budapest. His father was a rabbi. But his family called him Ehrie, which sounds sort of like Harry, and he named himself after a French magician named Eugene Robert-Houdin—a man he once admired but later despised.

Harry Houdini was probably the most famous magician who ever lived—and he knew just what to do so that people would always remember that name. Sid Fleischman, who knows how to tell a story about as well as anyone who ever did, tells us just how he became so famous—and how he was always willing to do more, to be the best, to keep people wondering and guessing all of his life.

After his family immigrated to the United States, Houdini grew up in Appleton, Wisconsin, but his parents were so poor that he ran away from home when he was only twelve. It took him a little while, but eventually he was really able to help out with the family finances.

He got on the stage doing magic tricks and became more and more famous—and better and better at getting publicity. He fell in love for good when he was only twenty years old, but he died long before his wife did. She befriended young magicians when she was an old woman, and Sid Fleischman was one of those kids she knew. He has a unique and original look at the famous story of the incredible man who was willing to try almost anything to stay on top of the game and get a lot of attention.

Show the picture of Houdini laughing at restraints on page 5.

***The Lost Colony of Roanoke* by Jean Fritz.**

Fritz, Jean. *The Lost Colony of Roanoke.* Illustrated by Hudson Talbott. G. P. Putnam's Sons, 2004. ISBN 0399240276. 58 p. Grades 3–6.

This is the story—and it is an amazing one—of the Roanoke colony as told by a fine writer who loves history.

Sir Walter Raleigh is the leading actor in the story. He had dreams of getting money from the colonies in the new land called America and of setting up those colonies himself. As long as Queen Elizabeth I was in charge of England, he was in good shape. He was one of her favorites, and she let him get away with a lot. (Except, of course, for the time he got married without her permission. She locked him and his new wife in prison. Elizabeth did not much like competition, but she let him out eventually.)

You can see in the fine map at the front of the book exactly when ships sailed to the colony on Roanoke Island. The trip that caused the biggest part of the mystery was the third voyage, the establishment of the first real colony on Roanoke Island, the one that took place in 1587. There were three ships with eighty-seven men, seventeen women, and eleven children on that voyage, and almost all of those people died or disappeared without leaving any real clues. We simply do not know what happened to them.

As the author says, "It is still hard for Americans to look at the country's history and see that hole right at the very beginning. And after more than four hundred years that hole is still there, although we are still looking much as we always have" (page 38).

There are lots of theories as to what happened. Maybe they went to live with the Native Americans. Maybe they were enslaved by them. Maybe they were massacred by them. Those are just three of the theories, and Fritz tells us several more. Read the book to find out about the colonists and to discover what archaeologists and historians are doing today to try to solve the mystery.

Vanished by **Judith Herbst.**

Herbst, Judith. *Vanished*. Lerner, 2005. ISBN 0822516314. 48 p. Grades 4–8.

People are fascinated when someone disappears without a trace. Vanishes. What happened? Where did the person go? How did he or she do it?

Judith Herbst tells us several fine stories about disappearances. She starts with Amelia Earhart, the daring female pilot who disappeared with her navigator, Fred Noonan, somewhere over the Pacific Ocean. Did she land on an island? Did she live for a long time? Or did she run out of gas and into the water, which most people think is much more likely? The Pacific Ocean is huge and incredibly easy to get lost in. What happened?

How about D. B. Cooper, who stole $200,000 after he hijacked a plane, and then, with four parachutes, jumped out of that plane over a wilderness area? Nine years later, an eight-year-old boy found $5,800 in a muddy packet near the place where Cooper jumped. Who was Cooper, and, more important, where was he?

And what about that Bermuda Triangle? Is it really almost a black hole where ships, planes, and people keep disappearing? And how about those three prisoners that actually escaped from Alcatraz Island—the island from which no one ever escaped? No one ever saw them again. Did they make it to San Francisco across the bay, or did they die in the icy waters before they ever got there?

These are intriguing stories. Read them and decide what *you* think.

***Fooled You! Fakes and Hoaxes through
the Years* by Elaine Pascoe.
Used by permission of Henry Holt & Co.**

Pascoe, Elaine. *Fooled You! Fakes and Hoaxes through the Years*. With illustrations by
   Laurie Keller. Henry Holt, 2005. ISBN 0805075281. 87 p. Grades 3–5.

Sometimes it is fun to fool people—and to be fooled. A hoax is when someone
fools a *lot* of people, deliberately, all at once. If that someone is never found out, people go on believing something that is not true.

This book tells us the true stories behind some famous attempts to fool people
throughout history. Maybe you have heard of some of them.

Would you like to see a real mermaid? Even if she was dead? Do you even believe
in mermaids? Well, you may have heard of Mr. P. T. Barnum. He had his own museum, and there he exhibited a mermaid. Well, it sort of looked like a mermaid—but
who could be sure? Had anyone ever seen a real one? How could you tell?

Would you like to see a photograph of a fairy? That is another thing people would
like to believe in. What if someone showed you actual photographs that they had taken
of a fairy? This was in 1917, when a lot of people did not understand how cameras actually worked. Read about the children who pulled off this hoax.

Just about everyone has heard of crop circles. Were they made by aliens? Did
aliens land in fields and make strange designs in them? How did it all work?

These are just a few of the fascinating stories told in this fun book.

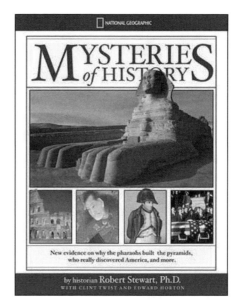

Mysteries of History **by Robert Stewart.**

Stewart, Robert, Ph.D., with Clint Twist and Edward Horton. *Mysteries of History.* National Geographic, 2003. ISBN 0792262328. 192 p. Grades 5–up.

One of the most exciting things about history is the information that we do *not* know. These mysteries drive historians (and many others) crazy. There are events that actually happened that we cannot explain, and learning whatever we can about them—and forming our own theories—is a great deal of fun.

This book, loaded with photographs and illustrations, tells us about a lot of historical mysteries, including the following:

- Why did the Pharaohs build the pyramids?
- Who built Stonehenge and why?
- Was there really a place called Troy, and did the Trojan War really happen?
- Did the Roman Empire really ever fall, or did it just sort of fade away?
- Did King Arthur really exist?
- Who *really* were the first to sail to North America? The Chinese?
- Who built the city of Great Zimbabwe?
- What really happened at Custer's Last Stand?
- What happened to the Roanoke Colony?

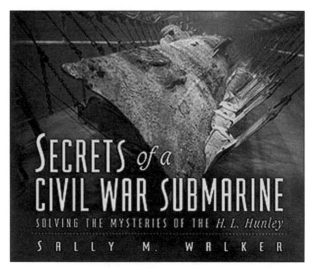

***Secrets of a Civil War Submarine: Solving
the Mysteries of the* H.L. Hunley
by Sally M. Walker.**

Walker, Sally M. *Secrets of a Civil War Submarine: Solving the Mysteries of the* H.L. Hunley. Carolrhoda Books, 2005. ISBN 1575058308. 112 p. Grades 4–up.

The *H.L. Hunley,* named after the man who paid for most of her construction, was the first submarine ever to sink a ship. It was an amazing first, and the story of the submarine is one of innovation, disaster, discovery, and unsolved mystery.

The Confederates needed her badly. Right in the middle of the Civil War, in 1863, the blockade the Union had created around their ports stopped ships from foreign countries, loaded with much-needed supplies, from getting through. The people in the south were hungry, and they needed all sorts of materials to live and to continue fighting successfully.

The Confederates had torpedoes, but they had no propellers. Most torpedoes just floated in the water. The hope was that an enemy ship would float too close, hit it, and blow up. This worked sometimes, but one problem was that any ship that got too close would blow up, including a Confederate ship. It was hoped that a submarine could carry a torpedo to a ship, sink that ship, and then return safely to shore. Parts of the plan worked, but the part about returning safely didn't work so well.

The *H.L. Hunley* was built in Mobile, Alabama, and brought to Charleston, South Carolina, an important port. Her designer, James McClintock, built a long, narrow submarine that was amazingly advanced for its time. It carried a crew of eight men, cramped tightly together—so tightly they could barely move. They sat in a row and turned the crankshaft to keep it moving. Show your audience the diagram on page 15.

Testing began immediately and did not go well. The ship could be maneuvered, but there were major problems from the first. On August 29, 1863, five crewmen died when the ship sunk. They brought it up and tinkered with it. On October 15, something went wrong and everyone on the *Hunley* died—including the man for whom it had been named. But they brought it up on October 18, and requisitioned ten slaves to clean out the ship, which must have been a horrifying job. By November 14, they were sure they had solved any problems, and they started practicing again. They got very good at it, and on February 17, they actually sank a Union ship, the USS

Housatonic—but then the submarine sank, this time for good, and even today no one is sure what happened except that all of the crew died.

This is an amazing story, made even more amazing by the fact that the *Hunley* was, like the *Titanic,* lost in the waters of the deep for a long, long time. It took more than 130 years for her to be found again. Not only do readers learn about the life and death of the ship, but also of the huge, expensive, fascinating rescue operation that was mounted to save and restore her, a restoration that is still in progress.

This is a wonderful read with an incredible combination of history and science.

Yolen, Jane, and Heidi Elisabet Yolen Stemple. *The Salem Witch Trials: An Unsolved Mystery from History.* Illustrated by Roger Roth. Simon & Schuster Books for Young Readers, 2004. ISBN 0689846207. Unpaged. Grades 3–5.

In the long, cold winter of 1692, a lot had been going on in the little Puritan village of Salem, Massachusetts. Everyone worked hard, and children had a lot of duties and work to do as well. Two girls who lived in the minister's house, his daughter and his niece, loved to hear the stories their father's slave Tituba told them.

It was a scary time. Relationships with the Native Americans had never been excellent, but now the natives were fighting back, attacking the settlers, and some people had been killed.

In February, both girls started having convulsions. They jerked around and shouted strange words. They hid behind chairs and acted scared to death. The doctor did not know what was the matter with them—but the girls eventually announced that three local women were witches and were bewitching them. One of the women they accused was Tituba. They started talking about seeing terrible, horrifying things, and Tituba confessed that she was, indeed, a witch. More girls claimed to be bewitched. The town went crazy. People were being arrested and thrown into jail and executed. Even a five-year-old girl was jailed, in chains. She confessed that she was a witch so she could stay with her mother, who was also accused.

One hundred forty-one people were arrested. The town had only a total population of 550. Nineteen people were hanged. Another man was pressed to death under a pile of rocks, and four people died in prison.

By the end of that year, it was all over, and this tells the story of how it ended. But the whole event remains a mystery to everyone alive today. How did all of those people go crazy?

There are a lot of theories, and the authors ask you, the reader, to think about them, and perhaps come up with one of your own.

NOT TO BE MISSED

Adams, Simon. *Titanic* (DK Eyewitness Books). DK, 1999. ISBN 078944724X. 60 p. Grades 4–8. *Gotcha Again.*

Browsing through this book is like eating peanuts. You can't put it down. Certainly, the sinking of the *Titanic* qualifies as one of the most famous disasters of all time, and almost one hundred years after the event it still commands our attention. This DK book is full of fine facts and photographs.

Armstrong, Jennifer. *Shipwreck at the Bottom of the World: The Extraordinary True Story of Shackleton and the* Endurance. Crown, 1998. ISBN 0517800144. 134 p. Grades 5–8. *Gotcha.*

Antarctica. 1914. Ernest Shackleton led an expedition to explore the area, and his ship, the *Endurance,* got stuck in ice, so stuck that the ice eventually crushed it. Although they were able to save a lot of supplies, they were stuck in the coldest place on Earth with not enough of anything. The crew needed help desperately—and in 1914, there was no way to communicate with the outside world in such a place. This is one of the most amazing true adventure stories of all time and is illustrated with magnificent photographs taken at that time.

Ballard, Robert D. *Exploring the* Titanic. Edited by Patrick Crean. Illustrated by Ken Marschall. A Scholastic/Madison Press Book, 1991. ISBN 0590442686. 64 p. Grades 4–7. *Gotcha.*

This is probably the best book about one of the most fascinating disasters of all time. The story of the sinking of the *Titanic* has it all—rich people, greedy people, death in icy waters, incompetence all over the place, inequality. And then the ship is lost for decades. Robert Ballard, the author of this book, lead the expedition that found the wreckage. Kids adore this book with its many wonderful photographs. Almost anyone who sees it wants to read it *right now*.

Ballard, Robert D. *Ghost Liners: Exploring the World's Greatest Lost Ships.* Little, Brown Young Readers 1998. ISBN 0316080209. 64 p. Grades 4–7. *Gotcha Again.*

Five twentieth-century ocean liners, the *Titanic,* the *Lusitania,* the *Empress of Ireland,* the *Britannic,* and the *Andrea Doria* sank in horrible disasters, and Ballard tells us about the ships and their fate. Illustrated with photographs and large paintings.

Ballard, Robert D. *The Lost Wreck of the* Isis. Archaeological and historical consultant Anna Marguerite McCann. A Scholastic/Madison Press Book, 1990. ISBN 0590438522. 64 p. Grades 3–7. *Gotcha.*

Ballard does it again in this interesting story of the discovery of a Roman merchant ship. No one really knows its name, but the *Isis* is what the discoverers decided to call it. The book is loaded with photographs and illustrations and makes guesses as to how the ship sank.

Bredeson, Carmen. *After the Last Dog Died: The True-Life, Hair-Raising Adventure of Douglas Mawson and His 1911–1914 Antarctic Expedition.* National Geographic, 2003. ISBN 0792261402. 64 p. Grades 4–8. *Gotcha Covered.*

Douglas Mawson was on a geological expedition to Antarctica when disaster struck, suddenly and unexpectedly. The story of his survival against almost impossible odds is accompanied by many fine photographs.

Calabro, Marian. *The Perilous Journey of the Donner Party.* Clarion Books, 1999. ISBN 0395866103. 192 p. Grades 5–8. *Gotcha Again.*

This ALA Notable Children's Book is the story of a westward journey, of bad decisions made whenever there was a possibility of doing so, and of ultimate disaster, when the traveling group was snowed in without food or decent shelter in the mountains. It even includes the gross, for the people who lived started eating the bodies of the people who died. This is compelling reading, but not a book for struggling readers.

Capuzzo, Michael. *Close to Shore: The Terrifying Shark Attacks of 1916.* Crown, 2003. ISBN 0375922318. 140 p. Grades 5–8. *Gotcha Covered.*

This page-turning thriller about a renegade shark who is starving and has somehow managed to find its way to the east coast of the United States is a surefire winner for good readers, or a fantastic read-aloud for a middle school audience. In 1916, there was a common belief that sharks did not eat human beings—so people weren't as afraid of them as we know now they should be.

Deem, James. *How to Hunt Buried Treasure.* Illustrated by True Kelley. Houghton Mifflin, 1992. ISBN 0395587999. 192 p. Grades 4–7. *Gotcha.*

The best place to look for buried treasure is the library. With this book in hand, readers already have a great start. Deem tells us what famous treasures remain undiscovered as well as step-by-step techniques for finding treasure.

Donkin, Andrew. *Atlantis: The Lost City?* DK, 2000. ISBN 0789466821. 49 p. Grades 3–5. *Gotcha Again.*

Everyone believes the ancient Greek philosopher Plato. So when he said that a magnificent city called Atlantis was destroyed in a horrible catastrophe, everyone started looking for the place where it had been—even though no one else in all of history ever said anything about it. It still drives people nuts, and this book is great for browsing about a riveting subject.

Donoughue, Carol. *The Mystery of the Hieroglyphs: The Story of the Rosetta Stone and the Race to Decipher Egyptian Hieroglyphs.* Oxford University Press, 1999. ISBN 0195215540. 48 p. Grades 5–9. *Gotcha Again.*

For centuries, no one could read any of the writing on paintings, art, and tombs from ancient Egypt. Everyone could tell that words were there, but no one could figure out what they meant. It took a major discovery and a lot of fantastic detective work to crack the code and start reading ancient Egyptian hieroglyphs. This is quite a tale.

Farman, John. *The Short and Bloody History of Highwaymen.* Lerner, 2000. ISBN 0822508400. 96 p. Grades 4–8. *Gotcha Covered.*

A common type of criminal in England in the 1700s was the highwayman. A lot of highwaymen were gentlemen who came from good families. But a good opportunity presented itself if you lost all your money or didn't inherit as much as you thought you would. You could become a person who robbed travelers on the highway—lone travelers as well as groups in coaches. There were not many roads, and there were not many travelers, so they could rob people and not worry too much about someone else stumbling in on the robbery. On the other hand, if they *were* caught, the future could be pretty grim. This is full of great and sometimes gory information.

Getz, David. *Purple Death: The Mysterious Flu of 1918.* Illustrations by Peter McCarty. Henry Holt, 2000. ISBN 080505751x. 86 p. Grades 4–8.

In World War I, 85 of every 100 American soldiers died not as a result of combat, but because they had gotten the influenza, sometimes called the swine flu or the

Spanish flu. They weren't alone. Scientists estimate that between twenty and forty *million* people died of that flu, and we still do not know what caused it—or whether it could happen again. This is a horrifying story of that pandemic, a disease that spreads very quickly and kills millions. Scientists are still trying to find out what it was.

Halley, Ned. *Disasters.* Kingfisher, 1999. ISBN 0753452219. 64 p. Grades 4–6. *Gotcha Again.*

Colorful illustrations depict many historical disasters, from the sinking of the *Titanic* to the nuclear disaster at Chernobyl, even including the grasshopper plague in Laura Ingalls Wilder's *On the Banks of Plum Creek.*

Holub, Joan. *How to Find Lost Treasure in All Fifty States and Canada Too!* Aladdin Paperbacks, 2000. ISBN 0689826435. 182 p. Grades 4–up. *Gotcha Again.*

It's just a small paperback, but it can tantalize readers for hours. Every state has some treasure supposedly lost there, and the author goes state by state and tells us what the story is behind that treasure. The best story of them all is the story of Oak Island in Nova Scotia.

Kent, Zachary. *The Mysterious Disappearance of Roanoke Colony in American History* (In American History). Enslow, 2004. ISBN 0766021475. 128 p. Grades 4–up. *Gotcha Covered.*

Going into the most detail of any of the Roanoke books, this one is for the serious researcher who has a lot of hard questions. An excellent look at the colony itself and the events surrounding its disappearance.

Leroe, Ellen. *Disaster! Three Real-Life Stories of Survival.* Hyperion Books for Children, 2000. ISBN 0786824743. 233 p. Grades 5–8. *Gotcha Again.*

Three little-known (at least to kids) disasters are highlighted in this account of the *Empress of Ireland*'s sinking in the Saint Lawrence Seaway, which killed 1,012 people, and two airship catastrophes.

Lourie, Peter. *Lost Treasure of the Inca.* Boyds Mills Press, 1999. ISBN 1563977435. 48 p. Grades 4–6. *Gotcha Again.*

Somewhere in the Llanganatis Mountains in Ecuador, the legends say, is at least 750 tons of gold treasure. When the Spaniards conquered the Incas, their king, Atahaualpa, bargained for his life, promising rooms full of gold in exchange for it. But the Spaniards killed him before it arrived, and it was hidden in the mountains. The author looked for it himself, and reproduces an old map to give readers an idea as to where to look.

Murphy, Jim. *An American Plague: The True and Terrifying Story of the Yellow Fever Epidemic of 1793.* Clarion Books, 2003. ISBN 0395776082. 165 p. Grades 4–8. *Gotcha Covered.*

This is a story told so well that it won the Sibert Medal for the best nonfiction book of the year. Most of us had never heard of the terrible epidemic that shut down both the city of Philadelphia and the government of the United States of America, but it happened, and this book is hard to put down. Good readers will enjoy this tale.

Murphy, Jim. *Blizzard: The Storm That Changed America.* Scholastic, 2000. ISBN 0590673092. 136 p. Grades 4–8. *Gotcha Again.*

The blizzard of 1888 was an unbelievably bad one. Temperatures hovered below zero and winds blew at seventy-five to eighty-five miles an hour. It blanketed the eastern seaboard of the United States, fueled by one storm blowing in from the west and another from the south. Many people died, and the government made changes to ensure that such a disaster would never happen again. This is a riveting story.

O'Brien, Patrick. *The* Hindenburg. Henry Holt, 2000. ISBN 080506415X Unpaged. Grades 2–4. *Gotcha Again.*

Until it caught on fire as it was landing in New Jersey, the *Hindenburg,* a German airship, looked as though it might be the future for aviation. People crossed the Atlantic in luxurious comfort, at a speed much faster than any ships could achieve. But its end was fiery and horrible. Good color illustrations help make this hard to put down.

Patent, Dorothy Hinshaw. *Lost City of Pompeii* (Frozen in Time). Benchmark Books, 2000. ISBN 0761407855. 64 p. Grades 4–8. *Gotcha Again.*

Amazingly, almost two thousand years after it occurred, we have an eyewitness account of the eruption of Mount Vesuvius and the destruction of the city of Pompeii. With that, and with the archaeological discoveries that have been made in the last three hundred years, we have a pretty good idea of what was like before the city was covered in lava and, also, what happened when it was destroyed. Good pictures flesh out the interesting text.

Patent, Dorothy Hinshaw. *Treasures of the Spanish Main* (Frozen in Time). Benchmark Books, 2000. ISBN 0761407863. 64 p. Grades 5–8. *Gotcha Again.*

In 1622, a Spanish ship laden heavily with treasure stolen from South America sank somewhere on the way home. No one knew exactly where, and every search effort was eventually abandoned. Then an American named Mel Fisher got interested, and he was sure he could find it. It took sixteen years, but he was right! Excellent photos show us some of the fabulous things he found.

Philbrick, Nathaniel. *The Revenge of the Whale: The True Story of the Whaleship Essex.* G. P. Putnam's Sons, 2002. ISBN 039923795x. Grades 4–up. 164 pages. *Gotcha Covered.*

By 1819, when the whaleship *Essex* headed out of Nantucket Island, whales were already getting scarce and hard to find. The ship headed out into a remote area in the Pacific Ocean, and there the ship ran into bad luck. An angry whale covered with scars rammed their ship and eventually sank it. The crew all survived, and they were able to prevent the ship from sinking and retrieve some provisions and navigation equipment in the first two days. But when it went down, they were left alone in the middle of the ocean in three small whaling boats. They were thousands of miles from land, and they were not very good at figuring out where they were. Would they starve to death or die of thirst? Would they have to eat each other? Would they ever find land? And, if they did, would they be eaten by cannibals?

This has a scholarly look to it, but its gruesome, thrilling story has huge appeal.

Preston, Diana. *Remember the* Lusitania! Walker, 2003. ISBN 0802788467. 95 p. Grades 4–8.

> On May 1, 1915, The German Imperial Embassy put an ad in the morning newspaper warning that Germany was at war with Britain and that British ships could be sunk. But the *Lusitania* was in New York, and a lot of Americans were on it. America was not yet in the war, and most people simply did not pay attention.
>
> They should have. A German U-boat hit the ship with a torpedo as it neared Ireland, and it was completely sunk in eighteen minutes. What happened was a true horror story. The people still alive were in agony. Some had been sucked into the smokestacks of the ship as it sank, and then were shot out like human cannonballs when the ship exploded. They were covered with soot and oil and some of them had their clothes ripped off. It's a gripping disaster well told.

Reid, Struan. *The Children's Atlas of Lost Treasures.* Millbrook Press, 1997. ISBN 0761302190. 96 p. Grades 5–8. *Gotcha.*

> Although some of the treasures have already been found, the locations of others remains a mystery. Reid discusses lost treasures all over the world, including the United States. Readers will want to start looking immediately.

Sandler, Martin W. *America's Great Disasters.* HarperCollins, 2003. ISBN 0060291079. 96 p. Grades 4–up. *Gotcha Covered.*

> If you were asked to name the most deadly American disasters of all, could you? What was the worst flood? Where was the worst earthquake? The most deadly disease? The worst hurricane and the worst blizzard? The worst fire? What shipwreck claimed the most lives? Most people's guesses would probably be wrong, because many of the worst disasters in our history are not as famous as others. This fills you in on the gory details.

Tanaka, Shelley. *Earthquake! A Day That Changed America: On a Peaceful Spring Morning, Disaster Strikes San Francisco.* Paintings by David Craig. Historical consultation by Gladys Hansen. Hyperion Books for Children, A Hyperion/Madison Press Book, 2004. ISBN 0786818824. 48 p. Grades 4–8. *Gotcha Covered.*

> San Francisco's earthquake was just the first of the horrors that struck the city in 1906. The breaking of the water mains, the fires that followed, and the impassable streets added to the catastrophe. Thousands of people were homeless without water or food. Lots of color illustrations add interest.

Vogel, Carole Garbuny. *Nature's Fury: Eyewitness Reports of Natural Disasters.* Scholastic, 2000. ISBN 0590115022. 121 p. Grades 5–8. *Gotcha Again.*

> Real people who have survived earthquakes, hurricanes, blizzards, tornadoes, fires, droughts, and floods tell their compelling stories.

Wood, Ted. *Ghosts of the West Coast: The Lost Souls of the* Queen Mary *and other Real-Life Hauntings.* Walker, 1999. ISBN 0802786685. 48 p. Grades 4–6. *Gotcha Again.*

> Spooky photographs illustrate this intriguing collection of (maybe?) real-life ghost stories from the West Coast of the United States. This delights ghosts aficionados.

Yolen, Jane, and Heidi Elisabet Yolen Stemple. *The Wolf Girls: An Unsolved Mystery from History.* Illustrated by Roger Roth. Simon & Schuster Books for Young Readers, 2001. ISBN 0689810806. Unpaged. Grades 2–5. *Gotcha Again.*

> In the early 1920s, a missionary in India claimed to find two girls abandoned in front of the door of his orphanage. He told a doctor that the girls had been raised in the jungle by wolves, and refused to wear clothing and growled and walked on all fours. The girls were in terrible health. So he said. But was he telling the truth? What really happened? Yolen, as always in this series, gives us several theories.

Yolen, Jane, and Heidi Elisabet Yolen Stemple. *The* Mary Celeste*: An Unsolved Mystery from History.* Illustrated by Roger Roth. Simon & Schuster Books for Young Readers, 1999. ISBN 0689810792. Unpaged. Grades 2–5. *Gotcha.*

> In 1872, the entire crew and all the passengers of an American ship, including the captain's family, disappeared. The ship kept floating on, in great shape, with supplies of food and water for six month. Nothing was a mess. There were no bodies. This mystery drives people crazy. People come up with unbelievable theories to explain the disappearance.

Yolen, Jane, and Heidi Elisabet Yolen Stemple. *Roanoke, the Lost Colony: An Unsolved Mystery from History.* Illustrated by Roger Roth. Simon & Schuster Books for Young Readers, 2003. ISBN 0689823215. Unpaged. Grades 3–5. *Gotcha Covered.*

> When the British founded Roanoke Colony in 1587, they had high hopes. In fact, the first British child born in North America was Virginia Dare, the granddaughter of the governor of he colony Edward White. But the colonials were not prepared for the difficulty of their new life, and White returned to England for more supplies—and was unable to return for three years. When he finally got back, the people he had left behind had all disappeared. More than four hundred years later, we still are mystified by what happened. Where did they go? Did they die? This has appealing illustrations and an unsolved mystery—a fine combination for amateur sleuths.

WORTH READING

Nonfiction books with "boy appeal" that have received positive reviews in *Booklist, Horn Book Guide,* and/or *School Library Journal.*

Ball, Jacqueline A. *Blizzard! The 1888 Whiteout* (X-treme Disasters That Changed America). Bearport, 2005. ISBN 1597160067. 32 p. Grades 2–4.

Ball, Jacqueline A. *Tornado! The 1974 Super Outbreak* (X-treme Disasters That Changed America). Bearport, 2005. ISBN 1597160791. 32 p. Grades 2–4.

Ball, Jacqueline A. *Wildfire! The 1871 Peshtigo Firestorm* (X-treme Disasters That Changed America). Bearport, 2005. ISBN 1597160113. 32 p. Grades 2–4.

Brunelle, Lynn. *Earthquake! The 1906 San Francisco Nightmare* (X-treme Disasters That Changed America). Bearport, 2005. ISBN 1597160083. 32 p. Grades 2–4.

1906 San Francisco Earthquake
by Tim Cooke.

Cooke, Tim. *1906 San Francisco Earthquake* (Disasters). Gareth Stevens, 2005. ISBN 0836844947. 32 p. Grades 5–8.

Deady, Kathleen W. *The* Hindenburg*: The Fiery Crash of a German Airship* (Disaster!). Capstone Press, 2002. ISBN 0736813217. 32 p. Grades 3–9.

Deady, Kathleen W. *The* Titanic*: The Tragedy at Sea* (Disaster!). Capstone Press, 2002. ISBN 0736813233. 32 p. Grades 3–9.

Dowswell, Paul. *Investigating Murder Mysteries* (Forensic Files). Heinemann Library, 2004. ISBN 1403448310. 48 p. Grades 4–8.

Dowswell, Paul. *The Chernobyl Disaster* (Days That Shook the World). Raintree, 2003. ISBN 0739860496. 48 p. Grades 4–8.

Myths and Monsters: Secrets Revealed
by Katie Edwards.

Edwards, Katie. *Myths and Monsters: Secrets Revealed.* Illustrated by Simon Mendez. Charlesbridge, 2004. ISBN 1570915814. 32 p. Grades 3–6.

Fahey, Kathleen. Challenger *and* Columbia (Disasters). Gareth Stevens, 2005. ISBN 0836844963. 32 p. Grades 5–8.

Fahey, Kathleen. Titanic (Disasters). Gareth Stevens, 2005. ISBN 0836844998. 32 p. Grades 5–8.

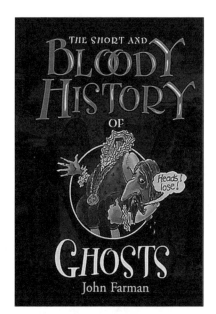

The Short and Bloody History of Ghosts
by John Farman.

Farman, John. *The Short and Bloody History of Ghosts*. Lerner, 2002. ISBN 0822508370. 96 p. Grades 4–8.

Green, Jen. *1993 Mississippi River Floods* (Disasters). Gareth Stevens, 2005. ISBN 0836844955. 32 p. Grades 5–8.

Green, Jen. *Hurricane Andrew* (Disasters). Gareth Stevens, 2005. ISBN 0836844971. 32 p. Grades 5–8.

Green, Jen. *Mount St. Helens* (Disasters). Gareth Stevens, 2005. ISBN 083684498x. 32 p. Grades 5–8.

***Spooky Riddles* by Marilyn Helmer.**

Helmer, Marilyn. *Spooky Riddles* (Kids Can Read). Illustrated by Eric Parker. Kids Can Press, 2003. ISBN 1553374479. 32 p. Grades K–3.

Higgins, Christopher. *Nuclear Submarine Disasters* (Great Disasters: Reforms and Ramifications). Chelsea House, 2001. ISBN 0791063291. 120 p. Grades 5–up.

Ingram, Scott. *Tsunami! The 1946 Hilo Wave of Terror* (X-treme Disasters That Changed America). Bearport, 2005. ISBN 1597160105. 32 p. Grades 2–4.

Krull, Kathleen. *What Really Happened in Roswell? Just the Facts (Plus the Rumors) about UFOs and Aliens.* Illustrated by Christopher Santoro. HarperTrophy, 2003. ISBN 0688172490. 54 p. Grades 4–7.

Latham, Donna. *Hurricane! The 1900 Galveston Night of Terror* (X-treme Disasters That Changed America). Bearport, 2005. ISBN 1597160717. 32 p. Grades 2–4.

Levey, Richard. *Dust Bowl! The 1930s Black Blizzards* (X-treme Disasters That Changed America). Bearport, 2005. ISBN 1597160075. 32 p. Grades 2–4.

Matsen, Brad. *The Incredible Quest to Find the* Titanic (Incredible Deep-Sea Adventures). Enslow, 2003. ISBN 0766021912. 48 p. Grades 3–6.

Matsen, Brad. The *Incredible Search for the Treasure Ship* Atocha (Incredible Deep-Sea Adventures). Enslow, 2003. ISBN 0766021939. 48 p. Grades 3–6.

Meltzer, Milton. *Case Closed: The Real Scoop on Detective Work.* Scholastic/Orchard, 2001. ISBN 0439293154. 88 p. Grades 5–9.

Nicolson, Cynthia Pratt. *Hurricane!* (Disaster). Kids Can Press, 2002. ISBN 1550749064. 32 p. Grades 3–6.

Nicolson, Cynthia. *Tornado!* (Disaster). Kids Can Press, 2003. ISBN 155074951x. 32 p. Grades 3–6.

Simon, Seymour. *Danger! Earthquakes* (See More Reader). North-South/Sea Star, 2002. ISBN 1587171392. 32 p. Grades K–3.

Simon, Seymour. *Super Storms* (See More Reader). North-South/Sea Star, 2002. ISBN 1587171376. 32 p. Grades K–3.

Streissguth, Tom. *The* Challenger: *The Explosion on Liftoff* (Disaster). Capstone Press, 2002. ISBN 0736813225. 32 p. Grades 3–9.

Vogt, Gregory L. *Disasters in Space Exploration.* Millbrook Press, 2003. ISBN 0761328955. 80 p. Grades 4–8.

White, Matt. *Storm Chasers: On the Trail of Deadly Tornadoes* (High Five Reading). Capstone Press, 2003. ISBN 0736895523. 48 p. Grades 3–9.

Woolf, Alex. *Investigating Fakes and Hoaxes* (Forensic Files). Heinemann Library, 2004. ISBN 1403448299. 48 p. Grades 4–8.

Woolf, Alex. *Investigating History Mysteries* (Forensic Files). Heinemann Library, 2004 ISBN 1403448302. 48 p. Grades 4–8.

Woolf, Alex. *Investigating Thefts and Heists* (Forensic Files) Heinemann Library, 2004. ISBN 1403448337. 48 p. Grades 4–8.

Chapter ——10

Hot Topics: Magic, Riddles, Games, and Puzzles, Art and Drawing, Fascinating Facts and Reference Books

MAGIC

The Book of Wizard Magic: In Which the Apprentice Finds Marvelous Magic Tricks, Mystifying Illusions and Astonishing Tales. Lark, 2003. ISBN 1579903452. 144 p. Grades 3–8.

Bull, Jane. *The Magic Book.* DK, 2002. ISBN 0789485354. 48 p. Grades 1–4.

Eldin, Peter. *Mind Tricks* (I Want to Do Magic). Millbrook/Copper Beech, 2002. ISBN 0761328246. 32 p. Grades 4–8.

Eldin, Peter. *Science Magic* (I Want to Do Magic). Millbrook/Copper Beech, 2002. ISBN 0761328505. 32 p. Grades 4–8.

Eldin, Peter. *Magic with Cards* (I Want to Do Magic). Millbrook/Copper Beech, 2002. ISBN 0761327541. 32 p. Grades 4–8.

Eldin, Peter. *Simple Magic* (I Want to Do Magic). Millbrook/Copper Beech, 2002. ISBN 0761327533. 32 p. Grades 4–8.

Ho, Oliver. *Card Tricks* (Young Magicians). Illustrated by Dave Garbot. Sterling, 2003. ISBN 1402700458. 48 p. Grades 1–4.

Ho, Oliver. *Magic Tricks* (Young Magicians). Illustrated by Dave Garbot. Sterling, 2003. ISBN 1402700466. 48 p. Grades 1–4.

Lakin, Patricia. *Harry Houdini: Escape Artist* (Ready-to-Read). Illustrated by Rick Geary. Simon/Aladdin, 2002. ISBN 0689853459. 32 p. Grades K–3.

RIDDLES, GAMES, AND PUZZLES

Agee, Jon. *Elvis Lives and Other Anagrams.* Collected and illustrated by Jon Agee. Farrar, Straus & Giroux, 2000. ISBN 0374321272. Unpaged. Grades 4–up. *Gotcha Again.*

Agee, Jon. *Palindromania.* Farrar, Straus & Giroux, 2002. ISBN 0374357307. 112 p. Grades 3–up.

Agee, Jon. *Sit on a Potato Pan, Otis! More Palindromes.* Farrar, Straus & Giroux, 1999. ISBN 0374318085. Unpaged. Grades 4–up. *Gotcha Again.*

Agee, Jon. *Smart Feller Fart Smeller and Other Spoonerisms.* Michael di Capua Books/Hyperion Books, 2006. ISBN 078683692X. Unpaged. Grades 4–up.

Agee, Jon. *Who Ordered the Jumbo Shrimp? And Other Oxymorons.* Michael Di Capua Books, HarperCollins, 1998. ISBN 0062051598. 80 p. Grades 4–up. *Gotcha Again.*

Ball, Johnny. *Go Figure! A Totally Cool Book about Numbers.* DK, 2005. ISBN 0756613744. 96 p. Grades 4–up.

Brewer, Paul. *You Must Be Joking! Lots of Cool Jokes.* Cricket, 2003. ISBN 0812626613. 107 p. Grades 3–7.

Cole, Joanna. *Crazy Eights: And Other Card Games.* Illustrated by Alan Tiegren. North-South/Sea Star, 2002. ISBN 0786276541. 76 p. Grades 3–6.

Ghigna, Charles. *Riddle Rhymes.* Illustrated by Julia Gorton. Hyperion Books for Children, 1995. ISBN 1562824791. Unpaged. Grades K–2. *Gotcha Again.*

Grambs, Alison. *Totally Silly Jokes.* Illustrated by Rob Collinet. Sterling, 2003. ISBN 1402703643. 96 p. Grades 1–4.

Gunter, Veronika Alice. *The Ultimate Indoor Games Book: The 200 Best Boredom Busters Ever!* Illustrated by Clay Meyer. Sterling/Lark, 2005. ISBN 1579906257. 128 p. Grades 3–5.

Helmer, Marilyn. *Yummy Riddles* (Kids Can Read). Illustrated by Eric Parker. Kids Can Press, 2003. ISBN 1553374460. 32 p. Grades K–3.

Horsfall, Jacqueline. *Funny Riddles* (Giggle Fit). Illustrated by Steve Harpster. Sterling, 2003. ISBN 1402708645. 48 p. Grades K–3.

Horsfall, Jacqueline. *Kid's Silliest Riddles.* Illustrated by Buck Jones. Sterling, 2003. ISBN 1402700059. 48 p. Grades 2–5.

Janeczko, Paul B. *Top Secret: A Handbook of Codes, Ciphers, and Secret Writing.* Illustrated by Jenna LaReau. Candlewick Press, 2004. ISBN 0763609714. 136 pages. Grades 4–8. *Gotcha Covered.*

Jones, Charlotte Foltz. *Eat Your Words: A Fascinating Look at the Language of Food.* Illustrated by John O'Brien. Delacorte Press, 1999. ISBN 0385325754. 87 p. Grades 4–6. *Gotcha Again.*

Keller, Charles. *Super Knock-Knocks* (Giggle Fit). Illustrated by Steve Harpster. Sterling, 2003. ISBN 1402708637. 48 p. Grades K–3.

***Games: Learn to Play, Play to Win*
by Daniel King.**

King, Daniel. *Games: Learn to Play, Play to Win.* Kingfisher, 2003. ISBN 0753455811. 64 p. Grades 4–9.

Lewis, J. Patrick. *Riddle-lightful: Oodles of Little Riddle Poems.* Illustrated by Debbie Tilley. Knopf, 1998. ISBN 0679887601. Unpaged. Grades 1–5. *Gotcha Again.*

Lupton, Hugh, Reteller. *Riddle Me This! Riddles and Stories to Challenge Your Mind.* Barefoot, 2003. ISBN 1841481696. 64 p. Grades K–3.

Marzollo, Jean. *I Spy Ultimate Challenger! A Book of Picture Riddles.* Photographs by Walter Wick. Scholastic/Cartwheel, 2003. ISBN 0439454018. 40 p. Grades K–3.

Mignon, Phillippe. *Labyrinths: Can You Escape from the Twenty-Six Letters of the Alphabet?* Firefly, 2002. ISBN 1552975592. 60 p. Grades 4–up.

Munro, Roxie. *Amazement Park.* Chronicle, 2005. ISBN 0811845818. 40 p. Grades 4–6.

Rissinger, Matt, and Philip Yates. *Wacky Jokes* (Giggle Fit). Illustrated by Steve Harpster. Sterling, 2003. ISBN 1402708629. 48 p. Grades K–3.

Rosenbloom, Joseph. *School Jokes* (Giggle Fit). Illustrated by Steve Harpster. Sterling, 2003. ISBN 1402704402. 48 p. Grades K–3.

Rosenbloom, Joseph. *Spooky Jokes* (Giggle Fit). Illustrated by Steve Harpster. Sterling, 2003. ISBN 1402704399. 48 p. Grades K–3.

Rosenbloom, Joseph, and Mike Artell. *Zany Tongue-Twisters* (Giggle Fit). Illustrated by Steve Harpster. Sterling, 2003. ISBN 1402708653. 48 p. Grades K–3.

Seckel, Al. *The Great Book of Optical Illusions.* Firefly Books, 2001. ISBN 1552976505. 304 p. Grades 4–up.

Slocum, Jerry, and Jack Botermans. *Tricky Optical Illusion Puzzles.* Sterling, 2002. ISBN 0806975679. 96 p. Grades 4–up.

Steig, William. *CDC?* Farrar, Straus & Giroux, 1984, 2003. ISBN 0374312338. 58 p. Grades 4–up. *Gotcha Covered.*

***Eye Guess: A Foldout Guessing Game*
by Phyllis Limbacher Tildes.**

Tildes, Phyllis Limbacher. *Eye Guess: A Foldout Guessing Game.* Charlesbridge, 2005. ISBN 1570916500. 36 p. Grades K–2.

Vecchione, Glen. *Sidewalk Games.* Illustrated by Blanche Sims. Sterling, 2003. ISBN 1402702892. 80 p. Grades K–4.

Wick, Walter. *Can You See What I See? Dream Machine: A Picture Adventure to Search and Solve.* Scholastic, 2003. ISBN 0439399505. 36 p. Grades K–3.

Wick, Walter. *Can You See What I See? Picture Puzzles to Search and Solve.* Scholastic/Cartwheel, 2002. ISBN 0439163919. 40 p. Grades K–3.

ART AND DRAWING

Bidner, Jenni. *The Kids' Guide to Digital Photography: How to Shoot, Save, Play with and Print Your Digital Photos.* Lark, 2004. ISBN 1579906044. 96 p. Grades 5–up.

Buckingham, Alan. *Photography* (Eyewitness Books). DK, 2004. ISBN 0756605431. 72 p. Grades 4–8.

De Rosamel, Godeleine. *Drawing with Circles* (Drawing Is Easy). Gareth Stevens, 2003. ISBN 0836836251. 24 p. Grades K–3.

De Rosamel, Godeleine. *Drawing with Nature* (Drawing Is Easy). Gareth Stevens, 2003. ISBN 083683626x. 24 p. Grades K–3.

De Rosamel, Godeleine. *Drawing with Objects* (Drawing Is Easy). Gareth Stevens, 2003. ISBN 0836836278. 24 p. Grades K–3.

Drawing with Your Fingerprints
by Godeleine De Rosamel.

De Rosamel, Godeleine. *Drawing with Your Fingerprints* (Drawing Is Easy). Gareth Stevens, 2003. ISBN 0836836286. 24 p. Grades K–3.

De Rosamel, Godeleine. *Drawing with Your Hands* (Drawing Is Easy). Gareth Stevens, 2003. ISBN 0836836294. 24 p. Grades K–3.

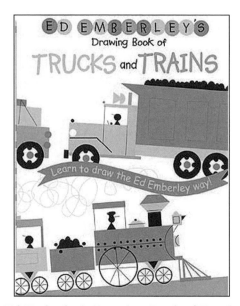

Ed Emberley's Drawing Book of Trucks
and Trains by Ed Emberley.

Emberley, Ed. *Ed Emberley's Drawing Book of Trucks and Trains*. Little, Brown, 2005. ISBN 0316789674. 32 p. Grades K–3.

**Ed Emberley's Drawing Book of Weirdos
by Ed Emberley.**

Emberley, Ed. *Ed Emberley's Drawing Book of Weirdos*. Little, Brown, 2002. ISBN 0316235466. 32 p. Grades K–3.

Lawrence, Colton. *Big Fat Paycheck: A Young Person's Guide to Writing for the Movies*. Bantam, 2004. ISBN 0553131222. 273 p. Grades 7-up.

**Ralph Masiello's Bug Drawing Book
by Ralph Masiello.**

Masiello, Ralph. *Ralph Masiello's Bug Drawing Book*. Charlesbridge, 2004. ISBN 1570915253. 32 p. Grades K–3.

Nguyen, Duy. *Creepy Crawly Animal Origami*. Sterling, 2003. ISBN 0806990120. 96 p. Grades 4–up.

Nguyen, Duy. *Origami Myths*. Sterling, 2005. ISBN 1402715501. 96 p. Grades 4–6.

Nguyen, Duy. *Under the Sea Origami*. Sterling, 2005. ISBN 1402715412. 96 p. Grades 4–6.

Robinson, Nick. *Making Paper Airplanes That Really Fly*. Sterling, 2005. ISBN 1402716303. 80 p. Grades 4–6.

Schmidt, Norman. *Great Paper Fighter Planes*. Sterling, 2004. ISBN 1895569842. 96 p. Grades 4–6.

Schmidt, Norman. *Incredible Paper Flying Machines*. Sterling, 2002. ISBN 1895569370. 96 p. Grades 4–8.

FASCINATING FACTS AND REFERENCE BOOKS

Many of these are updated regularly, so you may want to check for the most current edition.

Ash, Russell. *The Top Ten of Everything*. DK, 2005. ISBN 0756613221. 256 p. Grades 5–up. Revised and updated every year.

Bathroom Readers' Institute. *Uncle John's Bathroom Reader for Kids Only*. Bathroom Reader's Press, 2002. ISBN 1571458670. 288 p. Grades 4–8.

Bathroom Readers' Institute. *Uncle John's Top Secret Bathroom Reader for Kids Only*. Bathroom Reader's Press, 2004. ISBN 1592232310. 288 p. Grades 4–8.

Bobick, James E., and Natalie E. Balaban. *Handy Science Answer Book*. Visible Ink, 2002. ISBN 1578591406. 660 p. Grades 5–up.

Brown, Gerry, and Michael Morrison. *ESPN Information Please Sports Almanac 2006: The Definitive Sports Reference Book*. ESPN Books, 2005. ISBN 1933060042. 960 p. Grades 5–up. Revised every year.

Buckley, James E., Jr. *Scholastic Book of Firsts*. Scholastic, 2005. ISBN 043967607X. 320 p. Grades 3–7.

Choron, Sandra, and Harry Choron. *The Book of Lists for Teens*. Houghton Mifflin, 2002. ISBN 0618179070. 322 p. Grades 7–9.

Choron, Sandra, and Harry Choron. *The All-New Book of Lists for Kids*. Houghton Mifflin, 2002. ISBN 0618191356. 416 p. Grades 4–6.

Fulghum, Hunter S. *Don't Try This at Home: How to Win a Sumo Match, Catch a Great White Shark, Start an Independent Nation, and Other Extraordinary Feats for Ordinary People*. Broadway Books, 2002. ISBN 0767911598. 264 p. Grades 7 and up.

Guinness World Records 2006. Guinness, 2005. 288 p. Grades 5–up. Revised and updated every year.

Hare, Tony. *Animal Fact File: Head-to-Head Profiles of More than 90 Mammals.* Checkmark, 1999. ISBN 0816040168. 192 p. Grades 4–7.

Mooney, Julie, and the Editors of Ripley's Believe It or Not! *The Ripley's Believe It or Not! Encyclopedia of the Bizarre* (Ripley's Believe It or Not!). Black Dog & Leventhal, 2002. ISBN 1579122167. 320 p. Grades 5–8.

Mooney, Julie, and the Editors of Ripley's Believe It or Not! *The World of Ripley's Believe It or Not!* Black Dog & Leventhal, 1999. ISBN 1579120881. 159 p. Grades 5–8.

Morse, Jennifer Carr. *Scholastic Book of World Records, 2006.* Scholastic, 2005. ISBN 0439755182. 320 p. Grades 4–6. Revised and updated every year.

Parsons, Jayne. *Encyclopedia of the Human Body.* DK, 2002. ISBN 0789486725. 304 p. Grades 4–up.

Ripley's Believe It or Not! Special Edition 2006. Scholastic, 2005. ISBN 0439718309. 144 p. Grades 4–7. Revised and updated every year.

Robson, Graham. *The Illustrated Directory of Sports Cars.* Motorbooks, 2003. ISBN 0760314209. 480 p. Grades 5–up.

Scholastic Atlas of the World. Scholastic, 2003. ISBN 043952797X. 224 p. Grades 4–6.

The World Almanac and Book of Facts, 2006. World Almanac, 2005. ISBN 0886879647. 1,008 p. Grades 5–up. Revised and updated every year.

The World Almanac for Kids, 2006. World Almanac, 2005. ISBN 0886879604. 336 p. Grades 4–6. Revised and updated every year.

Visual Encyclopedia of Animals. DK, 2001. ISBN 0756607019. 526 p. Grades 4–7.

Znamierowski, Alfred. *The World Encyclopedia of Flags.* Lorenz, 2005. ISBN 0754814432. 256 p. Grades 5–up.

Acknowledgments

Chapter 1

Cover from *What If You Met a Pirate?* by Jan Adkins. Roaring Brook Press, 2004. Reprinted with permission.

Cover from *Pirates & Smugglers* by Moira Butterfield, 2005 © Kingfisher Publications.

Cover from *How to Be a Medieval Knight* by Fiona MacDonald. National Geographic, 2005. Reprinted with permission of the National Geographic Society.

Cover from *Remember World War II: Kids Who Survived Tell Their Stories* by Dorinda Makanaonalani Nicholson. National Geographic Society Children's Books, 2005. Reprinted with permission of the National Geographic Society.

Cover from *Adolf Hitler: Evil Mastermind of the Holocaust* by Linda Jacobs Altman. Enslow Publishers, Inc., 2005. Reprinted with permission.

Cover from *The D-Day Landings* by Sean Connolly. Heinemann Library, 2003. Reprinted with permission.

Cover from *The Colosseum* by Leslie DuTemple. Lerner, 2003. All covers are reprinted with the permission of Lerner Publications Company, a division of Lerner Publishing Group. All rights reserved. No part of the covers may be used or reproduced in any manner whatsoever without the prior written permission of Lerner Publications Company.

Cover from *Spies* by Clive Gifford. 2004 © Kingfisher Publications.

Cover from *Ancient Greek War and Weapons* by Haydn Middleton. Heinemann Library, 2002. Reprinted with permission.

Cover from *Pirates and Privateers of the High Seas* by Laura Lee Wren. Enslow Publishers, Inc., 2003. Reprinted with permission.

Chapter 2

Cover from *Freedom Riders: John Lewis and Jim Zwerg on the Front Lines of the Civil Rights Movement* by Ann Bausum. National Geographic, 2006. Reprinted with permission of the National Geographic Society.

Cover from *Kid Blink Beats* The World by Don Brown. Roaring Brook Press, 2004. Reprinted with permission.

The Battle of the Alamo © 2005 by Capstone Press. All rights reserved.

Cover from *Let It Begin Here! Lexington & Concord: First Battles of the American Revolution* by Dennis Brindell Fradin. Walker & Company, 2005. Reprinted with permission of Walker & Company.

Cover from *The Remarkable Benjamin Franklin* by Cheryl Harness. National Geographic, 2005. Reprinted with permission of the National Geographic Society.

Cover from *Onward: A Photobiography of African-American Polar Explorer Matthew Henson* by Dolores Johnson. National Geographic, 2006. Reprinted with permission of the National Geographic Society.

Cover from *Counting Coup: Becoming a Crow Chief on the Reservation and Beyond* by Joseph Medicine Crow with Herman J. Viola. National Geographic, 2006. Reprinted with permission of the National Geographic Society.

Cover from *The Journey of the One and Only Declaration of Independence* by Judith St. George. Philomel Books, 2005. Reprinted with permission.

Cover from *You're on Your Way, Teddy Roosevelt!* by Judith St. George. Philomel Books, 2004. Reprinted with permission.

Cover from *Read about Crazy Horse* by Stephen Feinstein. Enslow Publishers, Inc., 2005. Reprinted with permission.

Cover from *Wyatt Earp: Wild West Lawman* by Elaine Landau. Enslow Publishers, Inc., 2004. Reprinted with permission.

Cover from *True Tales of the Wild West* by Paul Walker. National Geographic Children's Books, 2002. Reprinted with permission of the National Geographic Society.

Chapter 3

Cover from *Boy, Were We Wrong about Dinosaurs* by Kathleen Kudlinski. Dutton Children's Books, 2005. Reprinted with permission.

Cover from *How Dinosaurs Took Flight: The Fossils, the Science, What We Think We Know, and the Mysteries Yet Unsolved* by Christopher Sloan. National Geographic, 2005. Reprinted with permission of the National Geographic Society.

Cover from *Feathered Dinosaurs of China* by Gregory Wenzel. Charlesbridge, 2004. Used with permission by Charlesbridge Publishing, Inc.

Cover from *Mammoths: Ice-Age Giants* by Larry D. Agenbroad. Lerner, 2002. All covers are reprinted with the permission of Lerner Publications Company, a division of Lerner Publishing Group. All rights reserved. No part of the covers may be used or reproduced in any manner whatsoever without the prior written permission of Lerner Publications Company.

Cover from *Pteranodon: The Life Story of a Pterosaur* by Ruth Ashby © 2005 Abrams Books for Young Readers.

Cover from *Dinosaur Discoveries* by Gail Gibbons. Holiday House, 2005. Reprinted with permission.

Cover from *Flying Giants of Dinosaur Time* by Don Lessem. Lerner Publishing Group, 2005. All covers are reprinted with the permission of Lerner Publications Company, a division of Lerner Publishing Group. All rights reserved. No part of the covers may be used or reproduced in any manner whatsoever without the prior written permission of Lerner Publications Company.

Cover from *Triceratops: Mighty Three-Horned Dinosaur* by Michael W. Skrepnick. Enslow Publishers, Inc., 2005. Reprinted with permission.

Cover from *National Geographic Prehistoric Mammals* by Alan Turner. National Geographic Children's Books, 2004. Reprinted with permission of the National Geographic Society.

Cover from *Little Book of Dinosaurs* by Cherie Winner. Two-Can Publishing, 2005. Reprinted with permission.

Chapter 4

Cover from *Fireworks* by Vicki Cobb. Millbrook Press, 2006. All covers are reprinted with the permission of Lerner Publications Company, a division of Lerner Publishing Group. All rights reserved. No part of the covers may be used or reproduced in any manner whatsoever without the prior written permission of Lerner Publications Company.

Cover from *Genius: A Photobiography of Albert Einstein* by Marfé Ferguson Delano. National Geographic, 2005. Reprinted with permission of the National Geographic Society.

Cover from *Guinea Pig Scientists: Bold Self-Experimenters in Science and Medicine* by Leslie Dendy and Mel Boring. Henry Holt and Company, 2005. Used by permission of Henry Holt & Co.

Cover from *Investigating Murders* by Paul Dowswell. Heinemann Library, 2004. Reprinted with permission.

Cover from *Home on the Moon: Living on the Space Frontier* by Marianne J. Dyson. National Geographic, 2003. Reprinted with permission of the National Geographic Society.

Cover from *In Your Face: The Facts about Your Features* by Donna M. Jackson. Viking, 2004. Reprinted with permission.

Cover from *Leonardo da Vinci* by Kathleen Krull. Viking, 2005. Reprinted with permission.

Cover from *Science Verse* by Jon Scieszka. Viking, 2004. Reprinted with permission.

Cover from *The Amazing International Space Station* by YES Magazine used by permission of Kids Can Press Ltd., Toronto, Canada. Cover photo courtesy of NASA.

Cover from *Tornadoes: Disaster and Survival* by Bonnie Ceban. Enslow Publishers, Inc., 2005. Reprinted with permission.

Cover from *Robotics* by Helena Domaine. Lerner Publishing Group, 2005. All covers are reprinted with the permission of Lerner Publications Company, a division of Lerner Publishing Group. All rights reserved. No part of the covers may be used or reproduced in any manner whatsoever without the prior written permission of Lerner Publications Company.

Cover from *Electricity and Magnetism Science Fair Projects: Using Batteries, Balloons, and Other Hair-Raising Stuff* by Robert Gardner. Enslow Publishers, Inc., 2004. Reprinted with permission.

Cover from *Forces of Nature: The Awesome Power of Volcanoes, Earthquakes, and Tornadoes* by Catherine Grace. National Geographic Children's Books, 2005. Reprinted with permission of the National Geographic Society.

Cover from *Robots Slither* by Ryan Ann Hunter. G. P. Putnam's Sons, 2004. Reprinted with permission.

Cover from *Planet Patrol* by Marybeth Lorbiecki. Two-Can Publishing, 2005. Reprinted with permission.

Cover from *An Extreme Dive under the Antarctic Ice* by Brad Matsen. Enslow Publishers, Inc., 2003. Reprinted with permission.

Cover from *Zzz...: The Most Interesting Book You'll Ever Read about Sleep* by Trudee Romanek and illustrated by Rose Cowles used by permission of Kids Can Press Ltd., Toronto, Canada. Cover © 2002 by Rose Cowles.

Cover from *Junk Lab* by Michael Elsohn Ross. Carolrhoda Books, 2002. All covers are reprinted with the permission of Lerner Publications Company, a division of Lerner Publishing Group. All rights reserved. No part of the covers may be used or reproduced in any manner whatsoever without the prior written permission of Lerner Publications Company.

Cover from *Why Does My Body Smell? And Other Questions about Hygiene* by Angela Royston. Heinemann Library, 2002. Reprinted with permission.

Cover from *Microscopic Life* by Richard Walker. 2004 © Kingfisher Publications.

Avalanches © 2003 by Capstone Press. All rights reserved.

Chapter 5

Cover from *Curse of the Pharaohs: My Adventures with the Mummies* by Zahi Hawass. National Geographic, 2004. Reprinted with permission of the National Geographic Society.

Cover from *Tutankahmun: The Mystery of the Boy King* by Zahi Hawass. National Geographic, 2005. Reprinted with permission of the National Geographic Society.

Cover from *Outside and Inside Mummies* by Sandra Markle. Walker & Company, 2005. Reprinted with permission of Walker & Company.

Cover from *Achoo! The Most Interesting Book You'll Ever Read about Germs* by Trudee Romanek and illustrated by Rose Cowles used by permission of Kids Can Press Ltd., Toronto, Canada. Cover © 2003 by Rose Cowles.

Cover from *What's Living in Your Bedroom?* by Andrew Solway. Heinemann Library, 2004. Reprinted with permission.

Bog Mummies: Preserved in Peat © 2002 by Capstone Press. All rights reserved.

Cover from *What's Living inside Your Body?* by Andrew Solway. Heinemann Library, 2004. Reprinted with permission.

Chapter 6

Cover from *A Platypus, Probably* by Sneed B. Collard III. Charlesbridge, 2005. Used with permission by Charlesbridge Publishing, Inc.

Cover from *Rickie and Henri: A True Story* by Jane Goodall. Putnam Young Readers Group, 2004. Reprinted with permission.

Cover from *The Best Book of Wolves and Wild Dogs* by Christiane Gunzi. 2003 © Kingfisher Publications.

Cover from *Great White Sharks* by Sandra Markle. Lerner Publishing Group, 2004. All covers are reprinted with the permission of Lerner Publications Company, a division of Lerner Publishing Group. All rights reserved. No part of the covers may be used or reproduced in any manner whatsoever without the prior written permission of Lerner Publications Company.

Cover from *Hyenas* by Sandra Markle. Lerner Publications Company, 2005. All covers are reprinted with the permission of Lerner Publications Company, a division of Lerner Publishing Group. All rights reserved. No part of the covers may be used or reproduced in any manner whatsoever without the prior written permission of Lerner Publications Company.

Cover from *Killer Fish* by Andrew Solway. Heinemann Library, 2004. Reprinted with permission.

Cover from *Exploring the Deep, Dark Sea* by Gail Gibbons. Little, Brown and Company, 1999. Reprinted with permission.

Cover from *Grey Wolf* by Jill Bailey. Heinemann Library, 2005. Reprinted with permission.

Cover from *Hermit Crabs* by Tristan Boyer Binns.

Cover from *Untamed: Animals around the World* by Steve Bloom © 2005 Abrams Books for Young Readers.

Cover from *Little Gorillas* by Bernadette Costa-Prades. Gareth Stevens, Inc., 2005. Reprinted with permission.

Cover from *Critter Riddles* by Marilyn Helmer and illustrated by Eric Parker. used by permission of Kids Can Press Ltd., Toronto, Canada. Cover © 2003 by Eric Parker.

Cover from *Powerful Predators* by Tim Knight.

Cover from *Gross and Gory* by Elizabeth Laskey. Heinemann Library, 2004. Reprinted with permission.

Cover from *Vultures* by Wayne Lynch. NorthWord Books for Young Readers, 2005. Reprinted with permission.

Cover from *Sea Creatures* by Tiffany Peterson. Heinemann Library, 2003. Reprinted with permission.

Cover from *Caribou* by Susan E. Quinlan. Carolrhoda Books, 2004. All covers are reprinted with the permission of Lerner Publications Company, a division of Lerner Publishing Group. All rights reserved. No part of the covers may be used or reproduced in any manner whatsoever without the prior written permission of Lerner Publications Company.

Cover from *Killer Carnivores* by Andrew Solway. Heinemann Library, 2005. Reprinted with permission.

Cover from *Gray Wolves* by Lynn M. Stone. Lerner Publishing Group, 2003. All covers are reprinted with the permission of Lerner Publications Company, a division of Lerner Publishing Group. All rights reserved. No part of the covers may be used or reproduced in any manner whatsoever without the prior written permission of Lerner Publications Company.

Cover from *Asian Elephant* by Matt Turner. Heinemann Library, 2005. Reprinted with permission.

Cover from *Wild Horses* by Julia Vogel. NorthWord Books for Young Readers, 2004. Reprinted with permission.

Cover from *Seahorses* by Sally M. Walker. Lerner Publishing Group, 2003. All covers are reprinted with the permission of Lerner Publications Company, a division of Lerner Publishing Group. All rights reserved. No part of the covers may be used or reproduced in any manner whatsoever without the prior written permission of Lerner Publications Company.

Vampire Bats © 2001 by Capstone Press. All rights reserved.

Chapter 7

Cover from *Outside and Inside Killer Bees* by Sandra Markle. Walker & Company, 2004. Reprinted with permission of Walker & Company.

Cover from *The Bumblebee Queen* by April Pulley Sayre. Charlesbridge, 2005. Used with permission by Charlesbridge Publishing, Inc.

Cover from *Mosquito Bite* by Alexandra Siy. Charlesbridge, 2005. Used with permission by Charlesbridge Publishing, Inc.

Cover from *Creepy Crawlies* by Jim Bruce. 2002 © Kingfisher Publications.

Cover from *Yellow Sac Spiders* by Eric Ethan. Gareth Stevens, Inc., 2004. Reprinted with permission.

Cover from *Lizards: Weird and Wonderful* by Margery Facklam. Little, Brown and Company, 2003. Reprinted with permission.

Cover from *Snakes* by Adrienne Mason and illustrated by Nancy Gray Ogle used by permission of Kids Can Press Ltd., Toronto, Canada. Cover © 2005 by Nancy Gray Ogle.

Cover from *Deadly Spiders and Scorpions* by Andrew Solway. Heinemann Library, 2005. Reprinted with permission.

Cover from *Everything Bug: What Kids Really Want to Know about Insects and Spiders* by Cherie Winner. NorthWord Books for Young Readers, 2004.

Chapter 8

Cover from *Young Thomas Edison* by Michael Dooling. Holiday House, 2005. Reprinted with permission.

Cover from *Freeze Frame: A Photographic History of the Winter Olympics* by Sue Macy. National Geographic, 2006. Reprinted with permission of the National Geographic Society.

Smokejumpers: Battling the Forest Flames © 2003 by Capstone Press. All rights reserved.

Cover from *Tae Kwon Do* by David Amerland. Gareth Stevens, Inc., 2004. Reprinted with permission.

Cover from *U.S. Army Fighting Vehicles* by Richard Bartlett. Heinemann Library, 2003. Reprinted with permission.

The World's Fastest Indy Cars © 2003 by Capstone Press. All rights reserved.

Extreme Mountain Biking Moves © 2003 by Capstone Press. All rights reserved.

Cover from *BMX* by Scott Dick. Heinemann Library, 2002. Reprinted with permission.

Cover from *An International Soccer Star* by Ben Godsal. Heinemann Library, 2005. Reprinted with permission.

Cover from *Attack Fighters* by Ian Graham. Heinemann Library, 2003. Reprinted with permission.

Cover from *Crime-Fighting Aircraft* by Henry M. Holden. Enslow Publishers, Inc., 2002. Reprinted with permission.

Cover from *Cars* by Nancy Smiler Levinson. Holiday House, 2004. Reprinted with permission.

Cover from *Trucks and Big Rigs* by Arlene Bourgeois Molzahn. Enslow Publishers, Inc., 2003. Reprinted with permission.

Cover from *Eureka! Great Inventions and How They Happened* by Richard Platt. 2003 © Kingfisher Publications.

Cover from *The Best Book of Martial Arts* by Lauren Robertson. 2002 © Kingfisher Publications.

Cover from *Scooters and Skateboards* by Wendy Sadler. Heinemann Library, 2005. Reprinted with permission.

Stunt Planes © 2003 by Capstone Press. All rights reserved.

The World's Fastest Pro Stock Trucks © 2003 by Capstone Press. All rights reserved.

Cover from *Transformed: How Everyday Things Are Made* by Bill Slavin used by permission of Kids Can Press Ltd., Toronto, Canada. Cover © 2005 by Bill Slavin.

Cover from *Karting* by Graham Smith. Heinemann Library, 2002. Reprinted with permission.

Cover from *How to Build Your Own Prize-Winning Robot* by Ed Sobey. Enslow Publishers, Inc., 2002. Reprinted with permission.

Bulldozers © 2004 by Capstone Press. All rights reserved.

Chapter 9

Cover from *The Lost Colony of Roanoke* by Jean Fritz. G.P. Putnam's Sons, 2004. Reprinted with permission.

Cover from *Vanished* by Judith Herbst. Lerner Publications Company, 2005. All covers are reprinted with the permission of Lerner Publications Company, a division of Lerner Publishing Group. All rights reserved. No part of the covers may be used or reproduced in any manner whatsoever without the prior written permission of Lerner Publications Company.

Cover from *Fooled You! Frauds and Hoaxes through the Years* by Elaine Pascoe. Henry Holt and Company, 2005. Used by permission of Henry Holt & Co.

Cover from *Mysteries of History* by Robert Stewart, Ph.D. with Clint Twist and Edward Horton. National Geographic, 2003. Reprinted with permission of the National Geographic Society.

Cover from *Secrets of a Civil War Submarine: Solving the Mysteries of the* H.L. Hunley by Sally M. Walker. Carolrhoda Books, Inc., 2005. All covers are reprinted with the permission of Lerner Publications Company, a division of Lerner Publishing Group. All rights reserved. No part of the covers may be used or reproduced in any manner whatsoever without the prior written permission of Lerner Publications Company.

Cover from *1906 San Francisco Earthquake* by Tim Cooke. Gareth Stevens, Inc., 2005. Reprinted with permission.

Cover from *Myths and Monsters: Secrets Revealed* by Katie Edwards. Charlesbridge, 2004. Used with permission by Charlesbridge Publishing, Inc.

Cover from *The Short and Bloody History of Ghosts* by John Farman. Lerner, 2002. All covers are reprinted with the permission of Lerner Publications Company, a division of Lerner Publishing Group. All rights reserved. No part of the covers may be used or reproduced in any manner whatsoever without the prior written permission of Lerner Publications Company.

Cover from *Spooky Riddles* by Marilyn Helmer and illustrated by Eric Parker used by permission of Kids Can Press Ltd., Toronto, Canada. Cover © 2003 by Eric Parker.

Chapter 10

Cover from *Games: Learn to Play, Play to Win* by Daniel King. 2003 © Kingfisher Publications.

Cover from *Eye Guess: A Foldout Guessing Game* by Phyllis Limbacher Tildes. Charlesbridge, 2005. Used with permission by Charlesbridge Publishing, Inc.

Cover from *Drawing with Your Fingerprints* by Godeleine De Rosamel. Gareth Stevens, Inc., 2003. Reprinted with permission.

Cover from *Ed Emberley's Drawing Book of Trucks and Trains* by Ed Emberley. Little, Brown and Company, 2005. Reprinted with permission.

Cover from *Ed Emberley's Drawing Book of Weirdos* by Ed Emberley. Little, Brown and Company, 2002. Reprinted with permission.

Cover from *Ralph Masiello's Bug Drawing Book* by Ralph Masiello. Charlesbridge, 2004. Used with permission by Charlesbridge Publishing, Inc.

Covers of Gareth Stevens books reprinted by permission of Gareth Stevens, Inc. To order copies, please contact the publisher at www.garethstevens.com.

Author/Illustrator Index

Ackerman, Diane, 128
Adams, Simon, 18, 211
Adkins, Jan, 1–2
Adler, David A., 10, 40, 175
Agee, Jon, 224
Agenbroad, Larry D., 59
Aldrich, Lisa, 84
Aldrin, Buzz, 67
Aliki, 10
Allan, Tony, 84
Allen, Thomas B., 40, 179
Altman, Linda Jacobs, 18–19
Amerland, David, 188
Anderson, Dale, 48
Armstrong, Jennifer, 15, 23–24, 179, 212
Arnold, Caroline, 51–52, 57, 59, 61, 128
Arnold, Katya, 138
Arnosky, Jim, 84, 128, 138, 163, 166
Artell, Mike, 226
Ash, Russell, 10, 230
Ashby, Ruth, 48, 59

Bagert, Brod, 104
Bailey, Jill, 138
Balaban, Natalie E., 230
Ball, Jacqueline A. , 217
Ball, Johnny, 224
Ballard, Robert D., 212
Bare, Colleen, 128
Barner, Bob, 57
Barr, Matt, 188
Barraclough, Sue, 166
Barrett, Jalma, 128
Barretta, Gene, 176
Bartlett, Richard, 188
Bartoletti, Susan Campbell, 2–3, 179
Batten, Mary, 129
Bausum, Ann, 24, 25
Beattie, Owen, 104
Beeler, Sally B., 40
Behler, Deborah, 167
Behler, John, 167

Bell, Lonnie, 189
Benchley, Peter, 138
Bergen, David, 59
Berger, Gilda, 10, 104–5
Berger, Melvin, 10, 79, 104–5, 138, 163
Bernard, Nancy Stone, 21
Betz, Adrienne, 118
Bidner, Jenni, 227
Bierman, Carol, 40
Binns, Tristan Boyer, 139
Birch, Robin, 167
Bircher, William, 40
Bishop, Nic, 129
Blacklock, Dyan, 10
Bledsoe, Glen, 189
Bledsoe, Karen, 189
Bloom, Steve, 139
Blumberg, Rhoda, 11, 40–41
Bobick, James E., 230
Bobrick, Benson, 25–26
Bonner, Hannah, 57, 61
Boring, Mel, 70–71, 73
Botermans, Jack, 226
Boyce, Natalie Pope, 63
Bradley, Kimberly Brubaker, 80
Bramwell, Martyn, 11
Brandenburg, Jim, 129
Branley, Franklyn M., 68, 80, 84
Branzei, Sylvia, 105
Bredeson, Carmen, 212
Brend, Stephen, 139
Brewer, Paul, 224
Briscoe, Diana, 184
Brown, Don, 26–27
Brown, Gerry, 230
Bruce, Jim, 167
Brunelle, Lynn, 217
Buckingham, Alan, 227
Buckley, James, 189, 230
Bull, Jane, 223
Burke, Jim, 176
Burnie, David, 60, 167

Butler, John, 140
Butterfield, Moira, 3–4
Buttitta, Hope, 84
Buxbaum, Susan Kovacs, 105

Calabro, Marian, 212–13
Califf, David J., 19
Campbell, Peter, 190
Camper, Cathy, 57
Caputo, Philip, 27
Capuzzo, Michael, 8, 213
Carlson, Laurie, 41
Carr, Karen, 57
Carrow, Robert, 185
Ceban, Bonnie J., 85
Cerullo, Mary M., 117, 129, 163
Chandra, Deborah, 25, 41
Charlip, Remy, 80
Chesterman, Barnaby, 190
Chin, Dr. Karen, 52, 61
Choron, Harry, 230
Choron, Sandra, 230
Chorlton, Windsor, 57, 61
Chottin, Ariane, 140
Chrisp, Peter, 19
Claybourne, Anna, 140
Clendening, John, 190
Cline-Ransome, Lesa, 41
Clinton, Catherine, 27–28, 41
Cobb, Vicki, 68, 73, 80
Coburn, Broughton, 11
Cohen, Daniel, 60
Coile, D. Caroline, 140
Cole, Joanna, 224
Collard III, Sneed B., 69, 115–16, 129
Collicutt, Paul, 190
Colman, Penny, 105
Colson, Mary, 85
Comora, Madeleine, 25, 41
Conniff, Richard, 116
Connolly, Sean, 19
Conrad, David, 105
Cook, Harry, 190
Cooke, Tim, 218
Cooper, Ilene, 41
Cooper, Margaret, 11
Cooper, Michael L., 41

Corbishley, Mike, 11
Coren, Stanley, 117
Costa-Prades, Bernadette, 140
Cotton, Jacqueline S., 140
Cowley, Joy, 159, 163
Crompton, Samuel Willard, 19
Crowe, Chris, 8, 15, 25, 41
Crutcher, Chris, 42
Curtis, Patricia, 130

Dahl, Michael, 80
Dahl, Roald, 105
Dalgliesh, Sharon, 140
Darling, Kathy, 130, 163–64
Davies, Nicola, 95–96, 99, 130
Davis, Gibbs, 130
Davis, Kenneth C., 60, 112
Day, Trevor, 106
De Rosamel, Godeleine, 227–28
de Souza, Philip, 13
Deady, Kathleen W., 140–41, 190, 218
Deem, James M., 96–97, 106, 213
Delano, Marfé Ferguson, 69–70, 73, 185
Demarest, Chris L., 176
Dendy, Leslie, 70–71, 73
Dick, Scott, 191
Diffily, Deborah, 52
DiSpezio, Michael A., 85
Dixon, Dougal, 60
Dixon, Norman, 167
Doeden, Matt., 28
Dolan, Edward F., 48
Domaine, Helena, 85
Donkin, Andrew, 213
Donoughue, Carol, 213
Dooling, Michael, 177
Doolittle, Michael J., 178–79
Dornfield, Margaret, 141
Dowswell, Paul, 48, 71–72, 218
Drez, Ronald. J., 11, 25, 179
Dunphy, Madeleine, 80
DuQuette, Keith, 130
Dussling, Jennifer, 80
DuTemple, Leslie A., 19–20
Dyson, Marianne J., 72–73

Earle, Sylvia A., 130–31

Edwards, Judith, 42
Edwards, Katie, 219
Eisenberg, Lisa, 62, 142
Eldin, Peter, 223–24
Emberley, Ed, 228–29
Estigarribia, Diana, 141
Ethan, Eric, 168

Facklam, Margery, 169
Fahey, Kathleen, 219
Faiella, Graham, 141
Farman, John, 20, 213, 219
Farmer, Jacqueline, 81
Farrell, Jeanette, 73–74
Feinstein, Stephen, 49
Filer, Joyce, 106
Fisher, David, 191
Fleischman, John, 99, 106
Fleischman, Sid, 205–6
Florian, Douglas, 118, 131, 169
Fradin, Dennis Brindell, 25, 29, 42, 73, 178
Fraser, Mary Ann, 141
Frattini, Stephanie, 118
Fredericks, Anthony D., 131
Freeman, Gary, 191
French, Vivian, 53
Frisch, Aaron, 191
Fritz, Jean, 206–7
Fulghum, Hunter S., 15, 230

Gail, Jarrow, 133
Ganci, Chris, 42
Gardner, Robert, 86
Gelman, Rita Golden, 105
George, Linda, 164
Gerstein, Mordicai, 43
Getz, David, 106, 213–14
Ghigna, Charles, 224
Gibbons, Gail, 60, 131–32, 141
Giblin, James Cross, 11–12, 29–30, 179
Gifford, Clive, 20, 191
Gigliotti, Jim, 191
Gilpin, Daniel, 169
Glaser, Jason, 185
Glass, Andrew, 43
Glidewell, Steve, 191
Godsal, Ben, 192

Goecke, Michael P., 61
Gold, Alison Leslie, 12
Goldin, Augusta, 132
Goldish, Meish, 86
Goodall, Jane, 119, 132
Goodman, Susan E., 8, 43, 86, 99, 106, 178–79
Gordon, Sharon, 141
Grace, Catherine, 87
Graham, Ian, 192
Graham-Barber, Lynda, 132
Grambs, Alison, 225
Grant, Neil, 20
Gray, Susan H., 61–62
Green, Jen, 220
Greenberg, Dan, 142, 169
Greenblatt, Miriam, 20
Greene, Meg, 43
Greenfield, Eloise, 43
Gunter, Veronika Alice, 225
Gunzi, Christine, 120, 169
Gutman, Bill, 169

Haduch, Bill, 107, 185
Hall, Katy, 62, 142
Halley, Ned, 214
Halls, Kelly Milner, 117, 132
Handford, Tom, 142
Hansen, Joyce, 43
Hare, Tony, 231
Harness, Cheryl, 4, 30–31
Harper, Cherise Mericle, 185
Harris, Nathaniel, 20
Harward, Barnaby, 20
Haskins, Jim, 43, 193
Hauser, Jill, 81
Hawass, Zahi, 97–99
Heathcote, Peter, 169
Hedlund, Stephanie F, 193
Hehner, Barbara, 40, 62
Heiligman, Deborah, 44, 164
Helmer, Marilyn, 112, 142, 220, 225
Hendrickson, Steve, 185
Herbst, Judith, 207
Hernandez-Divers, Sonia, 169
Hickman, Pamela, 132
Higgins, Christopher, 220

Hill, Lee Sullivan, 193
Hirschi, Ron, 142
Hiscock, Bill, 143
Ho, Oliver, 224
Hocking, Justin, 193
Hoena, B.A., 49
Hoena, Blake, 143
Holden, Henry M., 194
Holmes, Kevin, 143
Holmes, Thom, 52
Holub, Joan, 21, 132–33, 143, 170, 214
Holzer, Harold, 44
Hooper, Meredith, 21
Hoose, Phllip, xvi, 120–21
Hopkins, Lee Bennett, 133
Hopping, Lorraine Jean, 81
Horsfall, Jacqueline, 62, 225
Horsley, Andy, 194
Hort, Lenny, 53
Horton, Edward, 209
Howes, Chris, 194
Hunter, Ryan Ann, 87, 186
Hynes, Margaret, 21

Ichord, Loretta Frances, 99, 107
Ingram, Scott, 194, 220
Inskipp, Carol, 143
Iorio, Nicole, 170

Jackson, Donna M., 8, 15, 73–75, 81, 107,
    117, 121–22, 133, 164, 179
Janeczko, Paul B., 225
Jango-Cohen, Judith, 143, 194
January, Brendan, 49, 195
Janulewicz, Mike, 107
Jeffrey, Gary, 4–5
Jeffrey, Laura S., 143–44
Jenkins, Martin, 164
Jenkins, Priscilla Belz, 133
Jenkins, Steve, 12, 53, 61, 81, 122, 133–34,
    144, 179
Job, Chris, 195
Johnson, Dolores, 31–32
Jonas, Ann, 144
Jones, Charlotte Foltz, 225
Jones, Rebecca, 44
Jordan, Denise M., 195

Jurmain, Suzanne Tripp, 32

Kalz, Jill, 144
Kane, Karen, 144
Kaner, Etta, 144
Kaplan, William, 12
Katz, Susan, 75
Keller, Charles, 144, 225
Kelsey, Elin, 144
Kendall, Patricia, 144–45
Kennedy, Senator Edward M., 122
Kent, Deborah, 87
Kent, Peter, 12, 81
Kent, Zachary, 214
Kerrod, Robin, 87
King, Daniel, 225
Kirk, Daniel, 134
Kite, L. Patricia, 144, 164
Knight, Tim, 144
Koehler-Pentacoff, Elizabeth, 49
Koss, Amy Goldman, 87
Krull, Kathleen, 12–13, 25, 44, 76, 220
Kudalis, Eric, 107, 112
Kudlinski, Kathleen V., 54

Lakin, Patricia, 224
Lalicki, Tom, 44
Landau, Elaine, 49–50, 144, 165, 170
Landstrom, Lee Ann, 134
Langley, Andrew, 13
Lanier, Shannon, 44–45
Larson, Heidi, 21
Laskey, Elizabeth, 144–46
Lasky, Kathryn, 32–33, 165
Lassieur, Allison, 21
Latham, Donna, 220
Laubach, Cynthia, 146
Lauber, Patricia, 8, 99, 107, 117, 134
Lawrence, Colton, 229
Lawton, Clive, 5, 13
Leach, Michael, 146
Lekuton, Joseph Lemasolai, 13, 15
Leroe, Ellen, 214
Lessem, Don, 62–63, 107
Levey, Richard, 220
Levine, Ellen, 13
Levine, Michelle, 146

Levinson, Nancy Smiler, 195
Levy, Pat, 50
Lewin, Ted, 134
Lewis, J. Patrick, 226
Lichtenheld, Tom, 195
Lindsay, Judy, 99
Llewellyn, Claire, 170
Lockwood, Sophie, 146
Logan, Claudia, 13
Logan, Jim, 195
Lorbiecki, Marybeth, 88
Lourie, Peter, 13–14, 45, 214
Loy, Jessica, 88
Lupton, Hugh, 226
Lynch, Wayne, 147

Macaulay, David, 186
MacDonald, Fiona, 6, 88, 99–100, 108
MacLeod, Elizabeth, 88
MacQuitty, Miranda, 147
Macy, Sue, 180–81
Malam, John, 21
Malone, Caroline, 21
Mann, Elizabeth, 14–15, 181–82
Marie, Christiane, 147
Markle, Sandra, 100–101, 123–24, 134–35,
     147–48, 160, 170
Marquez, Heron, 195
Marrin, Albert, 58, 108
Martin, Patricia A. Fink, 165
Martin-James, Kathleen, 148
Marzollo, Jean, 226
Masiello, Ralph, 229
Masoff, Joy, 108
Mason, Adrienne, 148, 170
Mason, Paul, 195–96
Matsen, Brad, 88–89, 221
Matthews, Dawn, 135
Matthews, Rupert, 63
Matthews, Tom L., 186
McAuliffe, Emily, 170
McDaniel, Melissa, 148
McDonough, Yona Zeldis, 15, 33, 182
McGowan, Gary, 43
McKendry, Joe, 196
McKerley, Jennifer, 148
McLafferty, Carla Killough, 99, 108

McMillan, Bruce, 135
McMullan, Kate, 63
McNicholas, June, 148
McNulty, Faith, 76, 117, 135
Medicine Crow, Joseph, 34
Meltzer, Milton, 15, 221
Michael Morrison, 230
Middleton, Haydn, 21, 196
Mignon, Phillippe, 226
Miles, Bill, 35
Millard, Anne, 15
Miller, Debbie S., 45
Millman, Isaac, 7
Milton, Joyce, 108
Molzahn, Arlene Bourgeois, 196
Monroe, Lucy, 109
Montarde, Helen, 148
Montgomery, Sy, 117, 124–25, 135, 165,
     181
Mooney, Julie, 231
Moran, Chris, 188
Morley, Jacqueline, 112
Morris, Ann, 21
Morse, Jennifer Carr, 231
Muller, Eric, 81
Munro, Roxie, 226
Murawski, Darlyne A., 165
Murphy, Frank, 196
Murphy, Jim, 45–46, 181, 214–15
Murray, Julie, 148–49, 171
Murray, Peter, 149
Myers, Jack, 171
Myers, Walter Dean, 35, 46

Nelson, Kristin L., 149, 196
Nelson, Lisa, 59
Nelson, Pete, 15, 46
Nelson, Robin, 149, 171
Newquist, H.P., 89
Nguyen, Duy, 229–30
Nicholson, Dorinda Makanaonalani, 7–8
Nicolson, Cynthia Pratt, 221
Nir, Yehuda, 16
Nonnemacher, Klaus, 196
Nurosi, Aki, 82
Nye, Bill, 63, 82, 89, 149

O'Brien, Patrick, 35–36, 215
O'Connor, Jane, 16
Ogle, Belinda, 149
Orme, David, 149
Osborne, Ian, 196
Osborne, Mary Pope, 63, 109
Oxlade, Chris, 89, 197

Page, Debra, 135
Page, Robin, 122, 134
Parker Barbara, 150
Parker, Barbara Keevil, 150
Parker, Steve, 150
Parsons, Jayne, 231
Pascoe, Elaine, 208
Patent, Dorothy Hinshaw, 150, 166, 215
Paulsen, Gary, 15, 109
Penner, Lucille Recht, 36
Penny, Malcolm, 150
Perry, Phyllis J., 136
Peterson, Tiffany, 150, 197
Petty, Kate, 4–5
Pfeffer, Wendy, 82, 136, 160–61
Philbrick, Nathaniel, 215
Piehl, Janet, 150
Pinchuck, Amy, 197
Pitkin, Linda, 77
Piven, Hanoch, 46
Platt, Richard, 77, 171, 197
Powell, Ben, 197
Prelutsky, Jack, 78, 101
Preston, Diana, 216
Pringle, Laurence, 50, 136, 150, 171
Prior, Natalie Jane, 109
Provensen, Alice, 8–9
Putnam, James, 109
Pyers, Greg, 150, 171–72

Quinlan, Susan E., 151

Readhead, Lloyd, 197
Redmond, Shirley Ray, 151
Reed, Jennifer, 89
Reid, Struan, 22, 216
Reinhard, Johan, 109
Reinhart, Matthew, 172
Reiter, Chris, 156

Rhatigan, Joe, 89
Richardson, Adele, 151
Rielly, Robin, 197
Riley, Joelle, 151
Ripley, Esther, 197
Rissinger, Matt, 226
Rivera, Sheila, 197
Robbins, Ken, 136
Robertshaw, Andrew, 16
Robertson, Lauren, 198
Robinson, Nick, 230
Robson, Graham, 231
Rockwell, Anne, 151, 172
Rollins, Barbara B., 109
Romanek, Trudee, 89, 101–2, 198
Rosenbloom, Joseph, 226
Ross, Michael Elsohn, 90
Ross, Stewart, 9
Rounds, Glen, 151
Rowan, Dr. Pete, 82
Royston, Angela, 90–91
Rumford, James, 16
Ruth, Maria Mudd, 151
Ryder, Joanne, 136

Sadler, Wendy, 198
Salkeld, Audrey, 16
Sandler, Martin W., 216
Saunders, Ian G., 63
Savage, Jeff, 198–200
Sayre, April Pulley, 78, 161, 166
Schaefer, A.R., 200
Schaefer, Lola, 125, 151–52, 172
Schafer, Susan, 152, 172
Schanzer, Rosalyn, 25, 46–47
Schlaepfer, Gloria G., 152
Schmidt, Norman, 230
Schomp, Victoria, 63
Schwarz, Renee, 200
Schyffert, Bea Uusma, 82, 181
Scieszka, Jon, 79
Searle, Bobbi, 91
Seckel, Al, 226
Senior, Kathryn, 99, 110
Setford, Steve, 152
Settel, Joanne, Ph.D., 8, 110, 117
Seuling, Barbara, 73, 82

Severance, John B., 186
Shange, Ntozake, 200
Shapiro, Stephen, 21
Sherman, Josepha, 21, 200
Sherman, Paul, 133
Showers, Paul, 110
Silbaugh, John, 200
Silverstein, Alvin, 172
Silverstein, Laura, 172
Silverstein, Virginia, 172
Simon, Seymour, 22, 79, 82, 91, 110, 125, 152, 166, 172, 200, 221
Sims, Neil, 152
Singer, Marilyn, 102, 110
Siy, Alexandra, 117, 162
Skrepnick, Michael W., 64
Skurzynski, Gloria, 83
Slavin, Bill, 200
Sloan, Christopher, 8, 55, 58, 61, 110
Slocum, Jerry, 226
Smith, Graham, 201
Smith, Ryan A., 201
Snedden, Robert, 99, 110
Sobey, Ed, 201
Solheim, James, 111
Solway, Andrew, 22, 99, 103, 113, 126, 152–53, 172
Souza, D. M., 153
Spilsbury, Louise, 91
Spilsbury, Richard, 91, 153, 172
St. George, Judith, 16, 37–39, 47, 186
Stanley, Diane, 17
Stanley, Jerry, 47
Steele, Philip, 17
Stefoff, Rebecca, 136, 153
Steig, William, 226
Stein, Sara, 153
Steinberg, David, 113
Stemple, Heidi Elisabet Yolen, 8, 211, 217
Stewart, Mark, 50, 182, 202
Stewart, Melissa, 153, 173
Stewart, Robert, Ph.D., 209
Stier, Catherine, 47
Stone, Lynn M., 153–54
Streissguth, Tom, 221
Strong, Mike, 154
Sullivan, George, 83, 183

Sullivan, Jody, 154
Swain, Gwenyth, 47
Swanson, Diane, 73, 83, 111 136, 154, 173
Sweetman, Bill, 183
Swinburne, Stephen R., 137, 154, 173

Tanaka, Shelley, 12, 17, 39–40, 48, 58, 103–4, 111, 216
Taylor, Barbara, 187
Taylor, Leighton, 154
Teitelbaum, Michael, 202
Thomas, Keltie, 91
Thomson, Sarah L., 127, 155, 162–63
Tildes, Phyllis Limbacher, 137, 227
Tomecek, Stephen M., 73, 183–84
Torres, John, 91
Townsend, John, 155, 173
Trumble, Kelly, 111
Turner, Alan, 64
Turner, Matt, 155
Turner, Pamela S., 117, 127, 181
Twist, Clint, 209

Van Cleaf, Kristin, 202
Vecchione, Glen, 227
Vieregger, K.E., 202
Viola, Herman, 13
Vogel, Carole Garbuny, 216
Vogel, Julia, 156
Vogt, Gregory L., 221

Waldman, Neil, 22
Walker, Kate, 22
Walker, Paul, 50
Walker, Richard, 92
Walker, Sally M., 8, 25, 58, 61, 156, 173, 181, 210–11
Wallace, Karen, 137
Walters, John, 202–3
Warhol, Tom, 156
Warren, Andrea, 15, 17–18, 25, 48, 181
Waters, Jo, 156–57, 173
Watkins, Richard, 18
Watts, Claire, 92
Waxman, Laura Hamilton, 157
Weaver, Robyn, 137
Webb, Sophie, 157

Wechsler, Doug, 166
Wells, Robert E., 83
Welsbacher, Anne, 157, 173
Welsh, Nick, 203
Wenzel, Gregory, 56
Wheatley, Abigail, 22
Wheeler, Jill C., 203
Wheeler, Lisa, 127
White, Matt, 221
Whiteman, Dorit Bader, 9
Wick, Walter, 227
Wilcox, Charlotte, 112–13, 137
Williams, Judith, 56–57
Williams, Linda D., 203
Willingham, Bob, 190
Winner, Cherie, 65, 157, 173–74
Winter, Jonah, 203
Wolf, Alan, 83
Wood, Don, 203
Wood, Ted, 216

Woods, Bob, 204
Woodward, John, 157
Woolf, Alex, 22, 221
Worth, Richard, 22
Wren, Laura Lee, 22
Wright, Rachel, 18
Wulffson, Don L, 73, 187

Yates, Philip, 226
Ylvisaker, Anne, 92–93
Yolen, Jane, 8, 211, 217
Yoo, Paula, 204
Youngblood, Ed, 187

Zeaman, John, 117, 137–38
Zemlicka, Shannon, 157
Znamierowski, Alfred, 231
Zoehfeld, Kathleen Weidner, 65
Zubrowski, Bernie, 84
Zuehlke, Jeffrey, 204

Title Index

10,000 Days of Thunder: A History of the Vietnam War, 27

1906 San Francisco Earthquake, 218

1993 Mississippi River Floods, 220

A Baseball All-Star, A, 195

Achoo! The Most Interesting Book You'll Ever Read about Germs, 101–2

Actual Size, 133

Adolf Hitler: Evil Mastermind of the Holocaust, 18–19

AFC East, 204

AFC North, 189

AFC South, 189

AFC West, 202

African Animals, 128

After the Last Dog Died: The True-Life, Hair-Raising Adventure of Douglas Mawson and His 1911–1914 Antarctic Expedition, 212

Alamo: February 23-March 6, 1836, The, 50

Alamo: Surrounded and Outnumbered, They Chose to Make a Defiant Last Stand, The, 48

Albert Einstein: A Life of Genius, 88

Albino Animals, 117, 132

All about Frogs, 166

All About Rattlesnakes, 163

All about Sharks, 138

All about Turtles, 163

Alligator, 172

All-New Book of Lists for Kids, The, 230

Allosaurus, 60

Alpha Bravo Charlie: The Military Alphabet, 176

Always Inventing: A Photobiography of Alexander Graham Bell, 186

Amazement Park, 226

Amazing Aircraft, 200

Amazing Gorillas!, 155

Amazing International Space Station, The, 84

Amazing Snakes!, 162–63

Amazing Whales!, 127

American Curl Cats, 148

American League Central, 190

American League East, 189

American League West, 191

American Mastodon, 61

America's Great Disasters, 216

Amistad: A Long Road To Freedom, 46

An American Plague: The True and Terrifying Story of the Yellow Fever Epidemic of 1793, 214

An Extreme Dive under the Antarctic Ice, 88

An International Soccer Star, 192

Anacondas, 173

Ancient Egypt Revealed, 19

Ancient Greek War and Weapons, 21

Ancient Romans, The, 21

Ancient Rome, 9

Animal Fact File: Head-to-Head Profiles of More than 90 Mammals, 231

Animal Grossology, 105

Animal Jokes, 144

Animal Mummies: Preserved through the Ages, 113

Animal Talk: How Animals Communicate through Sight, Sound And Smell, 144

Animals Eat the Weirdest Things, 136

Animals Eating: How Animals Chomp, Chew, Slurp and Swallow, 132

Animals That Walk on Water, 165

Animals You Never Even Heard Of, 130

Ankylosaurus (by Daniel Cohen), 60

Ankylosaurus (by Matthew Rupert), 63

Ankylosaurus and Other Armored Plant-Eaters, 63

Ants, 166

Ants!, 168

Ants Up Close, 167

Apatosaurus (by Matthew Rupert), 63

Apatosaurus (by Susan Gray), 61

Apatosaurus and Other Giant, Long-Necked
    Plant-Eaters, 63
Arctic Babies, 130
Are We Alone? Scientists Search for Life in
    Space, 83
Armadillos (by Judith Jango-Cohen), 143
Armadillos (by Lola Schaefer), 151
Armored Dinosaurs, 62
Army Ant Parade, 166
Asian Elephant, 155
Assassination in Sarajevo: June 28, 1914, 22
Atlanta Braves, The, 202
Atlantis: The Lost City?, 213
Attack Fighters, 192
Attack on Pearl Harbor: The True Story of
    the Day America Entered World War II,
    48
Auschwitz, 13
Avalanches, 92
Awesome Obstacles: How to Build Your
    Own Skateboard Ramps and Ledges,
    193

Babe Ruth Saves Baseball!, 196
Bad Guys: True Stories of Legendary
    Gunslingers, Sidewinders, Fourflushers,
    Drygulchers, Bushwhackers,
    Freebooters, and Downright Bad Guys
    and Gals of the Wild West, 43
Bald Eagles, 153
Bananas!, 81
Basketball All-Star, A, 194
Bat Loves the Night, 130
Batboy's Day, A, 189
Bats (by Gail Gibbons), 141
Bats (by Margaret Dornfield), 141
Bats!, 141
Bats! Strange and Wonderful, 136
Bats: Shadows in the Night, 128
Battle of Actium, 19
Battle of Little Bighorn, The, 48
Battle of the Alamo, The, 28
Battle Stations! Fortifications through the
    Ages, 21
Beaks!, 129
Beaver, 151
Beavers: Big-Toothed Builders, 154

Becoming Best Friends with Your Iguana,
    Snake, or Turtle, 169
Bees, 166
Bees Up Close, 167
Bees!, 168
Beetle, 203
Beneath the Streets of Boston: Building
    America's First Subway, 196
Bengal Tiger, 153
Best Book of Early People, The, 21
Best Book of Endangered and Extinct
    Animals, The, 142
Best Book of Martial Arts, The, 198
Best Book of Pirates, The, 20
Best Book of Snakes, The, 169
Best Book of Wolves and Wild Dogs, The,
    120
Bicycle Stunt Riding, 185
Big Bugs, 172
Big Caribou Herd: Life in the Arctic
    National Wildlife Refuge, The, 143
Big Cats, 138
Big Fat Paycheck: A Young Person's Guide
    to Writing for the Movies, 229
Big Head!, 82
Bill Nye the Science Guy's Big Blue Ocean,
    82, 149
Bill Nye the Science Guy's Great Big Book
    of Tiny Germs, 89
Bill Nye the Science Guy's Great Big
    Dinosaur Dig, 63
Bill Pickett: Wild West Cowboy, 49
Billy the Kid: Wild West Outlaw, 49
Birdhouses, 200
Birds: How to Choose and Care for a Bird,
    143
Bizarre Bugs, 166
Black Bear: North America's Bear, 154
Black Soldier: 1492 to the Present, The, 41
Black Widow Spiders, 168
Blazing Bush and Forest Fires, 91
Blizzard! The 1888 Whiteout, 217
Blizzard: The Storm that Changed America,
    181, 215
Blizzards!, 81
Blood Evidence, 109
Blood-Feeding Bugs and Beasts, 164

Blood-Hungry Spleen and Other Poems about Our Parts, The, 83

Blue Whales, 148

BMX (by Chris Job), 195

BMX (by Scott Dick), 191

BMX Biking, 202

Bodies from the Ash: Life and Death in Ancient Pompeii, 96–97

Bodies from the Bog, 106

Body Noises, 105

Bog Mummies: Preserved in Peat, 112

Bone Detectives: How Forensic Anthropologists Solve Crimes and Uncover Mysteries of the Dead, The, 8, 15, 107, 179

Book of Lists For Teens, The, 230

Book of Wizard Magic: In Which the Apprentice Finds Marvelous Magic Tricks, Mystifying Illusions and Astonishing Tales, The, 223

Boss of the Plains: The Hat That Won the West, 41

Bottle-Nosed Dolphins, 148

Bottoms Up! A Book about Rear Ends, 110

Bound for the North Star: True Stories of Fugitive Slaves, 25, 42

bow wow meow meow: it's rhyming cats and dogs, 131

Boy, Were We Wrong about Dinosaurs, 54

Brachiosaurus, 60

Brown Recluse Spiders, 168

Bug Faces, 165

Bug Hunter, 167

Bug Scientists, The, 117, 164

Bugs, 167

Bugs before Time: Prehistoric Insects and their Relatives, 57

Building Beavers, 148

Building Big, 186

Built to Last: Building America's Amazing Bridges, Dams, Tunnels, and Skyscrapers, 183

Bulldozers, 203

Bumblebee Queen, The, 161

Buried in Ice: Unlocking the Secrets of an Arctic Voyage, 104

Burp! The Most Interesting Book You'll Ever Read about Eating, 73, 111

Burps, Boogers, and Bad Breath, 105

Bury the Dead: Tombs, Corpses, Mummies, Skeletons and Rituals, 110

Butterflies Up Close, 171

Calico's Cousins: Cats from Around the World, 137

Camaro, 203

Can You See What I See? Dream Machine: A Picture Adventure to Search and Solve, 227

Can You See What I See? Picture Puzzles to Search and Solve, 227

Cannibal Animals: Animals That Eat Their Own Kind, 131

Car, 197

Card Tricks, 224

Caribou, 151

Cars, 195

Case Closed: The Real Scoop on Detective Work, 221

Case of the Monkeys That Fell from the Trees: And Other Mysteries in Tropical Nature, The, 151

Cat Mummies, 111

Cats: How to Choose and Care for a Cat, 143

Caving, 194

CDC?, 226

Centipedes, Millipedes, Scorpions & Spiders, 169

Challenger and *Columbia*, 219

Challenger: The Explosion on Liftoff, The, 221

Chameleon, Chameleon, 159

Chameleons are Cool, 164

Chameleons: On Location, 163

Champion: The Story of Muhammad Ali, 193

Charlemagne and the Early Middle Ages, 20

Chattering Chipmunks, 150

Cheetah, 140

Cheetahs (by Barbara Parker), 150

Cheetahs (by Diana Estigarribia), 141

Cheetahs (by Jill Kalz), 144

Chernobyl Disaster, The, 218

Chicago Cubs, The, 202
Chicago White Sox, The, 202
Chihuahua, The, 137
Chief: The Life of Peter J. Ganci, A New
    York City Firefighter, 42
Child of the Warsaw Ghetto, 10
Children's Atlas of Lost Treasures, The, 216
Chimpanzees, 144
Chimpanzees I Love: Saving Our World and
    Theirs, The, 132
Chinchillas, 142
Choppers!, 86
Civil War Drummer Boy: The Diary of
    William Bircher 1861–1865, A, 40
Clever Camouflage, 157
Climbing Everest: Tales of Triumph and
    Tragedy on the World's Highest
    Mountain, 16
Close to Shore: The Terrifying Shark
    Attacks of 1916, 8, 213
Clydesdale Horses, 148
Cockatiels, 149
Cockroaches, 164
Cockroaches Up Close, 167
Coelophysis, 61
Colorful Illusions: Tricks to Fool Your Eyes,
    82
Colosseum, The, 19–20
Computer Evidence, 80
Cool Chemistry Concoctions: 50 Formulas
    That Fizz, Foam, Splatter & Ooze, 89
Copperheads, 171
Coral Reef, 85
Coral Reef: A City That Never Sleeps, 129
Corpses, Coffins, and Crypts: A History of
    Burial, 105
Counting Coup: Becoming a Crow Chief on
    the Reservation and Beyond, 34
Cows, 148
Coyote: North America's Dog, 137
Coyotes, 154
Crazy Eights: And Other Card Games, 224
Crazy Horse: American Indian Leader, 49
Creepy Crawlies (by Alvin Silverstein et al.),
    172
Creepy Crawlies (by Jim Bruce), 167
Creepy Crawly Animal Origami, 229

Creepy Cuisine: Revolting Recipes that
    Look Disgusting but Taste Divine, 109
Creepy Spiders, 170
Crime-Fighting Aircraft, 194
Critter Riddles, 142
Crocodile, 170
Crocodiles (by Judith Jango-Cohen), 143
Crocodiles (by Julie Murray), 171
Crocodiles (by Sally M. Walker), 173
Crocodiles (by Sandra Markle), 170
Crocodiles and Alligators, 166
Crushing Avalanches, 91
Curse of the Pharaohs: My Adventures with
    the Mummies, 97–98

Dallas Cowboys, The, 202
Danger! Earthquakes, 221
Danger! Volcanoes, 82
Darkness over Denmark: the Danish
    Resistance and the Rescue of the Jews,
    13
D-Day Landings, The, 19
D-Day: They Fought to Free Europe from
    Hitler's Tyranny: A Day That Changed
    America, 17
Deadliest Dinosaurs, The, 62
Deadly Reptiles, 172
Deadly Snakes, 172
Deadly Spiders and Scorpions, 172
Death and Disease, 22
Deer, 152
Demolition Derby Cars, 198
Destination: Space, 91
Detroit Pistons, The, 202
Did Dinosaurs Eat Pizza? Mysteries Science
    Hasn't Solved, 53
Did Dinosaurs Have Feathers?, 65
Dig a Tunnel, 186
Dino Dung: The Scoop on Fossil Feces, 52,
    61
Dino Riddles, 62
Dinosaur Bones!, 57
Dinosaur Discoveries, 60
Dinosaur Hunt: Texas 115 Million Years
    Ago, 57
Dinosaur Hunters, 63
Dinosaur Jokes, 62

Dinosaurs with Feathers: The Ancestors of Modern Birds, 59

Diplodocus: Gigantic Long-Necked Dinosaur, 64

Dirt Track Racing, 187

Disaster in the Indian Ocean: Tsunami, 91

Disaster! Three Real-Life Stories of Survival, 214

Disasters, 214

Disasters in Space Exploration, 221

Discovering Dinosaurs with a Fossil Hunter, 56–57

Discovering the Iceman: What It Was Like to Find 5,300 Year Old Mummy?, 111

Discovering the Inca Ice Maiden: My Adventures on Ampato, 109

Diving Dolphins, 157

Dog of Discovery: A Newfoundland's Adventures with Lewis and Clark, 50

Dogs, 153

Dogs ABC: An Alphabet Book, 143

Dogs Rule!, 134

Dogs: How to Choose and Care for a Dog, 143

Dolphin Talk: Whistles, Clicks, and Clapping Jaws, 136

Dolphins (by Patricia Kendall), 144

Dolphins (by Ron Hirschi), 142

Don't Know Much about Dinosaurs, 60

Don't Know Much about Mummies, 112

Don't Try This at Home: How to Win a Sumo Match, Catch a Great White Shark, Start an Independent Nation, and Other Extraordinary Feats (for Ordinary People), 15, 230

Dr. Jenner and the Speckled Monster: the Search for the Smallpox Vaccine, 108

Dramatic Displays, 144

Drawing with Circles, 227

Drawing with Nature, 227

Drawing with Objects, 227

Drawing with Your Fingerprints, 228

Drawing with Your Hands, 228

Dreadful Droughts, 91

Dream Builders: The World's Best Skate Park Creators, 193

Droughts, 92

Ducks Don't Get Wet, 132

Duel of the Ironclads: The *Monitor* vs. the *Virginia*, 35–36

Dump Trucks, 194

Dust Bowl! The 1930s Black Blizzards, 220

Eagles, 156

Earthmovers, 193

Earthquake! A Day That Changed America: On a Peaceful Spring Morning, Disaster Strikes San Francisco, 216

Earthquake! The 1906 San Francisco Nightmare, 217

Earthquakes, 68

Earthquakes: Disaster and Survival, 89

Earthworms, 166

Eat Your Words: A Fascinating Look at the Language of Food, 225

Eating the Plates: A Pilgrim Book of Food and Manners, 36

Ed Emberley's Drawing Book of Trucks and Trains, 228

Ed Emberley's Drawing Book of Weirdos, 229

Electricity and Magnetism, 91

Electricity and Magnetism Science Fair Projects: Using Batteries, Balloons, and Other Hair-Raising Stuff, 86

Elephants (by Gloria G. Schlaepfer), 152

Elephants (by Julie Murray), 149

Elephants can Paint Too!, 138

Elvis Lives and Other Anagrams, 224

Emperor's Silent Army: Terracotta Warriors of Ancient China, The, 16

Empire State Building, 181–82

Encantado: Pink Dolphin of the Amazon, 135

Encyclopedia of Preserved People: Pickled, Frozen and Mummified Corpses from Around the World, The, 109

Encyclopedia of the Human Body, 231

Enduro Racing, 185

Energy Makes Things Happen, 80

ER Vets: Life in an Animal Emergency Room, 15, 121–22

Escape from Saigon: How A Vietnam War Orphan Became an American Boy, 17

Escape! The Story of the Great Houdini, 205–6
ESPN Information Please Sports Almanac 2006: The Definitive Sports Reference Book, 230
Eureka! Great Inventions and How They Happened, 197
Everyday Life in Ancient Rome, 20
Everyday Life of the Celts, 20
Everything Bug: What Kids Really Want to Know about Insects and Spiders, 173
Everything Dolphin: What Kids Really Want to Know about Dolphins, 157
Everything I Know about Cars: A Collection of Made-Up Facts, Educated Guesses, and Silly Pictures about Cars, Trucks, and Other Zoomy Things, 195
Everything Reptile: What Kids Really Want to Know about Reptiles, 174
Exploding Ants: Amazing Facts about How Animals Adapt, 8, 110, 117
Exploring the Deep, Dark Sea, 131
Exploring the Ice Age, 11
Exploring the *Titanic*, 212
Extreme Freestyle Motocross Moves, 200
Extreme Mountain Biking Moves, 190
Extreme Rock Climbing Moves, 190
Extreme Wakeboarding Moves, 200
Eye Guess: A Foldout Guessing Game, 227

Face-to-Face with the Cat, 118
Facing the Lion: Growing Up Maasai on the African Savanna, 13, 15
Falcons, 147
Fantastic Feats and Failures, 73, 177–78
Farm Tractors, 196
Far-Out Science Projects with Height and Depth: How High Is Up? How Low Is Down?, 86
Fastest Dinosaurs, The, 62
Fearsome Alligators, 170
Feathered Dinosaurs, 58
Feathered Dinosaurs of China, 56
Ferocious Fighters, 144
Ferrets, 148
Fierce Cats, 144

Fight for Freedom: The Remarkable Revolutionary War, 25–26
Fighting for Honor: The Japanese-Americans and World War II, 41
Fire Trucks, 194
Fire-Fighting Aircraft and Smoke Jumpers, 194
Fireworks, 68, 73
Fish: How to Choose and Care for a Fish, 144
Flash, Crash, Rumble, and Roll, 80
Flashy Fantastic Rainforest Frogs, 166
Float Like a Butterfly, 200
Flying Giants of Dinosaur Time, 62–63
Flying Squirrels, 143
Follow the Trail: A Young Person's Guide to the Great Outdoors, 88
Food Rules! The Stuff You Munch, Its Crunch, Its Punch, and Why You Sometimes Lose Your Lunch, 107
Fooled You! Fakes and Hoaxes through the Years, 208
Football Pro, A, 194
Forces of Nature: The Awesome Power of Volcanoes, Earthquakes, and Tornadoes, 87
Forensics, 77
Fossil Fish Found Alive: Discovering the Coelacanth, 58, 61
Fossil Tales, 86
Foxes, 146
Freedom Riders: John Lewis and Jim Zwerg on the Front Lines of the Civil Rights Movement, 24–25
Freedom Roads: Searching for the Underground Railroad, 43
Freeze Frame: A Photographic History of the Winter Olympics, 180–81
Freshwater Fishes, 143
Freshwater Giants, Hippopotamus, River Dolphins, and Manatees, 136
Frogs, 171
From Head to Toe: The Amazing Human Body and How It Works, 73, 82
Frozen Man, 106
Funnel-Web Spiders, 168

Funny Riddles, 225
Fury on Horseback, 48

Games: Learn to Play, Play to Win, 225
Geckos, 169
Genius: A Photobiography of Albert
    Einstein, 69–70, 73
Gentle Giant Octopus, 137
George Did It, 32
George vs. George: The American
    Revolution as Seen from Both Sides, 25,
    46
George Washington's Teeth, 25, 41
Get on Board: The Story of the Underground
    Railroad, 43
Getting Away with Murder: The True Story
    of the Emmett Till Case, 8, 15, 25, 41
Gettysburg, 48
Gettysburg: July 1–3, 1863, 49
Gettysburg: The Legendary Battle and the
    Address that Inspired a Nation, 39–40
Ghost Liners: Exploring the World's
    Greatest Lost Ships, 212
Ghosts of the Nile, 4
Ghosts of the West Coast: the Lost Souls of
    the Queen Mary and Other Real-Life
    Hauntings, 216
Giant and Teeny, 144
Giant Armadillo, 61
Giant Children, 104
Giant Machines, 200
Giant Meat-Eating Dinosaurs, 63
Giant Panda, 140
Giraffes, 150
Gladiator, 18
Gladiator: Life and Death in Ancient Rome,
    21
Go Figure! A Totally Cool Book about
    Numbers, 224
Go Fly a Bike! The Ultimate Book about
    Bicycle Fun, Freedom & Science, 185
Go to Jail! A Look at Prisons through the
    Ages, 12
Go-Karts, 199
Gone A-Whaling: The Lure of the Sea and
    the Hunt for the Great Whale, 45

Good Brother, Bad Brother: The Story of
    Edwin Booth and John Wilkes Booth,
    29–30
Gorilla, 139
Gorilla Doctors: Saving Endangered Great
    Apes, 117, 127, 181
Gorillas (by Patricia Kendall), 144
Gorillas (by Seymour Simon), 152
Gorillas (by Judith Jango-Cohen), 143
Grasshoppers, 171
Grasshoppers Up Close, 171
Gray Wolves, 154
Great Book of Optical Illusions, The, 226
Great Brain Book: An Inside Look at the
    Inside of Your Head, The, 89
Great Expedition of Lewis and Clark by
    Private Reubin Field, Member of the
    Corps of Discovery, The, 42
Great Paper Fighter Planes, 230
Great Pets! An Extraordinary Guide to More
    than 60 Usual and Unusual Family Pets,
    153
Great Pyramid: The Story of the Farmers,
    the God-King and the Most Astounding
    Structure Ever Built, The, 14
Great Serum Race: Blazing the Iditarod
    Trail, The, 45
Great Wall: The Story of 4,000 Miles of
    Earth and Stone That Turned a Nation
    into a Fortress, The, 15
Great White Shark, 153
Great White Sharks (by Kathleen W.
    Deady), 140
Great White Sharks (by Sandra Markle), 123
Great Wonders of the World, 10
Grey Wolf, 138
Grierson's Raid: A Daring Cavalry Strike
    through the Heart of the Confederacy,
    44
Grizzly Bears (by Kathleen W. Deady), 141
Grizzly Bears (by Patricia Kendall), 144
Gross and Gory, 146
Grossology and You, 105
Grossology: The Science of Really Gross
    Things, 105
Growing Up Wild: Penguins, 134
Guess Who Bites, 141

Guess Who Dives, 141
Guess Who Hides, 141
Guess Who Hisses, 141
Guess Who Hops, 141
Guess Who Roars, 141
Guess Who Runs, 141
Guess Who Swoops, 141
Guinea Pig Scientists: Bold
    Self-Experimenters in Science and
    Medicine, 70–71, 73
Guinness World Records 2006, 230
Guts: Our Digestive System, 79
Guts: The True Stories Behind Hatchet and
    the Brian Books, 15, 109

Hammerhead Sharks, 149
Hammerin' Hank: The Life of Hank
    Greenberg, 182
Hamsters, Gerbils, Guinea Pigs, Rabbits,
    Ferrets, Mice, and Rats: How to Choose
    and Care for a Small Mammal, 144
Hands-On Grossology, 105
Handy Science Answer Book, 230
Harlem Hellfighters: When Pride Met
    Courage, 35
Harp Seal Pups, 135
Harry Houdini: Escape Artist, 224
Harvesting Hope: The Story of Cesar
    Chavez, 25, 44
Hawk Highway in the Sky: Watching Raptor
    Migration, 128
Hawks, 147
Hawks and Falcons, 151
Head Bone's Connected to the Neck Bone:
    The Weird, Wacky and Wonderful
    X-Ray, The, 99, 108
Head Lice Up Close, 167
Heat Hazard: Droughts, 92
Heavy-Duty Science Projects with Weight:
    How Much Does It Weigh?, 86
Heinrich Himmler: Murderous Architect of
    the Holocaust, 22
Hello, Fish! Visiting the Coral Reef, 130
Herbivores, 60
Here Is the Coral Reef, 80
Hermit Crabs, 139

Hero Dogs: Courageous Canines in Action,
    117, 133
Hidden Child, 7
Hidden Hibernators, 150
Hidden Under the Ground: The World
    Beneath Your Feet, 81
High Hopes: A Photobiography of John F.
    Kennedy, 44
Hilde and Eli: Children of the Holocaust, 10
Hindenburg, The, 215
Hindenburg: The Fiery Crash of a German
    Airship, The, 218
Hiroshima: The Story of the First Atom
    Bomb, 5
Hitler Youth: Growing up in Hitler's
    Shadow, 2–3, 179
Hmm? The Most Interesting Book You'll
    Ever Read about Memory, 83
Hobo Spiders, 168
Hold the Flag High, 27–28
Home Front in World War II, The, 50
Home on the Moon: Living on the Space
    Frontier, 72–73
Honeybees, 164
Hook, Line & Sinker: A Beginner's Guide to
    Fishing, Boating, and Watching Water
    Wildlife, 138
Horned Dinosaurs, 63
Horses (by Seymour Simon), 125
Horses (by Susan Schafer), 152
Horses: How to Choose and Care for a
    Horse, 144
Hottest Coldest Highest Deepest, 81
How Ben Franklin Stole the Lightning, 46
How Bright Is Your Brain? Amazing Games
    to Play with Your Mind, 85
How Dinosaurs Took Flight: The Fossils, the
    Science, What We Think We Know,
    and the Mysteries Yet Unsolved, 8, 55,
    61
How Smart Is Your Dog? 30 Fun Science
    Activities with Your Pet, 140
How the Wolf Became the Dog, 117, 137
How They Got Over: African Americans and
    the Call of the Sea, 43
How to Be a Medieval Knight , 6

How to Build Your Own Prize-Winning Robot, 201

How to Find Lost Treasure in All Fifty States and Canada Too!, 214

How to Hunt Buried Treasure, 213

How We Crossed the West: The Adventures of Lewis and Clark, 47

How Whales Walked into the Sea, 117, 135

Hurricane Andrew, 220

Hurricane!, 221

Hurricane! The 1900 Galveston Night of Terror, 220

Hurry Freedom: African Americans in Gold Rush California, 47

Hyenas, 124

I See a Kookaburra! Discovering Animal Habitats around the World, 122

I Spy Ultimate Challenger! A Book of Picture Riddles, 226

I Wonder Why Zippers Have Teeth and Other Questions about Inventions, 187

Ice Age Cave Bear: The Giant Beast that Terrified Ancient Humans, 62

Ice Age Sabertooth: The Most Ferocious Cat That Ever Lived, 62

Ice Mummies: Frozen in Time, 107

Ice Storms, 92

Iceman, The, 107

If I Were President, 47

If You Decide to Go to the Moon, 76

Iguanadon, 61

Illustrated Directory of Sports Cars, The, 231

Imaginative Inventions: The Who, What, Where, When, and Why of Roller Skates, Potato Chips, Marbles, and Pie and More!, 185

In the Line of Fire: Presidents' Lives at Stake, 47

In the Sky, 60

In the Time of Knights: The Real-Life Story of History's Greatest Knights, 17

In Your Face: The Facts about Your Features, 74–75

Incredible Amphibians, 173

Incredible Arachnids, 173

Incredible Birds, 155

Incredible Fish, 155

Incredible Insects, 173

Incredible Mammals, 155

Incredible Mollusks, 155

Incredible Paper Flying Machines, 230

Incredible Quest to Find the *Titanic*, The, 221

Incredible Record-Setting Deep-Sea Dive of the Bathysphere, The, 89

Incredible Reptiles, 155

Incredible Search for the Treasure Ship *Atocha*, 221

Incredible Submersible Alvin Discovers a Strange Deep-Sea World, The, 89

Indianapolis Colts, The, 202

Indoor Zoo, 90

Inline Skating, 191

In-line Skating, 202

Insect-lo-Pedia: Young Naturalist's Handbook, 172

Inside the Alamo, 46

Inside the Beagle with Charles Darwin, 88

Inside the Tomb of Tutankhamun, 112

Interrupted Journey: Saving Endangered Sea Turtles, 165

Inventing the Future: A Photobiography of Thomas Alva Edison, 185

Investigating Fakes and Hoaxes, 221

Investigating History Mysteries, 221

Investigating Murder Mysteries, 218

Investigating Murders, 71–72

Investigating Thefts and Heists, 221

Invisible Allies: Microbes that Shape our Lives, 73–74

Irish Elk, 61

It's about Time! Science Projects: How Long Does It Take?, 86

It's Disgusting—and We Ate It! Food Facts around the World and throughout History, 111

It's Not Magic, It's Science! 50 Science Tricks That Mystify, Dazzle & Astound!, 84

It's Snowing! It's Snowing! Winter Poems, 78

Jack Russell Terriers, 149
Jack: The Early Years of John F. Kennedy, 41
Javelinas, 152
Jefferson's Children: The Story of One
    American Family, 44–45
Jesse James: Wild West Train Robber, 49
Joe Louis: America's Fighter, 175
John Muir and Stickeen: An Alaskan
    Adventure, 49
John Muir: America's First
    Environmentalist, 32–33
Journey of the One and Only Declaration of
    Independence, The, 37
Journey to Ellis Island: How My Father
    Came to America, 40
Journey under the Sea, 77
Judo, 190
Julius Caesar: The Life of a Roman General,
    4–5
Jumping Kangaroos, 146
Jumping Spiders, 171
Junk Lab, 90
Jurassic Shark, 52

Kangaroo, 150
Karate, 190
Karate for Kids, 197
Karting, 201
Kickboxing, 196
Kid Blink Beats The World, 26–27
Kid Who Invented the Trampoline: More
    Surprising Stories about Inventions,
    The, 187
Kids' Guide to Digital Photography: How to
    Shoot, Save, Play with and Print Your
    Digital Photos, The, 227
Kid's Silliest Riddles, 225
Killer Bees, 144
Killer Carnivores, 152
Killer Cats, 153
Killer Fish, 126
Killer Whale, 143
Killer Whales (by Sandra Markle), 147
Killer Whales (by Seymour Simon), 152
King of the Mild Frontier: An Ill-Advised
    Autobiography, 42

Kingfisher Illustrated Dinosaur
    Encyclopedia, The, 60
Kitchen Lab, 90
Klondike Gold, 8–9
Knights, 17
Koala, 143
Komodo Dragon: On Location, 164
Komodo Dragons, 173

Labyrinths: Can You Escape from the
    Twenty-Six Letters of the Alphabet?,
    226
Ladybugs Up Close, 171
Land Speed Racing, 185
Landslides, 92
Leeches, 144
Left for Dead: A Young Man's Search for
    Justice for the USS Indianapolis, 15, 46
Lemurs: On Location, 130
Leonardo da Vinci, 76
Leopards (by Dan Greenberg), 142
Leopards (by Patricia Kendall), 144
Let It Begin Here! Lexington & Concord:
    First Battles of the American
    Revolution, 29
Lexington and Concord: April 19, 1775, 48
Life and Death of Adolf Hilter, The, 12, 179
Life in Ancient Rome, 18
Life of Benjamin Franklin: An American
    Original, The, 33
Life-Size Dinosaurs, 59
Lions (by Sandra Markle), 147
Lions (by Patricia Kendall), 144
Little Bighorn: June 25, 1876, 49
Little Book of Dinosaurs, 65
Little Elephants, 144
Little Foxes, 140
Little Giraffes, 147
Little Gorillas, 140
Little Leopards, 140
Little Panda: the World Welcomes Hua Mei
    at the San Diego Zoo, 136
Little Shark, 172
Little Wolves, 148
Lizards (by Dan Greenberg), 169
Lizards (by Julie Murray), 171
Lizards (by Lola Schaefer), 172

Lizards (by Peter Heathcote), 169
Lizards, Frogs and Polliwogs, 169
Lizards: Weird and Wonderful, 169
Lonek's Journey: The True Story of a Boy's Escape to Freedom, 9
Looking for Jaguar and Other Rain Forest Poems, 75
Lost Childhood: A World War II Memoir, The, 16
Lost City of Pompeii, 215
Lost Colony of Roanoke, The, 206–7
Lost Temple of the Aztecs, 17
Lost Treasure of the Inca, 214
Lost Wreck of the Isis, The, 212
Lowdown on Earthworms, 167
Lynx, 128

Machu Picchu: The Story of the Amazing Inkas and Their City in the Clouds, 14
Maggots, Grubs, and More: The Secret Lives of Young Insects, 173
Magic Book, The, 223
Magic Tricks, 224
Magic with Cards, 224
Magic … Naturally! Science Entertainments and Amusements, 80
Maiasaura, 61
Major Tyler: Champion Cyclist, 41
Make Amazing Toy and Game Gadgets, 197
Make Cool Gadgets for Your Room, 197
Making Paper Airplanes that Really Fly, 230
Malcolm X: A Fire Burning Brightly, 46
Mammalabilia, 131
Mammoths on the Move, 127
Mammoths: Ice-Age Giants, 59
Man o' War: Best Racehorse Ever, 148
Man Who Walked between the Towers, The, 43
Man Who Went to the Far Side of the Moon: The Story of Apollo 11 Astronaut Michael Collins, The, 82, 181
Manatee Morning, A, 128
Manatees: Peaceful Plant-Eaters, 151
Mary Celeste: An Unsolved Mystery from History, The, 8, 217
Masada, 22
Maserati, 203

Matthew Henson: Arctic Adventurer, 49
Medieval Castle, A, 99, 108
Meerkats, 137
Megalosaurus, 61
Mercedes-Benz, 203
Miami Heat, The, 202
Michael Phelps, 204
Michelangelo, 17
Microscopic Life, 92
Mind Tricks, 223
Mission to Mars, 84
Mississippi River: A Journey Down the Father of Water, 45
Mistakes That Worked, 186
Monkeys, 148
Monster Mall: And Other Spooky Poems, The, 113
Monster Trucks, 196
Moose, 146
Mosquito Bite, 117, 162
Mosquitoes, 166
Mosquitoes Up Close, 167
Motocross (by Aaron Frisch), 191
Motocross (by Gary Freeman), 191
Mount St. Helens, 220
Mountain Bikes, 199
Mountain Biking, 196
Mountain Gorillas, 144
Muhammad Ali: Meet the Champion, 195
Mummies, 108
Mummies of the Pharaohs: Exploring the Valley of the Kings, 104–5
Mummies, Bones, and Body Parts, 112
Mummies: The Newest, Coolest & Creepiest from around the World, 103–4
Mummy, 109
My Family Shall Be Free: The Life of Peter Still, 42
My Pet Hamster, 151
My Season with Penguins: An Antarctic Journal, 157
My Senator and Me: A Dog's-Eye View of Washington D.C., 122
Mysteries of History, 209
Mysterious Disappearance of Roanoke Colony in American History, The, 214
Mystery of the Egyptian Mummy, The, 106

Mystery of the Hieroglyphs: The Story of the Rosetta Stone and the Race to Decipher Egyptian Hieroglyphs, The, 213

Mystery of the Maya: Uncovering the Lost City of Palenque, The, 13

Myths and Monsters: Secrets Revealed, 219

Naked Mole Rats, 133

NASCAR, 189

National Geographic Prehistoric Mammals, 64

National League Central, 200

National League East, 202

National League West, 191

Nature Shockers, 91

Nature's Fury: Eyewitness Reports of Natural Disasters, 216

Nature's Yucky! Gross Stuff that Helps Nature Work, 134

New Dinos: The Latest Finds! Coolest Dinosaur Discoveries!, 58

New England Patriots, The, 182

New York Yankees, The, 202

NFC East, 203

NFC South, 195

NFC West, 203

Night the Martians Landed: Just the Facts (Plus the Rumors) about Invaders from Mars, The, 44

Nights of the Pufflings, 135

Nikola Tesla and the Taming of Electricity, 84

Now & Ben: The Modern Inventions of Ben Franklin, 176

Nuclear Submarine Disasters, 220

Octopus: Phantom of the Sea, The, 129

Octopuses (by Diane Swanson), 154

Octopuses (by Judith Jango-Cohen), 143

Octopuses (by Leighton Taylor), 154

Off the Wall: A Skateboarder's Guide to Riding Bowls and Pools, 193

Off-Road Vehicles, 192

Oh, Yuck! The Encyclopedia of Everything Nasty, 108

Old-Time Baseball: 1903 and the First Modern World Series, 190

Omnibeasts: Animal Poems and Paintings by Douglas Florian, 118

On the Trail of Lewis and Clark: A Journey Up the Missouri River, 45

On the Trail of the Komodo Dragon and Other Explorations of Science in Action, 171

One More Border: The True Story of One Family's Escape from War-Torn Europe, 12

Onward: A Photobiography of African-American Polar Explorer Matthew Henson, 31–32

Orangutan, 149

Orcas around Me: My Alaskan Summer, 135

Origami Myths, 229

Out of Sight: Pictures of Hidden Worlds, 110

Outside and Inside Bats, 134

Outside and Inside Big Cats, 147

Outside and Inside Giant Squid, 147

Outside and Inside Killer Bees, 160

Outside and Inside Mummies, 100–1

Oviraptor, 62

Owl, 147

Owls (by Adrienne Mason), 148

Owls (by Maria Mudd Ruth), 151

Owls (by Sandra Markle), 148

Owls: Flat-Faced Flyers, 151

Palindromania, 224

Panama Canal: The Story of How a Jungle Was Conquered and the World Made Smaller, The, 14

Pandas, 149

Peaceful Protest: The Life of Nelson Mandela, 15

Peanut Butter Party: Including the History, Uses, and Future of Peanut Butter, 80

Pearl Harbor: December 7, 1941, 48

Penguin, 136

Penguins, 152

Penguins Swim but Don't Get Wet and Other Amazing Facts about Polar Animals, 138

Penguins!, 141

Perilous Journey of the Donner Party, The, 212–13
Pesky Parasites, 157
Pet Fish, 149
Pet for Me: Poems, A, 133
Pet Frog, 171
Pet Guinea Pig, 149
Pet Hamster, 149
Pet Hermit Crab, 149
Philadelphia Eagles, The, 202
Phineas Gage: A Gruesome but True Story about Brain Science, 99, 106
Phoenix Spurs, The, 202
Photo by Brady: A Picture of the Civil War, 23–24
Photography, 227
Picture Book of Dwight David Eisenhower, A, 40
Pigs, 141
Pill Bugs Up Close, 171
Pink Snow and Other Weird Weather, 80
Piracy and Plunder: A Murderous Business, 15
Pirates & Smugglers, 3–4
Pirates and Privateers of the High Seas, 22
Plane, 197
Planet Patrol, 88
Platypus, Probably, A, 115–16
Polar Bears (by Jacqueline S. Cotton), 140
Polar Bears (by Sandra Markle), 148
Polar Bears (by Sophie Lockwood), 146
Polar Exploration: Journeys to the Arctic and Antarctic, 11
Pompeii: Lost and Found, 109
Poop: A Natural History of the Unmentionable, 95–96, 99
Porcupines, 154
Potbellied Pigs, 139
Pouncing Bobcats, 151
Powerful Predators, 144
Prairie Builders: Reconstructing America's Lost Grasslands, The, 69
Predator: Animals with the Skill to Kill, 152
Prehistoric Actual Size, 53, 61
President Has Been Shot! True Stories of the Attacks on Ten U.S. Presidents, The, 44

President Is Shot! The Assassination of Abraham Lincoln, The, 44
President of the Underground Railroad: A Story about Levi Coffin, 47
Prickly Porcupines, 157
Psittacosaurus, 62
Pteranodon: The Life Story of a Pterosaur, 59
Pterosaurs: Rulers of the Skies in the Dinosaur Age, 51–52, 61
Purple Death: The Mysterious Flu of 1918, 213–14
Put a Fan in Your Hat! Inventions, Contraptions, and Gadgets Kids Can Build, 185
Pyramids & Mummies, 22

Rabbits, Rabbits and More Rabbits!, 131–32
Race Cars, 192
Race to Save the Lord God Bird, The, xvi, 120–21
Raging Floods, 91
Ralph Masiello's Bug Drawing Book, 229
Ramps: A Skateboarder's Guide to Riding Half-Pipes, 193
Raptor! A Kid's Guide to Birds of Prey, 146
Rats, 148
Rats! The Good, the Bad, and the Ugly, 116
Rattlesnakes, 171
Reaching for the Moon, 67
Read about Crazy Horse, 49
Real Vikings: Craftsmen, Trades, and Fearsome Raiders, The, 10
Red-Eyed Tree Frog, The, 163
Remarkable Benjamin Franklin, The, 30–31
Remember D-Day: The Plan, the Invasion, Survivor Stories, 11, 25, 179
Remember Pearl Harbor: American and Japanese Survivors Tell Their Stories, 40, 179
Remember the Lusitania!, 216
Remember World War II: Kids Who Survived Tell Their Stories, 7–8
Rescue Helicopters and Aircraft, 194
Revenge of the Whale: The True Story of the Whaleship Essex, The, 215
Rhinoceroses, 143

Rickie and Henri: A True Story, 119

Riddel-lightful: Oodles of Little Riddle Poems, 226

Riddle Me This! Riddles and Stories to Challenge Your Mind, 226

Riddle Rhymes, 224

Rio Grande: From the Rocky Mountains to the Gulf of Mexico, 45

Ripley's Believe It or Not! Special Edition 2006, 231

Ripley's Believe It or Not! Encyclopedia of the Bizarre, The, 231

Rippin' Ramps: A Skateboarder's Guide to Riding Half-Pipes, 193

Rise of Hitler, The, 20

Roald Dahl's Revolting Recipes, 105

Roanoke, the Lost Colony: An Unsolved Mystery from History, 217

Roberto Clemente: Baseball's Humanitarian Hero, 195

Roberto Clemente: Pride of the Pittsburgh Pirates, 203

Robotics, 85

Robots Slither, 87

Rock Climbing (by Chris Oxlade), 197

Rock Climbing (by Kristin Van Cleaf), 202

Rolls-Royce, 203

Roman Army: The Legendary Soldiers Who Created an Empire, The, 10

Roman Colosseum: The Story of the World's Most Famous Stadium and Its Deadly Games, The, 14

Roman News, The, 13

Rome: In Spectacular Cross-Section, 22

Royal Mummies: Remains from Ancient Egypt, The, 112

Sabertooths and the Ice Age: A Nonfiction Companion to Sunset of the Sabertooth, 63

Safe Home for the Manatees, A, 133

Saladin: Noble Prince of Islam, 17

Salamanders (by Julie Murray), 171

Salamanders (by Peter Heathcote), 169

Salem Witch Trials: An Unsolved Mystery from History, The, 211

Sammy: Dog Detective, 128

San Antonio Spurs, The, 202

Scary Sharks, 144

Scholastic Atlas of the World, 231

Scholastic Book of Firsts, 230

Scholastic Book of World Records, 2006, 231

Scholastic Dinosaurs A to Z: The Ultimate Dinosaur Encyclopedia, 63

School Jokes, 226

Science Magic, 224

Science Verse, 79

Scimitar Cat, 61

Scooters and Skateboards, 198

Scruffy: A Wolf Finds its Place in the Pack, 129

Sea Creatures, 150

Sea Critters, 131

Sea Giants of Dinosaur Time, 63

Sea Hunters: Dolphins, Whales, and Seals, 153

Sea Otters, 146

Sea Turtles: Ocean Nomads, 163

Seahorses, 156

Seal, 150

Search for the Golden Moon Bear: Science and Adventure in the Asian Tropics, 124–25

Searching for Grizzlies, 142

Secrets from the Rocks: Dinosaur Hunting with Roy Chapman Andrews, 58

Secrets of a Civil War Submarine: Solving the Mysteries of the H.L. Hunley, 8, 25, 181, 210–11

Secrets of Animal Flight, The, 129

Secrets of the Mummies: Uncovering the Bodies of Ancient Egyptians, 111

Secrets of the Sphinx, 11–12

Seeker of Knowledge: The Man Who Deciphered Egyptian Hieroglyphs, 16

Shaky Ground: Earthquakes, 85

Shark Life: True Stories about Sharks & the Sea, 138

Shark! the Truth Behind the Terror, 154

Sharks! (Time for Kids Science Scoops Confident Reader 3), 118

Sharks and Other Scary Sea Creatures, 147

Sheep, 149

Shipwreck at the Bottom of the World: The Extraordinary True Story of Shackleton and the *Endurance*, 15, 179, 212

Shipwrecked: the True Adventures of a Japanese Boy, 11

Short and Bloody History of Ghosts, The, 219

Short and Bloody History of Highwaymen, The, 213

Short and Bloody History of Knights, The, 20

Short and Bloody History of Pirates, The, 20

Short and Bloody History of Spies, The, 20

Short-Faced Bear, 61

Sidewalk Games, 227

Signers: The Fifty-Six Stories Behind the Declaration of Independence, The, 25, 42

Simple Magic, 224

Sinister Snakes, 170

Sit on a Potato Pan, Otis! More Palindromes, 224

Sixteen Years in Sixteen Seconds: The Sammy Lee Story, 204

Skateboarding (by Ben Powell), 197

Skateboarding (by K. E. Vieregger), 202

Skating, 194

Skiing, 196

Skunks, 154

Skunks Do More than Stink!, 153

Skyscraper: From the Ground Up, 178–79

Skyscrapers: How America Grew Up, 186

Slave Young, Slave Long: The American Slave Experience, 43

Slinky Scaly Slithery Snakes, 166

Sloths, 153

Small Birds, 153

Smart Feller Fart Smeller and Other Spoonerisms, 224

Smartest Dinosaurs, The, 63

Smokejumpers: Battling the Forest Flames, 184

Snails Up Close, 150

Snake Pits, Talking Cures, and Magic Bullets: A History of Mental Illness, 87

Snake Scientist, The, 117, 165

Snakes (by Adrienne Mason), 170

Snakes (by Deborah Behler and John Behler), 167

Snakes (by Diane Swanson), 173

Snakes (by Sonia Hernandez-Divers), 169

Snakes (by Susan Schafer), 172

Snakes!, 168

Snakes! Strange and Wonderful, 171

Snakes: Biggest! Littlest!, 170

Snowboarding (by Matt Barr and Chris Moran), 188

Snowboarding (by Stephanie F. Hedlund), 193

So You Want to be an Explorer?, 16

So You Want to Be an Inventor, 186

So You Want to be President?, 47

Soda Science: Designing and Testing Soft Drinks, 84

Soldier's Life: A Visual History of Soldiers through the Ages, A, 16

Solo Sailing, 197

Sounds All Around, 82

Space Mania: Discovering Distant Worlds without Leaving Your Own, 85

Special Fate. Chiune Sugihara: Hero of the Holocaust, A, 12

Speedy and Slow, 146

Spiders (by Dan Greenberg), 169

Spiders (by Seymour Simon), 172

Spiders' Secrets, 171

Spiders Up Close, 167

Spiders! (by Editors of Time for Kids), 168

Spiders! (by Nicole Iorio), 170

Spies, 20

Spies and their Gadgets, 22

Spinning Spiders, 163

Spinosaurus, 62

Split-Second Science Projects with Speed: How Fast Does It Go?, 86

Spooky Jokes, 226

Spooky Riddles, 220

Sports Cars, 193

Spraying Skunks, 149

Spy Hops and Belly Flops: Curious Behavior of Woodland Animals, 132

Squirrels, 152

Stars Beneath Your Bed: The Surprising Story of Dust, 78

Stealth Bombers: The B-2 Spirits, 183
Stegosaurus and Other Plains Dinosaurs, 60
Stephen Biesty's Castles, 21
Stonehenge, 21
Storm Chasers: On the Trail of Deadly
    Tornadoes, 221
Storm Warning: Tornadoes, 89
Story of Coca-Cola, The, 189
Story of Harley-Davidson, The, 200
Story of Medicine from Acupuncture to X
    Rays, The, 99
Strange New Species: Astonishing
    Discoveries of Life on Earth, 144
Street through Time: A 12,000 Year Walk
    through History, A, 15
Stunt Planes, 199
Super Bowl, 189
Super Knock-Knocks, 225
Super Science Concoctions: 50 Mysterious
    Mixtures for Fabulous Fun, 81
Super Storms, 221
Superbike Racing, 187
Superbikes, 193
Superboats, 193
Supercroc and the Origin of Crocodiles, 58
Supercross Racing, 186
Supersonic X-15 and High-Tech NASA
    Aircraft, The, 194
Surprising Sharks, 130
Surviving Hitler: A Boy in the Nazi Death
    Camps, 15, 18, 181
Sweeping Tsunamis, 91
Switched On, Flushed Down, Tossed Out:
    Investigating the Hidden Workings of
    Your Home, 198

T. Rex, 53
Tae Kwon Do, 188
Take Me Out to the Ball Game, 176
Take the Lead, George Washington, 38–39
Taking Action: How to Get Your City to
    Build a Public Skate Park, 193
Tarantula Scientist, The, 117, 165, 181
Tarantulas (by Emily McAuliffe), 170
Tarantulas (by Eric Ethan), 168

Technical Terrain: A Skateboarder's Guide
    to Riding Skate Park Street Courses,
    193
Tentacles! Tales of the Giant Squid, 151
The 5,000-Year-Old Puzzle: Solving a
    Mystery of Ancient Egypt, The, 13
They Call Me Woolly: What Animal Names
    Can Tell Us, 130
They Saw the Future: Oracles, Psychics,
    Scientists, Great Thinkers, and Pretty
    Good Guessers, 12–13
Third Crusade: Richard the Lionhearted vs.
    Saladin, The, 19
This Book Really Sucks! The Science
    behind Gravity, Flight, Leeches, Black
    Holes, Tornadoes, Our Friend The
    Vacuum Cleaner, And Most Everything
    Else, 106
This Car, 190
Throw Your Tooth on the Roof: Tooth
    Traditions from Around the World, 40
Thunder on the Plains: the Story of the
    American Buffalo, 136
Thunderbird, 197
Tierra del Fuego: A Journey to the End of
    the Earth, 14
Tiger Sharks, 149
Tigers (by Lynn M. Stone), 154
Tigers (by Patricia Kendall), 144
Tigers (by Peter Murray), 149
Tigers (by Rebecca Stefoff), 153
Tigers (by Sarah L. Thomson), 155
Titanic (by Kathleen Fahey), 219
Titanic (by Simon Adams), 211
Titanic: The Tragedy at Sea, The, 218
To the Bottom of the Sea: The Exploration
    of Exotic Life, the Titanic, and Other
    Secrets of the Oceans, 83
Toilets, Bathtubs, Sinks and Sewers: A
    History of the Bathroom, 105
Tooth and Claw: Animal Adventures in the
    Wild, 134
Toothworms and Spider Juice: an Illustrated
    History of Dentistry, 99, 107
Top of the World: Climbing Mount Everest,
    The, 12, 179

Top Secret: A Handbook of Codes, Ciphers, and Secret Writing, 225
Top Ten of Everything, The, 230
Tornado!, 221
Tornado! The 1974 Super Outbreak, 217
Tornadoes: Disaster and Survival, 85
Totally Silly Jokes, 225
Toy Lab, 90
Toys! Amazing Stories behind Some Great Inventions, 73, 187
Trading Cards: From Start to Finish, 201
Trains, 193
Transformed: How Everyday Things Are Made, 200
Treasures of the Spanish Main, 215
Triceratops and Other Forest Dinosaurs, 60
Triceratops and Other Horned Plant-Eaters, 63
Triceratops: Mighty Three-Horned Dinosaur, 64
Tricky Optical Illusion Puzzles, 226
Triumph on Everest: A Photobiography of Sir Edmund Hillary, 11
Trucks and Big Rigs, 196
True Tales of the Wild West, 50
True-or-False Book of Dogs, The, 8, 117, 134
Truth about Great White Sharks, The, 117, 129
Truth about Poop, The, 8, 99, 106
Tsunami! The 1946 Hilo Wave of Terror, 220
Tsunami: Helping Each Other, 21
Turkey Riddles, 142
Turtle Tide: The Ways of Sea Turtles, 173
Tutankhamun: The Mystery of the Boy King, 98–99
Tyrannosaurus and Other Giant Meat-Eaters, 63
Tyrannosaurus Rex: Fierce King of the Dinosaurs, 64

U.S. Army Fighting Vehicles, 188
Ultimate Field Trip 4: A Week in the 1800s, 43
Ultimate Indoor Games Book: The 200 Best Boredom Busters Ever!, The, 225

Unbeatable Beaks, 137
Uncle John's Bathroom Reader for Kids Only, 230
Uncle John's Top Secret Bathroom Reader for Kids Only, 230
Under the Sea Origami, 230
Under the Wild Western Sky, 84
Universe, 87
Untamed: Animals around the World, 139
Usborne Introduction to Archaeology: Internet-Linked, The, 22

Valley of the Golden Mummies, 21
Vampire Bats (by Anne Welsbacher), 157
Vampire Bats (by Julie Murray), 149
Vanished, 207
Velociraptor and Other Small, Speedy Meat-Eaters, 63
Viking News, The, 18
Violent Skies: Hurricanes, 89
Vipers, 164
Visual Encyclopedia of Animals, 231
Vultures (by Sandra Markle), 148
Vultures (by Wayne Lynch), 147

Wackiest White House Pets, 130
Wacky Jokes, 226
Warthogs, 143
Wasps Up Close, 172
Watching Water Birds, 128
Water Hole, 92
Watercraft, 197
We Rode the Orphan Trains, 25, 48
Weimeraner, The, 137
Weird and Wonderful, 146
Whales (by Dan Greenberg), 142
Whales (by Graham Faiella), 141
Whales! Strange and Wonderful, 150
What a Day It Was at School!, 101
What a Great Idea: Inventions That Changed the World, 73, 183–84
What Do You Do When Something Wants to Eat You?, 144
What Do You Do with a Tail Like This?, 134
What Happens to a Hamburger?, 110
What If You Met a Pirate?, 1–2

What Presidents are Made of, 46

What Really Happened in Roswell? Just the Facts (Plus the Rumors) about UFOs and Aliens, 220

What Stinks?, 102

What You Never Knew about Tubs, Toilets, and Showers, 8, 99, 107

What's Up? What's Down?, 125

What's Faster than a Speeding Cheetah?, 83

What's Living in your Backyard?, 153

What's Living in Your Bedroom?, 99, 103

What's Living in Your Classroom?, 153

What's Living in Your Kitchen?, 153

What's Living inside Your Body?, 113

What's Living on Your Body?, 113

When Bugs Were Big, Plants Were Strange, and Tetrapods Stalked the Earth: A Cartoon Prehistory of Life before the Dinosaurs, 57, 61

When Mammoths Walked the Earth, 57

Where Are the Night Animals?, 141

Where Fish Go in Winter: And Other Great Mysteries, 87

While You're Waiting for the Food to Come: A Tabletop Science Activity Book: Experiments and Tricks That Can Be Done at a Restaurant, the Dining Room Table, or Wherever Food Is Served, 81

White-Out: Blizzards, 92

White-Tailed Deer, 150

Who Ordered the Jumbo Shrimp? And Other Oxymorons, 224

Whose Nose and Toes?, 140

Why Do Bones Break? And Other Questions about Movement, 90

Why Do Bruises Change Color? And Other Questions about Blood, 90

Why Do Cats Meow?, 132

Why Do Dogs Bark?, 133

Why Do Dogs Have Wet Noses?, 117

Why Do Horses Neigh?, 143

Why Do I Vomit? And Other Questions about Digestion, 90

Why Do Rabbits Hop? And Other Questions about Rabbits, Guinea Pigs, Hamsters, and Gerbils, 133

Why Do Snakes Hiss? And Other Questions about Snakes, Lizards, and Turtles, 170

Why Does My Body Smell? And Other Questions about Hygiene, 91

Why I Sneeze, Shiver, Hiccup and Yawn, 79

Why the Cat Chose Us, 138

Wiggling Worms at Work, 160–61

Wild Bears, 152

Wild Flamingos, 135

Wild Horses, 156

Wild Side of Pet Birds, The, 156

Wild Side of Pet Hamsters, The, 156

Wild Side of Pet Mice and Rats, The, 157

Wild Side of Pet Rabbits, The, 157

Wild Side of Pet Snakes, The, 173

Wild Water: Floods, 84

Wildfire! The 1871 Peshtigo Firestorm, 217

Wildlife Detectives: How Forensic Scientists Fight Crimes against Nature, The, 8, 73, 81

William Shakespeare & the Globe, 10

Windsurfing, 193

Winking, Blinking Sea: All about Bioluminescence, The, 129

With a Little Luck: Surprising Stories of Amazing Discoveries, 73, 178

Wolf, 146

Wolf Girls: An Unsolved Mystery from History, The, 217

Wolf Spiders, 171

Wolves (by Anne Welsbacher), 157

Wolves (by Dan Greenberg), 142

Wolves (by Sandra Markle), 148

Wolves: Growing Up Wild, 135

Woolly Rhinoceros, 61

Woolly Mammoth: Life, Death and Rediscovery, 57, 61

Working Dogs, 140

World Almanac and Book of Facts, The, 231

World Almanac for Kids, The, 231

World Encyclopedia of Flags, 231

World of Architectural Wonders, The, 11

World of Ripley's Believe It or Not!, The, 231

World-Class Boxer, A, 203

World-Class Gymnast, A, 197

World-Class Judo Champion, A, 195

World-Class Marathon Runner, A, 196
World-Class Mountain Biker, A, 195
World-Class Sprinter, A, 191
World-Class Swimmer, A, 196
World's Fastest Dragsters, The, 189
World's Fastest Indy Cars, The, 189
World's Fastest Pro Stock Trucks, The, 199
World's Fastest Stock Cars, The, 200
Wyatt Earp: Wild West Lawman, 50

Yellow Sac Spiders, 168
Yikes! Your Body, Up Close!, 107
York's Adventures with Lewis and Clark:
    An African-American's Part in the
    Great Expedition, 40–41
You Must Be Joking! Lots of Cool Jokes,
    224
You Wouldn't Want to Be an Aztec
    Sacrifice! Gruesome Things You'd
    Rather Not Know, 108

You Wouldn't Want to Be in a Medieval
    Dungeon! Prisoners You'd Rather Not
    Meet, 100
You Wouldn't Want to Be Sick in the 16th
    Century: Diseases You'd Rather Not
    Catch, 99, 110
You're on Your Way, Teddy Roosevelt!, 38
Youch! It Bites: Real-Life Monsters Up
    Close, 106
Young Thomas Edison, 177
Your Pet Iguana, 165
Your Travel Guide to Ancient Israel, 21
Yuck! A Big Book of Little Horrors, 99, 110
Yucky Riddles, 112
Yummy Riddles, 225

Zany Tongue-Twisters, 226
Zero Gravity, 83
Zoo's Who: Poems and Paintings by
    Douglas Florian, 118
Zzz...: The Most Interesting Book You'll
    Ever Read about Sleep, 89

About the Authors

KATHLEEN A. BAXTER served as the Coordinator of Children's Services in the Anoka County Library for over twenty-five years. She has written "The Nonfiction Booktalker" column for School Library Journal since 1997. She has presented at hundreds of national and state library and reading conferences all over the country. Kathleen has also taught classes in children's literature, served on the 2001 Newbery Committee, consults for publishers, and now presents all-day seminars on children's books for the Bureau of Education and Research.

MARCIA AGNESS KOCHEL has been a school media specialist in grades K-8 in North Carolina, Indiana, and Minnesota. She is currently Media Director at Olson Middle School in Bloomington, Minnesota. She has an undergraduate degree from The College of William and Mary in Virginia and a Masters of Science in Library Science from The University of North Carolina at Chapel Hill. She was a member of the 2006 Sibert Award Committee.